VICTORY IN EUROPE

TIME
LIFE ®
BOOKS

Other Publications:
PLANET EARTH
COLLECTOR'S LIBRARY OF THE CIVIL WAR
LIBRARY OF HEALTH
CLASSICS OF THE OLD WEST
THE EPIC OF FLIGHT
THE GOOD COOK
THE SEAFARERS
THE ENCYCLOPEDIA OF COLLECTIBLES
THE GREAT CITIES
HOME REPAIR AND IMPROVEMENT
THE WORLD'S WILD PLACES
THE TIME-LIFE LIBRARY OF BOATING
HUMAN BEHAVIOR
THE ART OF SEWING
THE OLD WEST
THE EMERGENCE OF MAN
THE AMERICAN WILDERNESS
THE TIME-LIFE ENCYCLOPEDIA OF GARDENING
LIFE LIBRARY OF PHOTOGRAPHY
THIS FABULOUS CENTURY
FOODS OF THE WORLD
TIME-LIFE LIBRARY OF AMERICA
TIME-LIFE LIBRARY OF ART
GREAT AGES OF MAN
LIFE SCIENCE LIBRARY
THE LIFE HISTORY OF THE UNITED STATES
TIME READING PROGRAM
LIFE NATURE LIBRARY
LIFE WORLD LIBRARY
FAMILY LIBRARY:
   HOW THINGS WORK IN YOUR HOME
   THE TIME-LIFE BOOK OF THE FAMILY CAR
   THE TIME-LIFE FAMILY LEGAL GUIDE
   THE TIME-LIFE BOOK OF FAMILY FINANCE

This volume is one of a series that chronicles
in full the events of the Second World War.
Previous books in the series include:

Prelude to War	The Road to Tokyo
Blitzkrieg	Red Army Resurgent
The Battle of Britain	The Nazis
The Rising Sun	Across the Rhine
The Battle of the Atlantic	War under the Pacific
Russia Besieged	War in the Outposts
The War in the Desert	The Soviet Juggernaut
The Home Front: U.S.A.	Japan at War
China-Burma-India	The Mediterranean
Island Fighting	Battles for Scandinavia
The Italian Campaign	The Secret War
Partisans and Guerrillas	Prisoners of War
The Second Front	The Commandos
Liberation	The Home Front: Germany
Return to the Philippines	Italy at War
The Air War in Europe	Bombers over Japan
The Resistance	The Neutrals
The Battle of the Bulge	

WORLD WAR II · TIME-LIFE BOOKS · ALEXANDRIA, VIRGINIA

BY GERALD SIMONS

AND THE EDITORS OF TIME-LIFE BOOKS

VICTORY IN EUROPE

Time-Life Books Inc.
is a wholly owned subsidiary of
TIME INCORPORATED

Founder: Henry R. Luce 1898-1967

Editor-in-Chief: Henry Anatole Grunwald
President: J. Richard Munro
Chairman of the Board: Ralph P. Davidson
Executive Vice President: Clifford J. Grum
Chairman, Executive Committee: James R. Shepley
Editorial Director: Ralph Graves
Group Vice President, Books: Joan D. Manley
Vice Chairman: Arthur Temple

TIME-LIFE BOOKS INC.

Editor: George Constable
Executive Editor: George Daniels
Board of Editors: Dale M. Brown, Thomas H. Flaherty Jr.,
Martin Mann, Philip W. Payne, John Paul Porter,
Gerry Schremp, Gerald Simons, Nakanori Tashiro,
Kit van Tulleken
Planning Director: Edward Brash
Art Director: Tom Suzuki
    Assistant: Arnold C. Holeywell
Director of Administration: David L. Harrison
Director of Operations: Gennaro C. Esposito
Director of Research: Carolyn L. Sackett
    Assistant: Phyllis K. Wise
Director of Photography: Dolores Allen Littles

President: Carl G. Jaeger
Executive Vice Presidents: John Steven Maxwell,
David J. Walsh
Vice Presidents: George Artandi, Stephen L. Bair,
Peter G. Barnes, Nicholas Benton, John L. Canova,
Beatrice T. Dobie, Carol Flaumenhaft,
James L. Mercer, Herbert Sorkin, Paul R. Stewart

WORLD WAR II

Editor: Thomas H. Flaherty Jr.
Victory in Europe was prepared under the supervision
of Time-Life Books by the following contributors:
Editors: Charles Osborne, Sheldon Cotler
Picture Editor: Peter D. Collins
Assistant Designer: Leonard Vigliarolo
Researchers: Vincent M. Badger, Ronald J. Fagan,
Jane Furth, Martha J. Mader, Josephine Reidy,
Starr Badger Shippee, John E. Taktikos
Writers: Cathy Beason, R. H. Cravens, Valerie
Moolman, Frederick King Poole, Eric Schurenberg,
Cinda Siler, E. Ogden Tanner, Bryce S. Walker
Editorial Manager: Felice Lerner
Editorial Assistants: Nicholas Goodman, Keith Nislow

Time-Life Books Editorial Staff for Victory in Europe
Researcher: Loretta Britten
Copy Coordinators: Ann Bartunek, Allan Fallow,
Barbara F. Quarmby
Art Assistant: Robert K. Herndon
Picture Coordinator: Betty Hughes Weatherley
Editorial Assistant: Andrea Reynolds

Editorial Operations
Production Director: Feliciano Madrid
    Assistants: Peter A. Inchauteguiz,
    Karen A. Meyerson
Copy Processing: Gordon E. Buck
Quality Control: Robert L. Young
    Assistant: James J. Cox
    Associates: Daniel J. McSweeney,
    Michael G. Wight
Art Coordinator: Anne B. Landry
Copy Room Director: Susan Galloway Goldberg
    Assistants: Celia Beattie, Ricki Tarlow

Correspondents: Elisabeth Kraemer (Bonn); Margot
Hapgood, Dorothy Bacon (London); Susan Jonas,
Lucy T. Voulgaris (New York); Maria Vincenza Aloisi,
Josephine du Brusle (Paris); Ann Natanson (Rome).
Valuable assistance was also provided by: Helga Kohl
(Bonn); Lois Lorimer (Copenhagen); Lynda Proud
(London); Felix Rosenthal (Moscow); Carolyn Chubet,
Miriam Hsia, Christina Lieberman, Cornelius Verwaal
(New York); Eva Stichova (Prague); Mimi Murphy
(Rome); Traudl Lessing (Vienna).

The Author: A long-time student of World War II,
GERALD SIMONS has been the editor of 14 titles in the
Time-Life Books World War II series. He is also the
author of Barbarian Europe in the Time-Life Books
Great Ages of Man series.

The Consultants: COLONEL JOHN R. ELTING, USA (Ret.),
was an intelligence officer with the 8th Armored Division in World War II. A former associate professor at
West Point, he is the author of Battles for Scandinavia
in the Time-Life Books World War II series and of The
Battle of Bunker's Hill, The Battles of Saratoga and
Military History and Atlas of the Napoleonic Wars.

EARL F. ZIEMKE, a research professor of history at the
University of Georgia, specializes in German history
and World War II. After wartime service as a U.S. Ma-
rine in the Pacific, he received his Ph.D. from the University of Wisconsin and worked as a supervisory historian for the Department of the Army in Washington,
D.C. He is the author of Stalingrad to Berlin: The German Defeat in the East, The U.S. Army in the Occupation of Germany 1944-1946, Battle for Berlin and, in
the Time-Life Books World War II series, The Soviet
Juggernaut.

Library of Congress Cataloguing in Publication Data

Simons, Gerald, 1923-
    Victory in Europe.

    (World War II; v. 36)
    Bibliography: p. 202
    Includes index.
    1. World War, 1939-1945—Campaigns—Germany.
2. World War, 1939-1945—Campaigns—Western. 3. World
War, 1939-1945—Campaigns—Eastern. 4. Germany—
History—1933-1945.   I. Time-Life Books.
II. Title.   III. Series.
D757.S48   940.54'21   81-18315
ISBN 0-8094-3403-2
ISBN 0-8094-3404-0 (lib. bdg.)
ISBN 0-8094-3406-7 (retail ed.)

For information about any Time-Life book, please write:

Reader Information
Time-Life Books
541 North Fairbanks Court
Chicago, Illinois 60611

CHAPTERS

PICTURE ESSAYS

CONTENTS

HARD-BOOTED LIBERATORS

Soviet troops marching on Vienna in April 1945 trample a Nazi flag. The Russians, making no distinction between Austrians and Germans, treated both harshly.

TRIUMPHAL THRUST OF A POLITICAL ARMY

Stalin's armies, advancing toward Germany through Nazi-dominated Eastern Europe, were as intent on asserting political dominance as they were on gaining military victory. Road signs and billboard slogans in German were quickly replaced by ones in Russian. And Soviet officers briefed their troops on the countries—from traditionally pro-Soviet Bulgaria to anti-Russian Poland—they were about to enter as friendly liberators and protectors.

Soviet troops received many a warm reception as they progressed toward Berlin. There were scenes of smiling soldiers accepting fruit from children, and giving them pocket knives in return. As the Russians neared one Bulgarian town, people turned out in their Sunday best, and the fire department hosed down the street to lay the dust; in another town the residents lined the route with red flags and built an archway over the main street with a sign of welcome.

In part, at least, the scenes of hospitality were the work of Soviet propagandists, and the friendly smiles were often forced. The Red Army's triumphal thrust through the collapsing German defenses stirred a powerful undercurrent of apprehension among some Eastern Europeans. Non-Communists in Poland, Rumania, Bulgaria and Hungary feared that the Russians came less as liberators than as conquerors. They dreaded the effect of the Russian presence on their religious beliefs, their property rights and the political future of their nations.

Even Yugoslavia's Josip Broz, the Communist Partisan leader known to his adherents as Marshal Tito, had misgivings about the Soviet Union's intentions. He insisted—successfully—that the Red Army leave Yugoslavia as soon as the Germans there had been defeated. For most of the liberated lands, however, Soviet influence was both immediate and far-reaching. In Poland, with Russian help, a pro-Soviet government was installed. In Hungary, a Budapest cabaret signaled the nation's future with a new floor show entitled "Leftward Ho!" But one Hungarian concluded that it was naïve to expect only a mere tilt to the left. "I knew," he wrote, "that the Russians had come to stay."

In northern Czechoslovakia a Red Army soldier, painting new road signs in Russian, puts finishing touches on an arrow pointing the way to Berlin.

Hawking a Communist newspaper that announces recent German defeats, a newsboy in Lublin, Poland, attracts a customer—a cheerful Soviet soldier.

Rumanian civilians, traditionally wary of the Soviet Union but disillusioned with their German alliance, welcome Russian soldiers to Bucharest with a show of warmth.

As Soviet troops roll through Sofia in September of 1944, Bulgarians respond with the clenched-fist Communist salute.

TWO NATIONS ON A TIGHTROPE

Rumanians and Bulgarians greeted the advancing Red Army with a complicated and often confusing mixture of emotions. Rumania, historically hostile to Russia, had joined Germany in its attack on the Soviet Union in 1941 to regain territory seized a few months earlier by the U.S.S.R. The Rumanians, however, felt no enmity toward the Western powers, and as Hitler's war became a losing cause, Rumania had sought—in vain—to negotiate a separate peace with Britain and the United States.

On the other hand, pro-Russian Bulgaria, allied with the Axis largely as a means to regain Balkan territory lost in World War I, had declared war on the West but not on the Soviet Union. The Bulgarian government maintained a loyally pro-Nazi posture until Russian troops neared the capital at Sofia, then did an abrupt about-face. Acknowledging the new Communist political structure it expected to live with, the government declared that "this war will certainly end with a large-scale social reorganization of mankind."

Soviet troops march through the old Polish city of Cracow in February 1945. The soldiers were shunned by many Poles, who remembered the Russian invasion of 1939.

A COLD GREETING, A STAGED WELCOME

The Red Army's welcome in Poland and in Yugoslavia was influenced by the capacity of each nation to resist. The Poles, prostrated ever since the Russo-German invasion of 1939, greeted their erstwhile Russian foes with skepticism when they reappeared as liberators. "We have been kicked around so much," said one weary Pole, "that the idea of a Russo-Polish alliance takes time to sink in."

In Yugoslavia, where partisan forces had been strong enough to tie down 10 German divisions, there was a Soviet-inspired pretense of solidarity. But the Red Army's entry into Belgrade was—by Yugoslav-Soviet agreement—only to help secure the capital. Once the city was safe from the Germans, the Russians moved out.

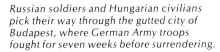
Russian soldiers and Hungarian civilians pick their way through the gutted city of Budapest, where German Army troops fought for seven weeks before surrendering.

In Vienna, a Soviet soldier removes a sign from a Nazi Party office wall. Written on the wall below the sign by a departed German is an ironic challenge: "We shall triumph."

WILTED HOPES AND PRUDENT APATHY

Hungary and Austria, once united in the old Habsburg Empire, had contrasting responses to the approach of the Russians: anticipation and fear. The Hungarians, allied with Hitler, were weary of his war; at first, many of them looked forward to the Soviets' arrival. But after the Red Army took Budapest in February 1945 following a 50-day siege, the brutality of the Soviet troops managed to unite the Hungarians against their conquerors.

In Austria, the Russians—who wanted to avoid a siege of the capital—called on the apprehensive citizens of Vienna to instigate a popular uprising. It never took place. Though the Soviets warned that retreating German troops intended to make a battleground of Vienna and wreck the fabled city, the Germans, as it turned out, left without much of a fight. Most Viennese stayed indoors as the Red Army took over on April 13, 1945.

Soviet artillerymen hear a political officer, standing at a map of Europe, remind them of their dual mission: Destroy the Nazis and win over the German people.

1

Minister of Propaganda Joseph Goebbels heard the news on his return to Berlin from a morale-building visit to the Eastern Front. He arrived at night during a British bombing raid and found members of his staff and a reporter waiting for him in the street when his car pulled up outside the Propaganda Ministry. The reporter cried, "Herr Reichsminister, Roosevelt is dead!"

"Goebbels jumped out of the car and stood for a moment as if transfixed," a secretary recalled. "I shall never forget the look on his face, which we could see in the light of Berlin burning." In that moment the thunderstruck Goebbels was sure that a historic miracle was being repeated: In 1762, when the fortunes of war were running so strongly against Frederick the Great of Prussia that he contemplated suicide, the King had been saved and his enemies, especially Russia, thrown into disarray by the sudden death of Elizabeth, the Russian Empress.

Goebbels hurried to his office and telephoned Adolf Hitler on their private line. "My Führer," he exclaimed, "I congratulate you. Roosevelt is dead!" He reminded Hitler that astrological charts kept in the research department of Reichsführer-SS Heinrich Himmler promised good things for the Führer and the Reich during the second half of April 1945. Then he said excitedly, "This is April the 13th! This is the turning point!"

Hitler instantly joined the celebration. He began babbling the news to everyone who entered his underground bunker in the Reich Chancellery garden, where he had lived like a mole since January. To enjoy a little gloating, he sent for his troublesome Minister of Armaments and War Production, Albert Speer, who had spread defeatist talk and even dared to oppose Hitler's scorched-earth policy. Hitler tolerated these transgressions only because he admired Speer's talents and ability.

Speer received the summons from the Führer after attending the last wartime concert of the Berlin Philharmonic Orchestra; at Speer's sardonic request, conductor Wilhelm Furtwängler had played the finale from Richard Wagner's opera *Götterdämmerung (Twilight of the Gods)*. "When I arrived in the bunker," Speer recounted, "Hitler rushed toward me with a degree of animation rare in him these days. He held a newspaper clipping in his hand. 'Here, read it!' His words came in a great rush. 'Here we have the miracle I

"WE SHALL NOT CAPITULATE"

always predicted. Who was right? The War isn't lost. Read it! Roosevelt is dead!' "

Speer was a perceptive man who fully appreciated the ironies of the scene. Hitler, the once-dynamic conqueror who had extended the German Reich from the Atlantic to the Volga and from the Arctic to the Sahara, had been reduced to a sick, shambling and prematurely senile man who clutched at historical and astrological straws in the hope of saving the remaining fragments of his domain. Speer wrote: "I was tempted to pity him, so reduced was he from the Hitler of the past."

In fact, Hitler's Germany was not merely dwindling fast; it had irremediably lost the War and was absorbing the worst defeat that had ever been inflicted on a major nation in modern times. The day after Roosevelt died, Vienna fell to the Red Army. More than six million Soviet soldiers were deployed along the Eastern Front; they held positions that included a 27-mile-long bridgehead on the west bank of the Oder River, less than 40 miles from Berlin (map, page 20). Two days earlier, the American vanguard of three million Allied troops had reached the Elbe River at a point just 53 miles southwest of Berlin.

Against these enormous and bountifully armed forces, the Germans could muster as many as five million men, but few were equipped to match their enemies. And the Germans were widely spread: They were attempting to hold not only the long Oder and Elbe lines but also southeastern Germany, western Austria, the northwestern corner of Yugoslavia, northern Italy, the western half of Czechoslovakia, all of Denmark and Norway, and a number of bypassed enclaves such as the so-called Courland pocket in Latvia and the Dodecanese Islands off Greece. Together these undertakings added up to an impossible task at which the Germans were failing daily.

The Third Reich was dying. German cities lay in ruins. Berlin, bombed almost every night in the 10 weeks since February 1, had been 75 per cent destroyed. German industry hardly deserved the name any longer. The once mighty factories of the Ruhr valley and their 350,000 defenders were surrounded by Americans. The latest trickle of war matériel was scarcely moving from factories in central and southern Germany along a transportation network already damaged by bombing and now further disrupted by the swift eastward advances of the Western Allies. In mid-March, Speer had calculated that "the final collapse of the German economy" should be expected within eight weeks, and conditions had worsened at an accelerated rate since that survey. Food shortages had become severe, particularly in the cities, where starvation threatened.

And still the War went on. It continued primarily because Hitler refused to surrender. "We shall not capitulate," he vowed time and again. "No, never! We may be destroyed, but if we are, we shall drag a world with us—a world in flames." He had always believed he could convince the Western nations that Germany was waging their battle against the "Bolshevik hordes" from the East, and he still hoped the Anglo-Americans would appreciate that fact in time to fight by his side. In any case, he expected Roosevelt's death to end what he called the "unnatural coalition" between the Anglo-Americans and the Russians, and to set them to cutting each other's throats. Meantime, Hitler urged the Germans to stand and fight to the last man. Of this sentiment his military chief of operations, General Alfred Jodl, later remarked, "For 80 million people, a fight to the death is not practicable."

The Wehrmacht—the Army, Navy and Luftwaffe—continued the fight primarily because its leaders believed they had no other choice. The only organized opposition to Hitler, which had crystallized in the Army's abortive bomb plot of July 1944, had been wiped out in a bloody purge; military and government leaders now followed orders mechanically, except for a handful of men who were negotiating individually with the Allies in hopes of salvaging their postwar careers. Actually, as the events of April would prove, even Hitler's private guard—the Schutzstaffel, or SS—not nearly so monolithic or uncompromising as the frightened Wehrmacht officers thought, was sagging under the pressure of defeat.

Many Germans—officers, soldiers and even civilians—continued to fight out of wrenching fear of the Russians. In savagery as well as scale, the war on the Eastern Front far exceeded the fighting in the West; German versus Slav was a war of ethnic extermination. During the long German scourging of the Soviet Union, at least seven million civilians had perished of all causes. About 10 million Soviet soldiers had been killed in action, and 3.5 million men had died as prisoners. As they swept into Prussia, Pomerania and Silesia, the Russians took vengeance in kind. German women were raped, crucified on barn doors or casually shot with their children. Long lines of fleeing Germans were deliberately run over by Soviet tanks. At first, the Soviet government unofficially encouraged the atrocious revenge, but later—officially—government leaders tried to curb the excesses, with only modest success.

All through February and March and into April, the German refugees from East Prussia and territories seized from Poland by Germany in 1939 streamed across the Oder and its tributary the Neisse. They brought tales of agony and gore, and the German military responded. Though many soldiers fled

or shucked their uniforms to survive the onslaught, many more chose to battle on to save their wives and families. These determined men, in desperate units that held out despite the reasonable assumption that they would be defeated or destroyed, inspired other officers and men. "To leave our comrades in the East in the lurch at this fateful moment," a veteran general wrote, "was impossible for any commander. We simply had to fight to give our eastern armies time to retreat into the British and American zones."

Because the Germans would not give up, a battle would have to be fought for Berlin and its surrounding territory. For the Third Reich, that sprawling struggle would make little difference—except to protract Germany's agony. For the Allies, the Berlin battle was to have serious repercussions on postwar Europe, as was the ensuing fight for Prague. Few as-

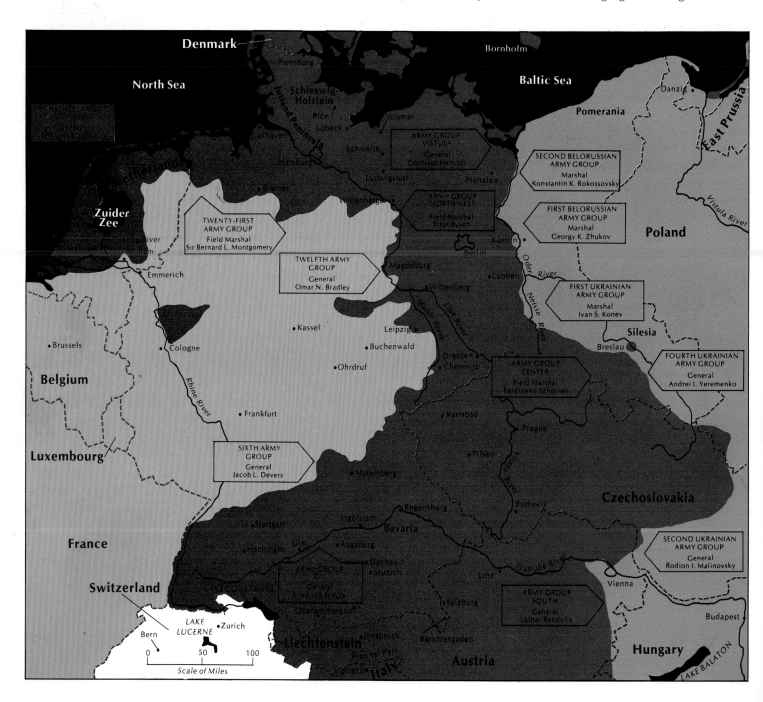

pects of World War II excited more controversy among the various Allied nations.

Such contention was already deeply embedded in relations among the Allies. As Hitler had predicted in his wishful, exaggerated way, the coalition against him was indeed breaking up. The United States, Great Britain and the Soviet Union were finding it ever harder to disguise—much less to resolve—their numerous political conflicts; it seemed likely that their hard-won wartime cooperation would end in angry peacetime alienation. The great battles for Berlin and Prague that were fought in the few nightmarish weeks that ended six years of world war would strike the trial balance for a new Europe.

The fate of Berlin caused no serious complications in the Allies' troubled dealings until the spring of 1945. Soviet, American and British diplomats, meeting in London as the European Advisory Commission (EAC) in November 1944, were assigned the task of working out postwar plans for the occupation of Germany. They agreed on the zones that each Allied power would occupy (page 25). They further agreed that the three great powers would jointly administer Berlin and that the surrounding territory as far west as the Elbe (and well beyond, in places) would lie in the Soviet zone of occupation.

These matters, vitally affecting the future of Europe and relations between the great powers, were discussed at the meeting in February 1945 of President Roosevelt, Prime Minister Winston Churchill and Soviet Premier Josef Stalin at Yalta, in the Crimea, where the leaders arrived at a general agreement on the subject of occupation zones.

The men who drafted the EAC agreement in 1944 had made no effort to allocate roles in an assault on Berlin, though it seemed likely at the time that the Russians would get there first. Independently, the Russians laid plans to take Berlin as part of their winter offensive, slated to start in January 1945. The British and Americans outlined as their climactic offensive, also in the early weeks of 1945, a drive from the western side of the Rhine northeast to the German capital. The Supreme Allied Commander in Western Europe, General Dwight D. Eisenhower, assured the British that, under Field Marshal Sir Bernard Law Montgomery, they would carry the main weight of the assault.

Events seemed to settle the question of who would take

Berlin. By late February 1945, Soviet armies had stormed across Poland and were drawing up along the Oder just a single day's march from the German capital. Meanwhile the Americans and British had been shaken by Hitler's surprise counteroffensive in the Ardennes region of Belgium and Luxembourg. Though they had recovered the ground lost in the Battle of the Bulge in time for the Yalta Conference, they were still some 350 miles from Berlin and much more concerned about forcing the Rhine. Apparently the Red Army was going to take Berlin at will. But Stalin was in no great rush; before assaulting Berlin, the Soviet leader wanted to consolidate territory he had occupied in the Balkans and liquidate the German armies on his forces' northern flank along the Baltic.

Trouble over the German capital finally erupted at the end of March, but it was not a quarrel between British and American leaders and the Soviet Union. Rather, it pitted Eisenhower against the British—specifically, Churchill and Montgomery. Churchill had always been in favor of an Anglo-American capture of the German capital as a matter of prestige: The world, he felt, would regard the conqueror of Berlin as the true victor in the War. He also believed that possession of Berlin would give the Western Allies an advantage over the Russians after the War. Montgomery, already able to imagine his triumphal entry into Berlin, was a most willing confederate.

Then, as the European Supreme Allied Commander, Eisenhower changed the game. The general decided to renounce Berlin as the final objective of the Western Allies. With his forces across the Rhine and set to strike rapidly eastward into central Germany, he shifted the main thrust of the advance from the British in the north to the Americans under General Omar N. Bradley in the center of the Western Front. Bradley would send his U.S. Twelfth Army Group due east to Leipzig and Dresden. The Russians, Eisenhower suggested, would meet Bradley's army group near that point and cut Germany in two.

Eisenhower made the change for reasons good and bad. He was right in believing that Berlin, capital of a country already defeated, had lost its strategic importance, and that as an objective it was not worth the 100,000 casualties he believed that fighting for it would claim. He intended to

On April 15, 1945, five major Russian formations (light red) confronted Germany along a 625-mile arc that stretched from Pomerania in the north to eastern Austria in the south. The major forces of the Western Allies (gray area) were two U.S. army groups and one British army group. The portions of Europe still in German hands (dark red) were defended by five army groups and an isolated Netherlands command.

shift the emphasis from Montgomery's drive to Bradley's in order to mop up war industries in central Germany and to counter any fanatical Nazi resistance in the mountains of southeastern Germany and western Austria. Eisenhower was correct about the desirability of finishing off Germany's industrial potential. But he was wrong about the rumored Alpine national redoubt—the supposed lair where a large force of diehard Nazis would resist until the bitter end. It did not exist.

A major factor in Eisenhower's decision probably was the character of his commanders. American generals such as Bradley and the Third Army's George S. Patton Jr. had shown a particular talent for the swift exploitation of breakthroughs; at this stage of Germany's collapse, the Americans seemed more likely to produce faster results than would Montgomery, with his genius for massive, relatively static battles such as the four-week siege of Caen in Normandy in the summer of 1944.

On March 28, Eisenhower sent an announcement to Major General John R. Deane, head of the U.S. Military Mission in Moscow, for delivery by hand to Stalin; in the message he executed the policy change that abandoned Berlin as an objective. In taking such a significant step without consulting

his superiors, Eisenhower believed he was acting within his authority as Supreme Commander. But if there should be any argument—as he was well aware there might be—he wanted to bring about a *fait accompli,* which he was certain his superiors would support. As the episode unfolded, Eisenhower's procedure turned out to have been an extremely shrewd move.

Deane was so startled by the radical change in plans that, while his staff translated the message into Russian, he sent an urgent wire for background information to Eisenhower's headquarters. Still-stronger reactions came from the British when Eisenhower informed them he had changed his plans. Churchill was furious, and in a telephone conversation he forced Eisenhower to defend his new plan point by point. Churchill argued that notwithstanding the general's writ of authority in dealing with the Russians in matters military, Eisenhower had not been empowered to make such a significant political decision. Eisenhower, he charged, had no right to address the head of the Soviet state directly on such a subject. Furthermore, fumed the Prime Minister, Eisenhower had foreclosed a plan that Churchill and his British colleagues considered vital to the success of negotiations with the Russians over the future of Europe.

Churchill wanted the Western Allies to capture as much

Wearing a white arm band, a member of the Volkssturm—the civilian home guard—aids a fellow Berliner wounded during an air raid in early 1945.

territory as possible from the areas earmarked by the EAC for Soviet occupation, then hold the ground until Stalin did what Britain and the United States wanted. Churchill was angry at the Americans for not sharing this viewpoint; the British considered Americans oblivious to European problems because they would not have to live in postwar Europe. After V-E Day, the British feared, the Americans would pull out as many troops as they needed to finish the war in the Pacific and would leave Western Europe at the Russians' mercy.

The U.S. Joint Chiefs of Staff, the Allied commander's American superiors, backed Eisenhower to the hilt: They agreed that because he was Supreme Commander, and because Stalin was military as well as political chief in the Soviet Union, Eisenhower was properly addressing Stalin as his Soviet counterpart in order to coordinate two gigantic converging assaults that were in danger of colliding.

Churchill did not fail to make his points directly to Roosevelt. But the American Commander in Chief, who could have reversed Eisenhower's decision, chose not to. Roosevelt, whose health was failing, lacked the strength for a fight with his military advisers—and even if he had been well, he probably would have balked at opposing them on an issue about which they felt so strongly.

It was not until March 31 that Deane, satisfied with the background briefing he had requested from Eisenhower's headquarters, and with a Russian translation of Eisenhower's March 28 message in hand, called on Stalin. The Soviet leader read the message on the spot and said, through a translator, that he would of course frame a written answer in full. But on first reading, Stalin declared, he agreed wholeheartedly with General Eisenhower's new plans; Berlin had lost its former importance, and as a consequence the Red Army would attack in the more southerly direction Eisenhower had indicated.

Josef Stalin, as Deane described him, had "all the attributes of a good poker player," and he had just played his cards very close to his vest. After the delegation left, Stalin scheduled a top-level military conference for the next day, Easter. An intensely suspicious man, Stalin apparently believed that Eisenhower's renunciation of Berlin meant that his intention was just the opposite—that the German capital would be the next Anglo-American objective. Stalin now would hurry to beat what he privately called the "little allies" into Berlin.

Allied relations with Stalin had been deteriorating for months. The Americans and British had been vainly striving to obtain Soviet compliance on a long list of matters already

Hitler and one of his aides survey bomb damage to a government building a short distance from the Führerbunker, Hitler's underground headquarters.

23

agreed upon. The Russians had become obstructive. What had happened? Was the change in Soviet policy due to some mysterious turn in Kremlin politics or to the fact that Stalin felt he no longer needed the Western Allies? At Yalta, Stalin had appeared to be in an expansive and amenable mood. To be sure, it seemed that the Soviet dictator had been conceded virtually everything he asked for, including consideration of a $10 billion German reparations payment to Russia after the War. But Stalin had made concessions to his Allies, too: He had agreed to their request for a French zone of occupation (to be carved out of the Anglo-American zones); he had agreed—conditionally—to enter the war against Japan within three months following the end of hostilities in Europe; and he had agreed to participate in the launching of the United Nations organization, President Roosevelt's most cherished project.

But as soon as the conference ended, it seemed that Stalin deliberately set out to break the Yalta agreements, and generally to oppose and bedevil the Western Allies in every way he could. For example, though Stalin had agreed at Yalta to let the Americans use the airfields that the Russians had captured in Hungary as bases from which to bomb southern Germany, the U.S. Air Force officers sent to inspect the bases were curtly turned away. A U.S. survey team, promised admission to the Soviet Far East to choose a bomber base for operations against Japan, was kept waiting in Alaska for visas; after 21 days, the group finally returned home in exasperation.

These Soviet affronts to the Western Allies were minor compared to the apparently systematic Soviet violation of another Yalta commitment. After the Germans retreated, it had been agreed, the governments of Poland, Bulgaria, Rumania and Hungary were to be de-Nazified and democratized; free elections were to be held at the earliest feasible dates. But the governments of Bulgaria, Rumania and Hungary were soon taken over by native Communists or converted to Communism under the guns of Red Army liberators. A control commission of officials from the three Allied powers was set up in each country to ensure fair play. But the Soviet members of each commission frustrated the activities of the British and American members—for example, by hampering their ability to travel in the countryside. The Allies pro-

tested in vain; the Soviets controlled the commissions. Only when the Russian delegations deemed that an election would be safe for their candidate was any balloting permitted; otherwise, they simply staged a coup.

Poland was a pitiable case. Since September 1939, a Polish government-in-exile had waited in London for the freeing of its homeland from German occupation; then, the exile government expected to be welcomed back to Poland, or at least to be given a chance, through a free election, to assume power. However, the Russians began locking the exile government out of postwar Polish politics even before the War had ended. In the summer of 1944, Soviet forces stood by on the east bank of the Vistula across from Warsaw while German SS units occupying the city crushed an uprising by a large Polish democratic underground that was a potential opponent not only of the Germans but also of the Soviets. After taking Warsaw and overrunning the western portion of Poland, the Russians installed a provisional government of hand-picked Polish Communists.

From then on, Stalin and his Foreign Minister, Vyacheslav M. Molotov, argued with the British and Americans over whether—and how—the provisional government should be expanded or reorganized to include the London Poles (or anyone else besides Moscow's own puppets). In the process, the Soviets managed to thwart any substantive change in the make-up of the Polish government. On April 7, 1945, Stalin declared himself satisfied with the status quo in a revealing message to Roosevelt: "Matters on the Polish question have really reached a dead end." The President, who often boasted that he could "handle Uncle Joe," had in fact been adroitly manipulated by Stalin.

In March, Stalin had informed Roosevelt that he simply could not spare Molotov to represent Russia at the upcoming United Nations convocation in San Francisco, the culmination of three years of international planning to establish a replacement for the moribund League of Nations. Sensing that the Soviet decision was a reaction to American attitudes on the postwar government of Poland, Roosevelt was particularly moderate in his dealings with Stalin on the problem. Ironically, only Roosevelt's death and a personal appeal by Averell Harriman, the American Ambassador to Moscow, persuaded Stalin to send Molotov to the U.N. convocation as a memorial gesture.

THE ALLIES' PLAN FOR CARVING UP THE REICH

Planned in late 1944, the division of Germany into occupation zones placed Berlin well within the sector assigned to the Soviet Union.

The final weeks of fighting in Europe were influenced on both sides by an Allied postwar occupation plan. The plan divided Germany—as well as the city of Berlin—into three separate zones of occupation, each assigned to one of the major Allies. (French zones were later carved out of the British and American zones.) Austria and Vienna were partitioned along the same lines.

The plan had an unintended effect on the battle for Berlin. By the middle of April, elements of the U.S. Ninth Army had reached the Elbe River, well inside the Russian zone. That put the German capital approximately half-way between the rapidly advancing Americans and the Russians, poised on the Oder and Neisse Rivers.

But Eisenhower ordered his commanders to halt. An Anglo-American drive on Berlin would be costly, and he was not prepared to sacrifice the lives of American troops to capture territory that he believed he would then have to hand over to the Russians. In effect, the occupation plan had helped ensure that Berlin would fall solely to the Red Army.

The German High Command knew of the occupation plan from a copy that had been captured in January of 1945; a letter found with it spoke of unconditional surrender and the dismemberment of Germany. The Allies' uncompromising intentions stiffened Germany's resistance, and probably prolonged the War.

Harriman at the same time was taking the brunt of an especially virulent quarrel with the Russians over Operation *Sunrise*, a complex and sometimes ludicrous effort by agents of the U.S. Office of Strategic Services (OSS) to arrange for the surrender of German forces in northern Italy. *Sunrise* was an effort worth making, for Italy was a cruel, dead-end theater. Since their invasion of southern Italy in July 1943, the Allies had suffered about 300,000 casualties and had advanced north only 350 miles—an average rate of less than 18 miles a month. The Germans, who had been crowded back into the hilly southern edge of the Po River valley, still fielded nearly a million troops. One of the German units, Army Group C, commanded by Field Marshal Albert Kesselring, was probably the strongest force now available to Hitler.

The *Sunrise* operation started in February 1945, when SS General Karl Wolff sent out word that he would like to discuss a German surrender with responsible Allied authorities. The highest-ranking SS officer in Italy, Wolff was the military plenipotentiary in charge of security and other occupation matters in the German rear areas, and the watchdog over the puppet Fascist republic that was the relic of Benito Mussolini's fallen regime. To transmit his message, Wolff sent an ingratiating Italian baron named Luigi Parrilli to Bern, Switzerland, where Allen Dulles, head of U.S. intelligence operations in Europe, had his headquarters. Although skeptical at first, Dulles gradually became interested in Wolff's offer, and he assigned his right-hand man in Europe, a German-American named Gero von Schulze Gaevernitz, to talk to Parrilli.

A meeting with Parrilli was set up by Major Max Waibel, a friend of Dulles' in the Swiss intelligence service. Because Swiss financiers had major economic interests in northern Italy that might be destroyed in the course of all-out fighting between the Germans and the Allies, Waibel was acting with the tacit blessing of his government. In early March, one of Waibel's men arranged to meet with Wolff's personal representative, Eugen Dollmann, at Lugano, near the Italian border. Dollmann was an SS colonel who had lived in Italy for years before the War.

Waibel's man escorted Dollmann and an associate to a private room in a restaurant, where they were kept waiting for several hours before a Dulles agent showed up. While he waited, Dollmann was curtly told to inform Wolff that the only terms available were unconditional surrender, and that Wolff would get nowhere if he tried to play the Western Allies against the Soviet Union. When the OSS agent arrived, Dollmann was also told that Dulles would appreciate a gesture of good faith—the release of two captured Italian partisan leaders.

Within five days, Wolff had responded. He had not only released the partisans but was hurrying, in civilian clothes, to Switzerland to talk personally with Dulles. After an appropriate amount of undercover maneuvering, Dulles met with Wolff and Gaevernitz in a Zurich apartment, beside a blazing hearth. (Dulles swore by the ingratiating effect of a wood fire, which seemed appropriate now that Wolff was demonstrating good faith.)

Since the first contact, the Americans had learned very little about Wolff; they might well have refused to deal with him if they had known more. They knew that Wolff had been liaison officer between the SS top command and Hitler's headquarters, that he had been favored with rapid promotions, and that he had been affectionately called "Wolffchen" by Himmler. They did not know, however, that as Himmler's adjutant Wolff had been involved in planning the death camps in Poland, or that he had written to an SS "transportation" official expressing his "special joy now that 5,000 members of the Chosen People are going to Treblinka every day." (The letter was unearthed after the War and was used in Wolff's war-crimes trial to convict him; he was sent to prison for 15 years.) Nor did the Americans pause to consider that Wolff's police detachments in Italy routinely tortured suspected partisans, executed hostages, and had been responsible for massacres of whole villages. To the Americans, Wolff was a clean-cut, intelligent officer who sounded no false notes and who seemed genuinely eager to avoid pointless bloodshed and destruction.

At the fireside meeting with Dulles, Wolff offered an alluring and concrete program that featured a proposal to surrender 200,000 troops. Most of these were Italian Fascists who had not surrendered to the Allies when Italy capitulated in 1943, but they also included 80,000 German police and occupation troops. Most important, Wolff would persuade Field Marshal Kesselring, who commanded 500,000 men, to join him in surrender. From conversations with Kesselring, Wolff—who acted as a political adviser to the field marshal—believed that he could be persuaded to support a peace effort.

Listening to Wolff, Dulles caught *Sunrise* fever. After the conference he sent his OSS superiors in Washington a highly optimistic report describing Wolff as a ''distinctive'' and ''dynamic'' personality. Wolff's proposals also raised hopes of a cease-fire in British Field Marshal Sir Harold Alexander, the Allied commander in chief in Italy, who was planning a spring offensive but would have been glad to avoid it. However, Dulles' optimism and Alexander's hopefulness were premature. Wolff's plans were quickly disrupted when Kesselring was called to Berlin to receive an assignment as commander of the Western Front.

The personnel shift meant that Wolff would be required to proselytize Kesselring's replacement, General Heinrich-Gottfried von Vietinghoff. Although Vietinghoff proved to be anxious to bring an end to the War, he had scruples: Because he believed that he was only a temporary substitute for Kesselring (whom he had served for years as a deputy and subordinate commander), he was loath to commit Army Group C in his own name.

During these preliminaries, the Allies' Combined Chiefs of Staff decided to send their own representative to the talks; at Churchill's suggestion, they also considered apprising the Russians of the situation. Influenced by the Americans, excited by the possibilities of a U.S.-sponsored German surrender in Italy, but convinced that Soviet participation in the early talks would ruin any chance of success, the Chiefs arrived at a consensus: inform the Russians but keep them from participating, on the reasonable ground that this was a local military surrender of the sort that the Soviet Union had accepted on the Eastern Front without bothering to tell the Western Allies.

The Soviets already knew that something was afoot; the mysterious comings and goings of Wolff and others across the Swiss-Italian border had been observed by Russian intelligence agents in the area and had aggravated their chronic suspiciousness. They believed that Operation *Sunrise* was an Anglo-American plot to negotiate a separate peace with the Reich that would release German troops to fight against the Soviet Union.

The news of Operation *Sunrise* reached the Russians officially on March 11 when, at the Combined Chiefs' behest, Harriman broached the subject of the talks in a memorandum to Molotov. Harriman immediately got a reply from Molotov appointing three Soviet officers to attend the talks. The Western Allies promptly refused to let the Russians into the meetings, a response that Molotov described as ''utterly unexpected and incomprehensible.'' There should be no meetings at all, he said, unless Soviet representatives were allowed to attend.

The Western Allies attempted to assuage Stalin's fears by sending Moscow reports on every development in *Sunrise*. Unfortunately there was little to report. Wolff visited Kesselring on the Western Front, and the field marshal agreed to recommend surrender to Vietinghoff. (But, Kesselring told Wolff, he would not surrender his new Western Front command, not while his Army oath of personal loyalty to Hitler was still in force.)

Stalin refused to believe that he was being kept informed about the true progress of *Sunrise*. On April 3, he sent a message to Roosevelt that imputed double-dealing on the part of the Americans and British: ''My military colleagues, on the basis of data which they have on hand, do not have any doubts that the negotiations have taken place, and that they have ended in an agreement with the Germans, on the basis of which the German commander on the Western Front, Field Marshal Kesselring, has agreed to open the front and permit the Anglo-American troops to advance to the east, and the Anglo-Americans have promised in return to ease the peace terms for the Germans. I think my colleagues are close to the truth.''

President Roosevelt, his health failing fast, fired back a strong note, written for him by U.S. Army Chief of Staff General George C. Marshall and by Admiral William Leahy, Roosevelt's personal chief of staff and acting chairman of the Joint Chiefs. ''It is astonishing,'' the message said, ''that a belief seems to have reached the Soviet government that I have entered into an agreement with the enemy without first obtaining your full agreement. . . . It would be one of the great tragedies of history if, at the very moment of the victory now within our grasp, such distrust, such lack of faith should prejudice the entire undertaking after the colossal losses of life, matériel and treasure involved. Frankly, I cannot avoid a feeling of bitter resentment toward your informers, whoever they are, for such vile misrepresentations of my actions or those of my trusted subordinates."

This angry statement elicited a temperate reply from Stalin: "We Russians think that in the present situation on the fronts, when the enemy is faced with inevitable surrender, if the representatives of any one ally ever meet the Germans to discuss surrender, the representatives of another ally should be afforded an opportunity of participating in such a meeting. In any case, this is absolutely essential if the ally in question asks for such participation."

The Russians now seemed willing to let the matter drop, and Roosevelt was only too glad to oblige; Field Marshal Alexander's spring offensive had been launched in the Po valley on April 9 and was sweeping forward steadily. The whole thorny matter eventually resolved itself on May 2, 1945, when the surrender of German forces in Italy took place after fitful negotiations—conducted with a Soviet delegate in attendance.

On April 1, Stalin held his staff meeting to react to Eisenhower's message about Berlin. Seven members of the powerful Soviet State Defense Committee attended the meeting. So did two of the Soviet Union's most prominent generals, the men who would command the main assaults in the offensive on Berlin: Marshal Georgy K. Zhukov and Marshal Ivan S. Konev. Each commanded an army group (the Russian word for it translates as "front") named for the area of the Soviet Union that it had been given the mission of liberating in 1944. Zhukov led the First Belorussian Army Group, Konev the First Ukrainian.

Zhukov and Konev had been cast in the same mold. Both were sons of peasants. Both were ethnic Russians, a factor of no small importance in their careers: Russian officers, products of the largest of the Soviet Union's hundred-odd ethnic groups, held the great majority of top posts in the Red Army, and they were a clannish lot. Though Zhukov was short and Konev tall, both marshals were thick-chested, broad-shouldered, square-faced men in their late forties; besides being physically imposing, each had a reputation for toughness verging on callousness.

(Konev once bragged, speaking of a battle during the Dnieper campaign: "We let the Cossacks cut as long as they wished. They even hacked off the hands of those who raised them in surrender.")

Through his first nine years in the Red Army, which he joined at its inception in 1917, Konev had served as a commissar—a Communist Party official who was assigned to monitor political behavior and ideological reliability in a military unit. He became a regular field officer in 1926 after studying the military sciences at Frunze Academy, the Red Army school in south central Russia. Konev was promoted regularly thereafter, rising to command an army by the start of World War II.

Zhukov's reputation as a hard man rested on his attitude not only toward an enemy but toward his own subordinates. On one occasion, Zhukov had reduced a general to junior rank and sent him to his death in a suicidal bayonet charge—acting on a snap judgment, disputed by the general's immediate superior, that the general had performed weakly. Despite such excesses, Zhukov had become a popular hero by stopping the German blitzkrieg at the gates of Moscow in the winter of 1941-1942. As a combat commander and as campaign coordinator for the Soviet high command, Zhukov had won many battles, from Stalingrad

A German poster demands revenge for inhabitants of the East Prussian village of Metgethen, a site of atrocities allegedly committed by the Red Army. Nazi propagandists exploited reports of rape and massacre to stiffen the resistance of the exhausted and outnumbered German Army.

onward. The German generals judged him the best of the Russian commanders, though hardly a subtle tactician. At an advanced stage of the War, Zhukov was simply more forceful than others in the use of the Soviet Union's increasing advantage in manpower, massed artillery and tanks.

Relations between these two military giants were poor—as might have been expected. Konev's success irritated Zhukov and other field officers, who considered commissars second-class soldiers—often with good cause, since they were chosen primarily for their political rather than military skills. To Konev (and a number of other Soviet generals), the eminence of Zhukov was too much the result of good luck and an undisguised favoritism on the part of Stalin. Konev meant to make the most of the Berlin offensive, which he regarded as a last chance to even the score with Zhukov in a competition that Stalin, a shrewd judge of men, had long fostered as a means of goading both generals to greater achievements.

With Stalin presiding, the meeting of the Defense Committee began on a note of secrecy and conspiracy. At a signal from Stalin, General Sergei M. Shtemenko, the operations chief of the General Staff, read a revealing telegram from an anonymous spy. The message outlined the Allied campaign that had been in preparation before Eisenhower's change of plans; it called for an attack on Berlin. Stalin made no reference to Eisenhower's letter of March 25 abjuring Berlin as an Anglo-American objective. When Shtemenko finished reading, Stalin put the obvious question: "Well, then, who is going to take Berlin, we or the 'Allies'?"

In his memoirs, Konev gives himself the next line: "It is we who will be taking Berlin, and we shall take it before the Allies." Stalin thereupon told Zhukov and Konev to develop their attack plans with the General Staff for his approval and return to the front as soon as possible to get the redeployment started. With that, he left the room.

Zhukov and Konev went to work immediately with high-ranking members of the General Staff. Apparently Zhukov was supposed to coordinate the entire operation—a difficult task made harder by the fact that Marshal Konstantin K. Rokossovsky, commander of the Second Belorussian Army Group assigned to cover the northern flank of the Berlin offensive, was absent, mopping up German resistance along the Baltic coast. These northern cleanup activities, it was obvious, would preclude his joining any attack westward until fairly late in April.

The plans that emerged called for a massive yet essentially simple operation. The three Soviet army groups were to destroy the two armies of German Army Group Vistula and one army of Army Group Center that were defending eastern Germany. In the process, the Russian forces would overrun all of the territory from the Oder-Neisse line to the Elbe-Mulde line, from the Baltic to the border of Czechoslovakia. In the north, along the lower Oder, Rokossovsky's army group was to attack westward, then wheel northward. In the center, Zhukov's armies, which were ranged along the middle Oder bracketing Berlin, would strike straight westward at Army Group Vistula and surround the capital. Konev's force would drive west and northwest, then mount a secondary attack southwest toward Dresden that was to develop into an assault on Prague against Army Group Center. Zhukov and Konev determined that April 16 was the earliest date on which they could open the offensive. At that, they would be starting their attack a few days before Rokossovsky could begin his.

When the plan was presented to Stalin, he drew a boundary line between Zhukov's and Konev's army groups, and blurred the seemingly routine distinction in the most significant way. The line that he drew ran west well to the south of Berlin, apparently reserving the capital as the prize for Zhukov. But Stalin extended the dividing line only as far as Lübben—45 miles southeast of Berlin—a town that Konev was supposed to reach on the third day of the offensive. Konev instantly realized that Stalin was challenging him to veer north from Lübben to beat Zhukov into Berlin, and Konev sensed that Zhukov had the same understanding. Stalin later told General Shtemenko, "Whoever reaches Berlin first—let him take it."

From the Kremlin, the two commanders sped to Moscow Central Airport to return to their headquarters; they were in the air within two minutes of each other. Thereafter, as Konev reported, quoting a Russian folk saying, "We hardly had time to look for our hats and gloves."

In the next two weeks the Red Army completed its fastest large-scale redeployment of World War II, under the supervision of Marshal Zhukov. Even though most of his own force had been encamped along the Oder since February, Zhukov had to move two armies into position to reinforce his northern flank, which would remain exposed following the launching of his attack, until the armies under Rokossovsky could force the Oder and break out of bridgeheads along its west bank.

Konev had much more unit-shuffling to do. His troops had scarcely finished a hard fight across Silesia in southern Poland when Stalin announced the Berlin offensive; the German garrison at Breslau still held out (Konev eventually left it to starve). Because the direction of his drive had been toward Czechoslovakia, Konev needed to move numerous divisions in order to swing his main force north into position for the new assault. He also had to arrange many replacements for heavy casualties; to achieve this, Stalin reinforced Konev with two armies that had been assigned to the eastern Baltic.

The logistical demands of the offensive were immense, and their fulfillment was a phenomenal accomplishment. The only direct rail line into Germany from the Soviet Union was the Moscow-Berlin road that the Germans destroyed as they withdrew; it had to be rebuilt by the Soviets. Most supplies—including U.S. Lend-Lease goods entering the U.S.S.R. through the Persian Gulf, Murmansk and the Far East—had to clear the Soviet capital, then rumble 1,000 miles to depots near the Oder, there to be redistributed northward and southward. Zhukov later wrote, with a fine eye for popularizing detail, that the supply trains would, if parked end to end, stretch 750 miles, and that it took 78,000 carloads to transport the 7,147,000 artillery shells that had been allocated for the opening phases of the offensive. The supply work was done by uncounted thousands of support troops and civilian laborers who also helped dig gun emplacements (170 to a mile) on Zhukov's line, build bridges and storage facilities, and lay numberless miles of telephone wire.

Soviet General Headquarters set up a special training program for the offensive. A large scale model of greater Berlin—all 340 square miles of it—had been built by Red Army engineers, and all Army commanders, corps commanders, chiefs of staff, artillery commanders and political officers were required to take the headquarters course.

HITLER'S LAST REFUGE

On January 16, 1945, Hitler moved his headquarters from Bad Nauheim, west of Berlin, into a bunker that he had ordered constructed under the Reich Chancellery garden near the center of the capital city. Cramped and badly ventilated, its communication system consisting of one radio receiver, one radio telephone and one telephone switchboard, the *Führerbunker* seemed an absurd choice for the Reich's supreme headquarters. Yet Hitler preferred it to his generals' sophisticated OKW command bunker at Zossen, 20 miles away—a preference based, perhaps, on a mistrust of his generals following the attempt to assassinate him the previous summer.

Whatever its shortcomings as a headquarters or a home, the *Führerbunker* was virtually impregnable—both from Allied bombs and from German plotters. The roof was 16 feet of concrete, the walls were six and a half feet thick, and the entire structure was buried six feet underground. Its main weakness was the marshy ground of Berlin, which had a high water table; if a large bomb had exploded close enough to the bunker to crack its walls, all the occupants of the structure might have drowned. Inside the bunker, the thunder of war was only a faint rumble—though after a near miss the structure would tremble and the overhead lamps would sway. All visitors, regardless of rank, were disarmed, searched, then required to show passes at SS checkpoints.

The bunker had 19 rooms. Besides Hitler, it housed a few guards, aides, personal servants and physicians. After mid-April, the residents included the Führer's mistress, Eva Braun, and Nazi propaganda chief Joseph Goebbels.

Though almost everyone else, including Eva, escaped the oppressive atmosphere of the bunker periodically, "Der Chef" left very rarely and then for a few hours at most. The last formal occasion was April 20, to attend a celebration in the Reich Chancellery in honor of his 56th birthday. Ten days later, back in the bunker, he took his own life, one of more than 50 million victims of the war he had started almost six years before.

Hitler's Bedroom

Situation Room

Hitler's Sitting Room

Hitler's Study

Hitler's Bath and Dressing Rooms

Toilets

Eva Braun's Bed-Sitting-Room

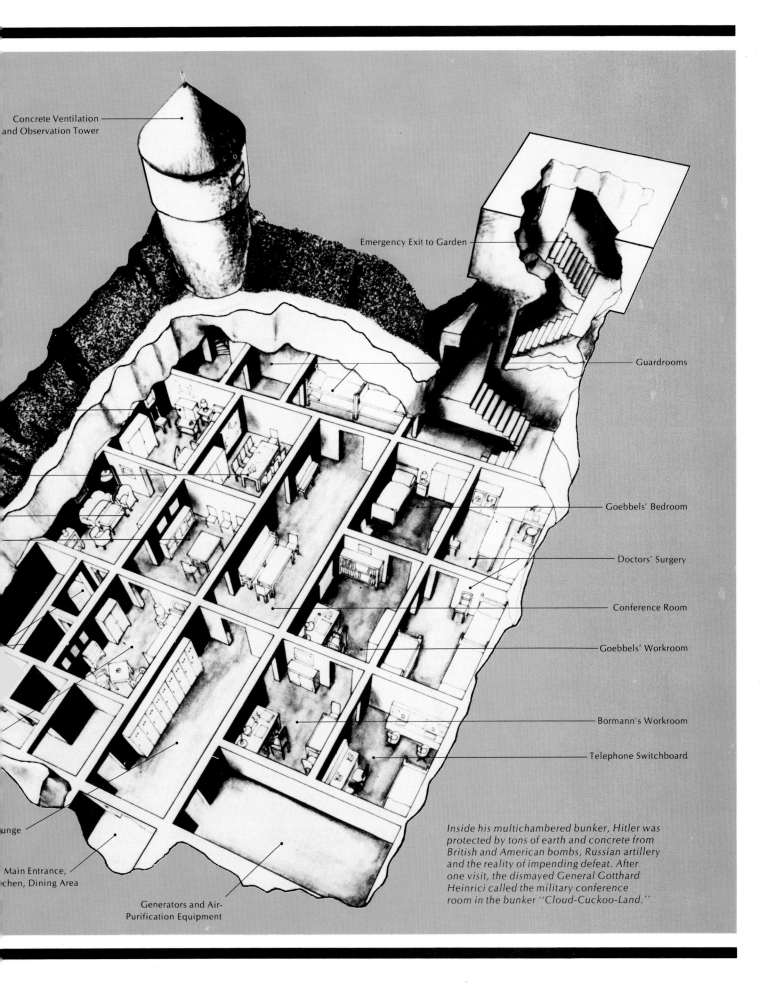

Concrete Ventilation and Observation Tower

Emergency Exit to Garden

Guardrooms

Goebbels' Bedroom

Doctors' Surgery

Conference Room

Goebbels' Workroom

Bormann's Workroom

Telephone Switchboard

...unge

Main Entrance, ...chen, Dining Area

Generators and Air-Purification Equipment

Inside his multichambered bunker, Hitler was protected by tons of earth and concrete from British and American bombs, Russian artillery and the reality of impending defeat. After one visit, the dismayed General Gotthard Heinrici called the military conference room in the bunker "Cloud-Cuckoo-Land."

Combat units were briefed on the defenses and enemy tactics they would have to deal with; toward the middle of April they began acquiring practical experience during battalion-strength reconnaissance missions conducted west of the Oder, expeditions that usually led to fierce fights with the defending German forces. Zhukov used these forays to expand his bridgehead north and south of the town of Küstrin to a belt of marshy land as much as 10 miles deep; he needed the room for all the forces and matériel that had to be ready on the west bank of the Oder for his first great lunge forward on April 16.

By the end of the two weeks of intense preparation, the Soviet forces along the Oder-Neisse line had substantially increased their huge advantages over the three German armies facing them. Zhukov had 77 rifle divisions and seven armored corps to the German Ninth Army's 14 infantry and panzer divisions; 3,155 tanks and self-propelled guns to the Ninth's 512; 16,934 guns and mortars (the Russians counted heavy mortars as artillery) to about 700 guns for the Ninth. Rokossovsky had 33 rifle divisions and four armored corps to the Third Panzer Army's 11 assorted divisions; 951 tanks and self-propelled guns to 242; 6,642 guns and mortars to 600-odd artillery pieces. Konev boasted a superiority over the Fourth Panzer Army of between three and five to one in men, tanks and guns.

The Russians' machines were of good quality. Though Soviet armor was crudely finished and usually unpainted, the 52-ton Stalin heavy tanks, T-34 medium tanks and self-propelled, long-range SU 122mm guns were the equal of anything in the Germans' worn and depleted arsenal. Together, the three Soviet army groups had nearly 100,000 trucks, virtually all American, for bringing up replacement troops; some Soviet troops were airlifted. In aircraft, the Luftwaffe Messerschmitts and Focke-Wulfs were hamstrung by fuel shortages and had lost their technical edge to new and improved Soviet fighter planes, notably the Yak-9 and the La-7. The Luftwaffe aces who once had run up 200 kills and more were now dead or had been promoted to ground commands, and their half-trained successors would be overwhelmed by the three Soviet air armies that were supporting the ground forces.

The Germans, their manpower depleted and their factories stilled, could not muster anything like a comprehensive counter to the Soviet build-up. Hitler's misjudgment of Soviet plans and his mismanagement of available manpower and matériel had further crippled his last-ditch stand.

In the three months before the Berlin offensive, the Führer could have assembled several hundred thousand more troops to defend the Oder-Neisse line—or any German border—if he had agreed with his generals' advice to evacuate territories, such as Norway and northern Italy, that could not be held against an Allied onslaught in any case. But to Hitler, any retreat was anathema. His insistence on defending the Baltic region against Rokossovsky, instead of pulling his armies there back across the Oder, cost him tens of thousands of men killed or taken prisoner. In a pointless attempt to recapture Budapest, taken by the Russians on February 12, 1945, Hitler sent the Sixth SS Panzer Army from the Western Front to Hungary's Lake Balaton area, where its four divisions were bled copiously during vain attacks on huge Soviet forces.

Then, having done nothing to strengthen the Oder-Neisse defenses, Hitler actually began taking men from them. On April 2 and 3, he transferred a panzer division and a panzer grenadier division to Army Group South in order to defend Vienna—too late. Earlier, toward the end of March, he had sent a panzer division to Army Group Center for the purpose of defending Prague from a suspected Soviet attack—too early.

The commander of Army Group Center was pleased but not surprised by Hitler's gift of panzers, and he was delighted but not overwhelmed by his promotion from general to field marshal during his visit to Berlin the same day. His name was Ferdinand Schörner, he was a well-known veteran of the Eastern Front, and he stood confident in the knowledge that he was just the sort of soldier his Führer admired—a tall, tough, vociferously Nazi officer who knew how to drive his soldiers hard.

Many considered Schörner an untalented brute. A much-put-upon staff officer wrote that the field marshal "spread fear and alarm by his blustering and stern appearance, no matter where he turned up. Details in the sphere of command did not interest him." A somewhat friendlier general gave Schörner decent marks for practical tactics—others gave him credit for taking good care of his men and for personal courage—but conceded that working with the man was a trial.

Whatever Schörner's merits as a fighter and tactician or as a thinker and strategist, he only compounded Hitler's mistakes. While Konev was shifting his strength north, Schörner, instead of using the transferred panzer division to shore up his weak Fourth Panzer Army opposite the Soviet units along the Neisse, sent the division 50 miles to the southeast. There, the panzers were in a superb position to block any Soviet move toward Prague, but they were well outside the area that would soon become Konev's immediate attack zone.

The three armored divisions that Hitler had sent south came from the skimpy reserve of General Gotthard Heinrici of Army Group Vistula, on Schörner's left flank opposite Zhukov. Not surprisingly, Heinrici was just the sort of soldier that Hitler intensely disliked. He sprang from a family of military aristocrats—a class Hitler hated for leading Germany to defeat in World War I—and he had spent 40 of his 58 years in the Army, serving with solid professionalism but in almost impenetrable obscurity. He was short and unobtrusive, taciturn but uncomfortably blunt when he spoke, and—worst of all from the Nazis' standpoint—he attended church regularly in spite of warnings that conventional religious practices, long discouraged by the Nazis, were intolerable in an officer of his rank.

To his own chagrin, Heinrici's best battles had all been defensive or rearguard fights. Most memorable was his work as commander of the Fourth Army in front of Moscow in the terrible winter of 1941-1942. His soldiers, equipped only for a quick summer campaign, froze to death by the hundreds, but Heinrici managed to hold his army together through dint of leadership. And in fighting on the long retreat of 1943 following the German defeat at Stalingrad, his soldiers held their ground well, knowing that Heinrici would never throw away their lives uselessly, as Hitler often demanded. His men respectfully referred to him as "our tough little bastard."

Heinrici's retreat with the Army had been interrupted at Smolensk in 1943. He was accused by Reich Marshal Hermann Göring of criminally failing to follow an all-embracing scorched-earth policy that had been ordered by Hitler; in particular he was charged with leaving the landmark Smolensk Cathedral standing—the implication being that he had disobeyed orders to destroy it because of his religious scruples. Heinrici escaped a court-martial, but he was declared to be in poor health and was dispatched to a nursing home in Czechoslovakia.

Eight months passed before Heinrici was recalled to duty,

as commander of the First Panzer Army in Hungary. Then in March 1945, the latest of Hitler's Army Chiefs of Staff, General Heinz Guderian of panzer fame, demanded Heinrici's services as commander of Army Group Vistula.

Like many generals before him, Heinrici quickly learned that the world of the *Führerbunker* was strangely unreal. In a bizarre early April meeting, Heinrici appealed to Hitler to replace the panzer divisions he had taken away from Army Group Vistula. Immediately Hitler approved in principle, and the commanders in chief of his various services began vying to impress Hitler with their offers of men. Heinrici was astonished to realize that each commander in chief, like a feudal lord, possessed untapped reserves of a size unknown even to Hitler and to his household generals of the OKW (Armed Forces High Command), Field Marshal Wilhelm Keitel, OKW chief, and operations chief Jodl.

"My Führer," said Göring, "I place at your disposal 100,000 men of the Luftwaffe. They will be at the Oder front within a few days."

"My Führer," said Himmler in his high-pitched voice, "the SS furnishes 25,000 fighters for the Oder front."

Grand Admiral Karl Dönitz made a modest donation: "My Führer, the Navy is in a position to send another 12,000 men to the Oder. They will be on their way within a day or two."

"There you are," Hitler announced to Heinrici. "That's 12 divisions."

Fighting for self-control, Heinrici ventured to say that those men had no training in ground warfare and would be slaughtered. Göring quickly interpreted the remark as a slur on his men's fighting qualities, and Hitler declared that the transferred troops should be placed in rear areas where they could learn gradually by experience as reserves, becoming splendid soldiers in due time—time, of course, that was not available to Heinrici.

Of the 137,000 men Hitler had promised to Heinrici, about 35,000 appeared within three days after the *Führerbunker* meeting, arriving at the headquarters of Army Group Vistula near Prenzlau, 60 miles northeast of Berlin. The majority had been civilians until recently, and were either very young or nearing old age. Few of them had any training. Not many had weapons or uniforms; a couple of men who had apparently been shanghaied from a formal party wore tuxedos. Heinrici sent a message to the *Führerbunker* saying that the men could do useful service only in pick-and-shovel gangs; he was told to stop complaining and arm them. By conducting a thorough canvass, Heinrici managed to collect 1,000 rifles of various ages and calibers, among them some antiquated models for which ammunition was nearly impossible to obtain.

Heinrici and the commanders of his two armies—Lieut. General Hasso von Manteuffel of the Third Panzer Army and Lieut. General Theodor Busse of the Ninth Army—had to make do with what little equipment Heinrici managed to find or requisition. They acquired a number of reconditioned tanks from Berlin repair shops, and with Hitler's permission Heinrici took 88mm guns from the Berlin antiaircraft defenses, where they had done no great good, and distributed them as antitank weapons along his main line—the second of three tiers of defense that he had set up several miles behind his front line.

Heinrici was called in on *Führerbunker* discussions of the close-in defense of Berlin, for which his army group was to be given oversight on April 15. The idea of fighting inside the city was repugnant to him and to most commanders. The only slight chance of avoiding defeat depended on holding the enemy along the line of the Spree River, whereas costly street fighting could delay the end by just a few days at the most.

All the same, the Führer wanted no one to think that Berlin would not be defended block by block. On March 9, Hitler dashed off a directive, *The Basic Order for the Preparations to Defend the Capital,* which was sent out under the signature of the commandant of Berlin, Major General Hellmuth Reymann. The order decreed that the battle for Berlin was to be fought with "fanaticism, imagination, every means of deception, cunning and deceit" from "every block, every house, every store, every hedge, every shell hole." What counted most, naturally, was a "fanatical desire to fight."

Until the last moments, nothing much was done to prepare the capital to withstand a ground attack. Not until March did troops and civilians inside the city bestir themselves and begin digging trenches and erecting roadblocks in streets and parks. This activity gave rise to many versions of a cynical joke. A Berlin resident, watching a work gang build a barricade, remarked that it would take the Russians two hours and five minutes to destroy the roadblock. When asked about the odd length of time, the observer replied that the Russians would spend two hours laughing at the barricade and five minutes tearing it down. In accounts of the battle, however, the Soviet generals did not scoff; they claimed, partly to puff their own feats and partly because the Germans fought so hard, that 400,000 Berliners had toiled on the defenses, probably 10 times more than the actual number.

The Germans sensed that the attack was near. Citizens in the eastern suburbs of Berlin reported hearing gunfire from the Oder as Zhukov's forces ran their battalion-strength patrols on the nights of April 12, 13 and 14. On April 15, Hitler wrote—and Goebbels heavily edited—a prebattle exhortation to the troops on the Eastern Front, to be read aloud by their platoon commanders when the Red Army struck. It was a tired message, repeating yet again the strained rhetoric and the few simple ideas that had been shouted so often before. The Russians were the "Jewish-Bolshevik" foe, who aimed "to reduce Germany to ruins and to exterminate our people." Any soldier who did not do his duty was a "traitor to our people," but "thanks to your resolution and fanaticism," the enemy assault would be stopped, "choked in a bath of blood." The only new thought Hitler added was his closing reference to the death of "the greatest war criminal of all time"—Roosevelt.

Death was in the air. Attorneys were besieged by Berliners wanting to make out their wills. Many Germans planned to commit suicide if the Russians broke into the city, and they sought out government officials, doctors, dentists and laboratory workers to obtain pistols, rat poison and capsules of potassium cyanide. Doctors discussed and disseminated information on the relative merits of various methods of ending one's own life. When Hitler's mistress, Eva Braun, arrived in the *Führerbunker* despite his orders to remain safe in Bavaria, the denizens of the bunker knew instinctively that she had come to share his fate. They thought of her as the "Angel of Death."

A German officer inspects a light machine-gun post west of the Oder River in late March of 1945. Army Group Vistula, assigned to defend the river line, was critically short of weapons—artillery in particular— with which to counter the coming Russian onslaught.

FORTRESS BERLIN

the last weeks of the War, the Führer and Hitler Youth leader Arthur Axmann review teen-age Eastern Front veterans, typical of the units left to defend Berlin.

THE STUBBORN ILLUSION OF A DIEHARD DEFENSE

A Volkssturm member trains with a Panzerfaust; derided by one official as a "primitive weapon," it was most effective in Berlin street fighting.

In the Nazis' glory years, and even in the years of retreat, no one had seriously prepared for an attack on Berlin. Not until March 1945—with the Russians only 50 miles to the east—did a comprehensive defense plan take shape. Hitler designated Berlin a "fortress"—a place to be defended until no one remained alive to fight. The capital was the last of a string of such fortresses, beginning with Stalingrad in 1942.

Propaganda Minister Joseph Goebbels, who also served as gauleiter, or Nazi governor, of the Berlin district, blamed the lack of preparation on the military. As Hitler's representative he instituted weekly meetings of Army commanders to solidify defense steps, but at the same time he undermined the defense plan by basing it on nonexistent pools of fresh troops and supplies. The mostly old men of the *Volkssturm,* or home guard, along with women and children, were put to work piling up barricades and digging trenches to trap Russian tanks. But military professionals, like the city's commandant, Major General Hellmuth Reymann, saw the preparations as mere illusion.

Reymann calculated that it would take at least 200,000 experienced troops to put up a creditable last stand in Berlin, and most of the men who might have made up such a force were already facing overwhelming Soviet numbers on the Oder-Neisse line. What Reymann had to work with in the city was the Hitler Youth—the last call-up had included 15-year-olds—and *Volkssturm* members, 60,000 of whom had been organized into scratch infantry units by the political officials who controlled them. Many had no uniforms, a third were unarmed, and the rest carried either *Panzerfäuste,* the one-shot grenade launchers, or rifles for which there was frequently no ammunition. In Berlin, no tanks, no fighter planes, and little artillery remained; motor fuel and barbed wire were in critically short supply.

Leaving one of Goebbels' weekly meetings, Reymann remarked to his chief of staff, Colonel Hans Refior, "I only hope that some miracle happens to change our fortunes, or that the War ends before Berlin comes under siege. Otherwise, God help the Berliners!"

Joseph Goebbels discusses Berlin's defense. From Berlin Army commandant Hellmuth Reymann, he said, "no extraordinary output can be expected."

In the heart of Berlin, construction workers set girders as tank traps (left) in the shadow of the Brandenburg Gate, traditional symbol of German military glory. At right, workers dig an underground bunker in the suburbs as part of Berlin's outer defense perimeter.

DOWNTOWN BARRICADES, SUBURBAN TRENCHES

All over Berlin, Joseph Goebbels noted enthusiastically in his diary, everyone was working "feverishly," and "barricades are to be seen mushrooming." Yet even Goebbels allowed that a drive in his car through the city already half-destroyed by Allied bombs "shatters me somewhat."

The hastily developed plan that Goebbels and the Army agreed upon called for a series of fallback positions: first a ring tracing the autobahn that belted the city about 20 miles from its center, reinforced by a second ring, approximately 10 miles out, along the route of Berlin's mass transit elevated railway, known as the *S-Bahn*. For the last stand, planners drew a small inner ring, encompassing most of the main government buildings and the park called the Tiergarten. They designated this area the "Citadel."

Throughout the defense system, people were to be deployed at "fortified places." Overturned trucks, streetcars and railway cars weighted with bomb debris were to link jerry-built concrete walls, the shells of bombed buildings, trenches, and the natural barriers provided by Berlin's rivers, lakes and canals.

The fortification effort temporarily lent heart to the defenders, but when the men and artillery needed to hold the strong points failed to materialize, the task of defending the city assumed an aura of gloom. An Army report that was circulated internally during the first week of April declared: "The population has given up all hope. Press and propaganda efforts meet ever-stronger mistrust. 'Where are the new weapons, the new air defenses?' they ask. Morale is at zero."

der close supervision, Berlin's defenders, including men once considered unfit to fight, pile scrap and rubble into barricades for a last line of defense.

A woman answering Hitler's eleventh-hour plea to join the fight is shown how to handle a Panzerfaust. No formal combat units of women were ever form

TRAINING STOPGAP SOLDIERS

Following the example of the Russians in defense of Moscow, Hitler decided that in addition to old men and children, women would fight in the ultimate battle. "The Führer is of the opinion," Goebbels noted, "that, provided they volunteer, they will undoubtedly fight fanatically. They should be placed in the second line; then the men in the front line will lose all desire to withdraw."

As for the arms that the women—and men—had to fight with, there was no miracle in sight, despite a year of talk about secret weapons that would dramatically change the course of the War. One-man submarines had still been under development when the Normandy invasion came, and a scheme to create manned rockets that would destroy Allied bombers by ramming them never got out of the laboratory. The only device available to Berliners in any quantity as the final attack drew near was the *Panzerfaust,* which fired only one shot and was then discarded.

"It's madness!" exclaimed one professional officer. "How are these people supposed to fight after they fire their single round? What does Headquarters expect them to do—use their empty weapons like billy clubs?"

While his comrades in the background wait their turns, a uniformed Hitler Youth learns how to fire the throwaway antitank weapon.

TOO LATE, A SCRAMBLE TO GET READY

Constructing fortifications for Berlin was child's play compared to the nightmare of organizing the few weapons that were available. By this stage of the War, General Reymann later recalled, the weapons were an eclectic assortment "from every country that Germany had fought with or against. Besides our own issues, there were Italian, Russian, French, Czechoslovakian, Belgian, Dutch, Norwegian and English guns."

Finding ammunition to match some 15 different types of rifles and 10 different types of machine guns was often impossible. Although certain Belgian rifles could use Czech bullets, for example, the Czech pieces would not take the Belgian rounds.

Compounding the shortages of fighting men and serviceable arms was a disappointing turnout of civilian labor volunteers. The defense plan was based on the assumption that 100,000 workers would be available to build the fortifications, but only 30,000 of the traditionally skeptical Berliners answered the call.

Earlier in the War elaborate fortifications—the Atlantic Wall along the French coast, the Gustav Line in Italy and the Siegfried Line along the western border of Germany—had effectively slowed, if not stopped, the Germans' enemies. The Berlin bulwarks bore little resemblance to these. General Max Pemsel, who had been in Normandy on D-Day, inspected Berlin's preparations and pronounced them "utterly futile, ridiculous!"

Odd lots of small arms are unloaded at a Berlin railroad station. The few defenders who were issued rifles received an average of only five bullets ea

In a German propaganda picture, civilians, many of them young women, smile as they hike off to dig antitank ditches.

A trench line intended to halt Soviet tanks zigzags across farmland along the approaches to Berlin.

Defenders of Berlin, their Panzerfäuste at the ready, await the approach of Soviet tanks. When the picture was made, Hitler was still boasting that the

Russians would "bleed to death" trying to take the German capital. The photograph was heavily touched up for publication in German newspapers.

THE RUSSIAN ONSLAUGHT

ockets from Red Army launchers—nicknamed Stalin Organs by German troops—stab through the predawn darkness to open the final offensive on Berlin.

ATTACKING THE LAIR OF THE "FASCIST BEAST"

The night of April 15 seemed endless to the 1.3 million veteran soldiers of the Red Army waiting along the rivers Oder and Neisse in eastern Germany. They were poised for the great assault on Berlin—the "final hour of vengeance," as Marshal Georgy K. Zhukov called it. It was the chance to pay back the hated Germans for the rape of the Russian homeland, for Leningrad and Stalingrad, for the deaths of loved ones and friends. A slogan scrawled on one of the waiting tanks read "50 kilometers to the lair of the fascist beast." Victory was close enough to taste.

In a command bunker overlooking the Küstrin bridgehead at the center of the Oder line, Zhukov and his aides sipped strong, hot tea as they watched the crawling hands of the clock. Farther south, along the Neisse, where Marshal Ivan S. Konev was in command, the waiting was equally tense. Before dawn on the 16th, the onslaught began.

Along the Oder signal flares burst high over the river; instantly the foggy darkness was split by the thundering flashes of thousands upon thousands of heavy guns. For more than half an hour the cannonade continued; then the Russians hurled themselves into the attack. On the Neisse, the crossing proceeded under a dense smoke screen.

The Germans were waiting in strength. Anticipating the bombardment, the German commander on the Oder, General Gotthard Heinrici, during the night had pulled his men out of front-line positions to Seelow Heights, a formidable crescent of bluffs set back several miles from the river's west bank. (When one of his officers protested the withdrawal, Heinrici responded: "You don't put your head under a trip hammer, do you? You pull it back in time.") Now, with the Russians floundering across the marshy terrain below the highlands, he hit them with everything he had.

As the attack became mired in the mud, Zhukov angrily ordered his two tank armies into action ahead of schedule to force the issue by sheer weight of arms—but he succeeded only in creating a gigantic traffic jam. By the end of the first day—and the second—his hammer blow at Germany's heart was still bogged down in the Oder swamps.

Screened by a canopy of camouflage netting, a Soviet 203mm howitzer mounted on a tracked carriage blasts away at a target west of the Oder River

53

The crews of 76mm self-propelled guns—the lightest such Soviet weapon—wait in their open compartments for the order to move out against the Ger-

ARMIES PRIMED TO STORM THE SKY ITSELF"

While Zhukov's forces fell upon Seelow Heights, the First Ukrainian Army Group to the south, led by Konev, was making more impressive progress. Aided by a 40-minute artillery bombardment, and by a smoke screen laid by fighter planes racing up the Neisse River valley, Konev's troops quickly seized bridgeheads on the western bank of the river; soon Soviet tanks rumbled through pine forests set ablaze by the shelling, smashing fierce counterattacks along an 18-mile front.

While Stormovik attack bombers blasted targets ahead of the ground forces, the Third and Fourth Guards Tank Armies raced toward Lübben, terminal point of the boundary between Konev's and Zhukov's zones of operation. Konev knew that the one who reached Lübben first would be in a commanding position to move on Berlin, and he was determined to beat his rival there—his determination reinforced by the knowledge that his men were "in very high fighting spirits," and that most of them had three years of battle experience under their belts. "With such soldiers," he later observed, "we could have stormed the sky itself."

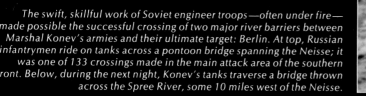

The swift, skillful work of Soviet engineer troops—often under fire—made possible the successful crossing of two major river barriers between Marshal Konev's armies and their ultimate target: Berlin. At top, Russian infantrymen ride on tanks across a pontoon bridge spanning the Neisse; it was one of 133 crossings made in the main attack area of the southern front. Below, during the next night, Konev's tanks traverse a bridge thrown across the Spree River, some 10 miles west of the Neisse.

CLOSING THE PINCERS AROUND THE CAPITAL

Marshal Konev arrived at the Spree River early on April 17. He stood on the riverbank admiring the crossing his tank commanders were conducting, and reviewing their plans for advancing the 25 miles to Lübben. At first the Germans had counterattacked fiercely, but then their resistance had faded. Now if he could reach Lübben quickly, Konev believed that Stalin would give him marching orders for Berlin.

That night at his new headquarters, a baronial castle at Cottbus on the bank of the Spree, Konev received more good news: His tank spearhead was advancing westward against little opposition. He put in a direct call to Josef Stalin in Moscow to report his successes. Against the background sounds of distant artillery, Konev heard the order he had been hoping for: Drive for Berlin.

Maneuvering to envelop Berlin, a Russian column moves along a wooded road southwest of the capital toward Potsdam, where it would converge with encircling armies from the north.

Infantrymen of Konev's army group make their way through a dusty field. Ahead, a radio man in the German command center at Zossen, 20 miles south of Berlin, was signing off: "Ivan is almost at the door."

attempted to achieve pinpoint fire control, the Russians relied on the massing of artillery to obliterate their targets with heavy concentrations of shells.

2

THE BLOW DELIVERED

In the early-morning darkness of April 16, the 11 armies of Marshal Zhukov's First Belorussian Group and the seven armies of Marshal Konev's First Ukrainian Group braced themselves along the line of the Oder and Neisse Rivers for the start of the Berlin offensive, scheduled for 5 a.m. As the last few Soviet units moved into their assigned attack positions, commanders made final reports on the combat readiness of their outfits.

The troops—more than 1.25 million of them—were not left alone to contemplate their chances. Commissars, political officers of the Communist Party, moved among the men, instructing them on their duty and commending the honorableness of patriotic sacrifice. On orders from Moscow, every man was required to swear an oath on the Soviet flag to fight with special zeal for the motherland, the Communist Party and final victory. Many soldiers joined the party on the spot in order to assure themselves of a benefit that was not provided by the Army: Their relatives would be notified if they were killed in action.

On the other side of the Oder-Neisse line *(map, page 64)*, two German armies of approximately 400,000 men waited tensely for the onslaught. The attack would come around dawn—such was the prediction of General Heinrici, the commander of Army Group Vistula, comprising the German Ninth Army and the Third Panzer Army. Heinrici, a grim, gray little man, exuded competence to all but those who admired strutters and table-thumpers. He had already saved the lives of hundreds and perhaps thousands of German soldiers by ordering his forward units to draw back before their positions were devastated by the opening Soviet artillery bombardment.

But Heinrici's operations officer, Colonel Hans-Georg Eismann, thought that nothing would help much at this stage of the conflict. "The Army Group," he wrote, "could be compared to a rabbit, watching spellbound for a snake to strike and devour it." The Fourth Panzer Army, stationed 75 miles southeast of Berlin under Field Marshal Schörner's Army Group Center, was similarly vulnerable.

The Russians could hardly lose the battle for Berlin, so greatly did they outnumber the Germans in men (5 to 1), guns (15 to 1), tanks (5 to 1) and planes (3 to 1). Yet the ambitions, rivalries, blunders and misconceptions of the leaders on both sides of the conflict would make for an unpredictable battle—and a bloody one, fueled by mutual hate and marked by atrocities.

The holding of misconceptions began at the top. Because Stalin believed, wrongly, that the Western Allies would try to beat him into Berlin, his offensive was planned for maximum speed. The three army groups involved—Marshal Rokossovsky's Second Belorussian Army Group, ranged on the northern sector of the front, was to become the third unit to join the battle, on April 20—were expected to crush all opposition and occupy all territory from the Oder-Neisse line west to the Elbe-Mulde line in 12 days, certainly in no more than 15 days. The unwarranted haste of this schedule, met by whipping and driving fiercely competitive front commanders, would make for great waste. The Red Army would match its war-long casualty rate of four Soviet soldiers killed for one German fatality, even though the Wehrmacht was now only a tattered travesty of its blitzkrieg-era legions.

Hitler, who never lacked for misplaced optimism, clung to his favorite latter-day delusion that, if he held out a little longer, the Russians and the British and Americans would soon start cutting each other's throats. Increasingly Hitler lived in his fevered imagination, deploying nonexistent divisions and sending real units to die for no discernible reason. Far from deploring German casualties, he wanted more of them, in order to punish Germany for failing him, and he despised the survivors. "Only those who are inferior will remain after the struggle," Hitler said, "for the good have already been killed."

The fight for Berlin was to be Hitler's greatest battle, immense, gory and pointless, killing half a million people and strewing wreckage over one quarter of Germany.

To launch his 750,000-man, 1,800-tank offensive, Marshal Zhukov made his way through the predawn fog and dark to the command post of the Eighth Guards Army. Located on the west bank of the Oder River in a bridgehead named for Küstrin, the nearest sizable town, the command post was an elaborate hillside dugout not far from the village of Reitwein. The post was the marshaling area for Zhukov's main attack, and overlooked the shortest route to Berlin. Just north of the post, the Küstrin-Berlin highway crossed the broad Oder valley, half-flooded by spring rain and scored with overflowing canals and streams.

At the village of Seelow across the valley, the highway climbed up to Seelow Heights, a 28-mile line of fortified hills and bluffs. The heights were the strongest sector of the 90-mile-long German defense system facing Zhukov, but Zhukov planned to take the whole Seelow line on the first day of the offensive, then penetrate the eastern boundaries of Berlin with the left wing of his force and envelop the city from the north with his right wing in the days following. To initiate the plan, Zhukov had packed the bridgehead with two tank armies and three mixed (or field) armies—mostly infantry integrated with tank teams. In addition to the Eighth Guards Army, the force comprised the First and Second Guards Tank Armies, and the Third and Fifth Shock Armies.

The commanding officer of the Eighth Guards Army, the outspoken General Vasily I. Chuikov, was annoyed by the unexpected visit of his celebrated superior. He considered Zhukov arrogant and meddlesome, and Chuikov wanted no interference with his own decisions and orders. He and his army had come too far, he believed, to be manipulated for the political advantage of Zhukov, who sought a position at or close to Stalin's right hand.

Chuikov had begun his career as a Soviet general by commanding a previously undistinguished army, the Sixty-second; under his leadership the army had won its honorific Guards designation by holding the Germans at bay for five months in the ruins of Stalingrad. Later, the army had taken part in the liberation of Odessa and then had led Zhukov's forces all the way across Belorussia, also known as White Russia, and through Poland to this soggy spot. Now his army had its last chance for glory, and Chuikov wanted to be left alone to execute his key assignments: to take Seelow village, to punch a hole in the German line for the First Guards Tank Army behind him, and finally to break down the eastern door to Berlin.

At exactly 5 a.m., Zhukov gave the signal to fire the flares that started the artillery bombardment. Nearly 17,000 field guns, mortars and Katyushas—multiple rocket launchers, called "Stalin Organs" by the Germans—let loose with a volley heard as far away as eastern Berlin, about 40 miles distant. The thunder of the close-set guns was literally ear-splitting; some of the gunners began bleeding from the ears, although their ears were stuffed with wadding to reduce the effect of the blasts.

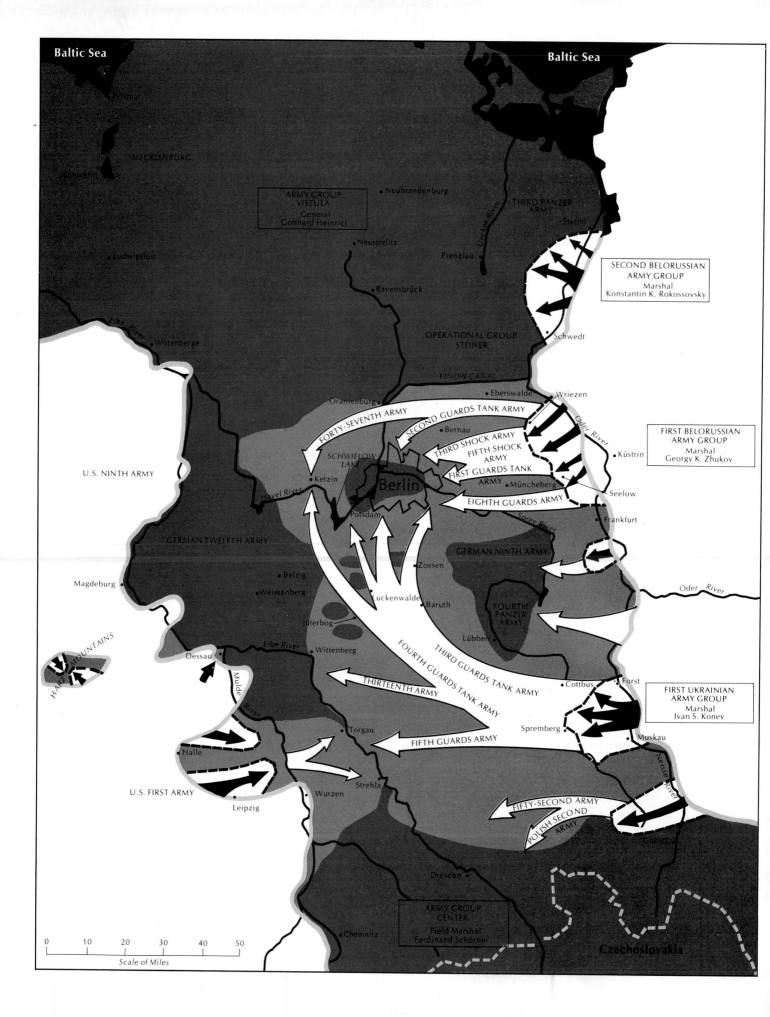

Baltic Sea

Baltic Sea

Wismar

MECKLENBURG

Schwerin

Neubrandenburg

ARMY GROUP
VISTULA
General
Gotthard Heinrici

THIRD PANZER
ARMY

Stettin

Ludwigslust

Neustrelitz

Prenzlau

SECOND BELORUSSIAN
ARMY GROUP
Marshal
Konstantin K. Rokossovsky

Ravensbrück

Elbe River

Wittenberge

OPERATIONAL GROUP
STEINER

Schwedt

FINOW CANAL

Eberswalde

Wriezen

Oranienburg

FORTY-SEVENTH ARMY

SECOND GUARDS TANK ARMY

Bernau

Oder River

U.S. NINTH ARMY

SCHWIELOW
LAKE

THIRD SHOCK ARMY
FIFTH SHOCK
ARMY

Küstrin

FIRST BELORUSSIAN
ARMY GROUP
Marshal
Georgy K. Zhukov

Ketzin

Berlin

FIRST GUARDS TANK
ARMY

Müncheberg

Seelow

Havel River

Potsdam

EIGHTH GUARDS ARMY

Frankfurt

GERMAN TWELFTH ARMY

Spree River

Belzig

Zossen

GERMAN NINTH ARMY

Magdeburg

Weissenberg

Luckenwalde

Baruth

Oder River

FOURTH
PANZER
ARMY

Jüterbog

Lübben

HARZ MOUNTAINS

Dessau

Elbe River

Wittenberg

THIRD GUARDS TANK ARMY

FOURTH GUARDS TANK ARMY

Cottbus

Forst

FIRST UKRAINIAN
ARMY GROUP
Marshal
Ivan S. Konev

Mulde River

THIRTEENTH ARMY

Torgau

Spremberg

Muskau

Halle

FIFTH GUARDS ARMY

Neisse River

U.S. FIRST ARMY

Wurzen

Strehla

Leipzig

FIFTY-SECOND ARMY

POLISH SECOND
ARMY

Görlitz

Dresden

ARMY GROUP
CENTER
Field Marshal
Ferdinand Schörner

Chemnitz

Czechoslovakia

0   10   20   30   40   50
Scale of Miles

For half an hour the bombardment continued, plowing up trenchworks, obliterating whole villages, and raising gushers of earth and rubble along Seelow Heights. And this was just a small part of the day's gunnery; the artillerymen of the two fronts would fire 1,236,000 shells that day and shower the enemy with 98,000 tons of hot steel.

At 5:30 a.m. the three mixed armies—the Eighth Guards Army, and the Third and Fifth Shock Armies—lurched forward side by side, and Zhukov introduced a fancy new tactic. He had collected 140 powerful antiaircraft searchlights, and now he had them switched on, along with the lights of hundreds of trucks and tanks. Zhukov's purpose was twofold: to light the way for his troops and to blind the enemy gunners across the valley. He later wrote with innocent enthusiasm of turning night to day with the intensity of a billion candle power. Actually, his searchlights were more hindrance than help: The beams bounced off clouds of dust and gunsmoke and disoriented his own units. As Chuikov saw it, the net effect was as much of a handicap as full darkness would have been. "On many sectors," he later wrote, "the troops came to a halt in front of streams and canals, waiting for the light of dawn to show them more clearly the obstacle they had to overcome."

Slowly, suspiciously, the infantrymen passed the enemy's vacated front lines. The absence of dead Germans in areas that had been heavily shelled suggested to the troops that they were moving into a trap, and the impression was reinforced by the silence of the enemy artillery. The Soviets kept moving forward, their tanks following the roads to avoid the swampy flats.

All along Seelow Heights, in front of the hills and on them, the Germans waited patiently, conserving their scant supplies of ammunition. The line of hills—indeed the entire 35-mile center of the eastern defense system—was held by the strongest of the three German armies, General Busse's Ninth Army. For all its relative strength, however, the defense had several weak links, and one of them was the 9th Parachute Division, formerly an elite outfit but now composed largely of odds and ends from the Luftwaffe—unemployed aircraft ground crewmen with planeless pilots for officers. The division, half-trained and untested, had properly been relegated at the outset to secondary defense. However, when Heinrici had evacuated his forward positions to

keep his armies beyond the reach of Soviet artillery bombardment, the 9th Parachute Division had found itself manning the front line, directly in the path of Marshal Chuikov's crack 67th Division.

The young Germans, entrenched in the valley in the vicinity of Seelow village, had shown early indications of soldierly skill; they had dug in deep, and had weathered the opening bombardment well. And they were keyed up to fight when, in the colorless first light, they made out waves of infantry sweeping toward them and columns of tanks approaching on the roads.

When the Russians had come well within range, the German artillery in the hills commenced firing. Dozens of Soviet tanks exploded, and the infantrymen riding their decks were tossed in the air like broken matchsticks. The 9th Parachute Division opened up with machine guns, rifles and submachine guns, mowing down the Russians and knocking out additional tanks with grenades fired from *Panzerfäuste*. For a while, a continuous stream of Soviet riflemen trotted forward, only to be shot down by the Germans. But then the advance stopped.

The Germans, surprised and elated by their success, savored their new status as veterans. Though they knew the Russian advance would start again, they no longer worried—they felt like world-beaters.

At about the same time that the men of the 9th Parachute Division were winning their brief clash, Marshal Konev began his opening bombardment on a front that stretched 243 miles south from the juncture of the Neisse and the Oder. Using seven armies—500,000 men and 1,400 tanks—Konev planned two assaults. The first, spearheaded by the mixed armor and infantry of the Fifth Guards Army and the Thirteenth Army, with the Third and Fourth Guards Tank Armies following up, would head for the Elbe and a linkup with the Americans; as a secondary mission, the tank armies were to support Zhukov south of Berlin. The second assault, with the Fifty-second Army and the Polish Second Army, would veer toward Dresden. (This Polish unit had been recruited from among prisoners of war whom the Russians had been holding since they divided up Poland with Germany in 1939, and from citizens in areas of Poland that the Russians had reoccupied in 1944.)

The assault by the Soviets on Berlin unfolded in two phases. The first, indicated by black arrows, lasted from April 16 until April 18, and coincided with American mop-up operations against forces in Leipzig, Dessau and the Harz Mountains. The second phase of the Russian attack, which occurred between April 18 and April 25, involved encirclement as well as penetration of the city (white arrows). (Dark red enclaves are large concentrations of German troops.) Russian and American troops eventually met on the Elbe River in the west.

Unlike Zhukov's force, the First Ukrainian Group had no bridgehead, and the Neisse was a swift, broad river—in some places 150 yards wide—across which Konev had to push his assault. For the dangerous crossing of the Neisse, Konev had decided to wait for daylight. To deceive the enemy as to his main attack area, Konev had ordered his supporting aircraft to lay a thick smoke screen over the full length of the Neisse valley. Shellbursts and bombs started fires in the dense pine forest that grew on the west bank, and the fire added to the dense smoke from the shelling.

After 40 minutes of bombardment, Konev's engineers began crossing the Neisse. Using motor launches, teams towed prefabricated assault bridges to the far side. As soon as each bridge was made fast, infantrymen raced across and attacked enemy troops along the river. The crossings fo-

cused on two targets: the 18-mile sector between Forst and Muskau, where the teams carved out 133 individual bridgeheads for the main assault, and the area about 30 miles to the south around Görlitz, the launching site for the secondary thrust aimed at Dresden.

Tanks that were too heavy for the early assault bridges were ferried across on pontoons; in some places, 85mm antitank guns were dragged through the water on the ends of cables. Armed with these weapons, and with a heavy barrage rolling ahead of them, attack units moved steadily westward from the river. By 8:35 a.m. the engineers had built more than 20 bridges strong enough to bear the 30- and 60-ton loads of armored vehicles, and the two tank armies began their day-long crossing operation.

The Fourth Panzer Army, which faced Konev on the Ger-

STALIN'S FIGHTING GENERALS

Marshal Georgy K. Zhukov
Stalin awarded to Zhukov, his favorite general, the choice assignment in the battle for Berlin, placing Zhukov's First Belorussian Army Group on the closest approach to the German capital. A one-time cavalryman, Zhukov pursued an aggressive strategy that was a major factor in smashing Hitler's invasion of Russia, and helped earn him the title Savior of Moscow. Zhukov in fact was widely regarded as the heir apparent of Premier Stalin.

Marshal Ivan S. Konev
Called "the general who never retreated" because he gave less ground than others early in the 1941 German invasion, Konev was appointed to lead the First Ukrainian Army Group on Zhukov's south flank—an opportunity, as Konev saw it, to beat Zhukov to Berlin. Exacting, abstemious and cultured—even in the field he carried such classics as Tolstoy's *War and Peace* and Livy's *History of Rome*—Konev was considerate of his officers and men.

Marshal Konstantin K. Rokossovs
The protection of Zhukov's north was assigned to the Second Belsian Army Group, led by the maveRokossovsky. Rokossovsky hated ing for orders and argued—even Stalin—over tactics. His flashing n teeth replaced those lost to NKVE terrogators when Stalin purged the Army in 1937-1938. Reinstated in to vindicate his unorthodoxy, he ceived honors second only to Zhuk for his part in the battle of Moscow

man side of the Neisse, was stunned by the assault; German intelligence analyses had projected a Soviet attack farther south, in the direction of Prague. The Fourth Panzer Army forces and its reserve units soon found themselves encountering Russians far to the west of the Neisse and all along their flanks. In some places the defenders counterattacked; elsewhere they formed islands of resistance that seemed to stem the enemy's westward thrust.

The Fourth Panzer Army's first combat report to Army Group Center said: "Our own lines maintained their position in general." However, as the report was being transmitted, Konev's northern thrust had ripped an 18-mile hole in the German defenses and was aproaching Spremberg, a town on the Spree River 75 miles southeast of Berlin—to the rear of the main German defense line.

From the Seelow Heights area just to the north of the Fourth Panzer Army, the Ninth Army's first report on the fighting was also encouraging but it had an ominous overtone. "The attack has been repulsed; fighting for some positions is still going on. Losses are very heavy." From the German point of view, the situation could have been a lot worse. Though Soviet units had made penetrations of a few miles, they had mostly conquered undefended swamps.

Zhukov was furious. In what Lieut. General Nikolai Popel, a member of the marshal's staff, called "a stream of extremely forceful expressions," the marshal dressed down Chuikov for failing to take Seelow. Like Popel, Chuikov was well acquainted with Zhukov's temper, and he tried to calm him, saying, "Comrade Marshal, the offensive will surely succeed." But the marshal was not mollified.

...eral Vasily I. Chuikov
...spearhead of Zhukov's First Be-
...ssian Army Group was the Eighth
...rds Army, commanded by Chui-
..., whose performance at Stalingrad
...ked it as early as 1943 for the honor
...torming Berlin. The Eighth Guards
...major attacks "like a boxer," Chui-
...boasted, "called on to go from one
...to another." Chuikov was known
...soldier's soldier, never far from the
...t, and was famed for his use of ar-
...in swift, overwhelming attacks.

General Pavel S. Rybalko
Commander of the Third Guards Tank Army under Konev, Rybalko—a general who rated high among Soviet tank tacticians—led the pivotal drive west of the Spree River in the race to Berlin. Konev prized Rybalko's attention to the details of logistics and vehicle maintenance that are so crucial in tank warfare, and respected his ability to discern the decisive moments in battle. Rybalko, said Konev, "knew exactly when and where he should be."

General Dmitri D. Lelyushenko
Commander of the Fourth Guards Tank Army, Lelyushenko led Konev's second armored spearhead toward Berlin. Only 41 in 1945, he was a robust, enthusiastic soldier whose forthright manner had charmed the former American Presidential candidate Wendell Willkie during his 1942 visit to Russia. Asked how much of the 2,000-mile Russian front was Konev's to defend, the general replied, "Sir, I am not defending. I am attacking."

By 2 p.m. on April 16, with his mixed armies clearly falling behind schedule in their mission to punch holes in the German line, Zhukov decided not to wait any longer to unleash his two tank armies. He ordered the armor into action—on roads already clogged by the trucks and tanks of the Eighth Guards Army on the left, and the Fifth and Third Shock Armies in the center and on the right.

The two tank armies rolled forward—into utter confusion. That part of the Oder valley facing Seelow Heights was soon a shambles of stalled vehicles and milling soldiers. Only the forward military units were beyond the traffic jams and capable of fighting, and these the Germans were able to hold off.

Indeed, General Busse felt he could hold the heights indefinitely if reinforced. From Ninth Army headquarters he reported late in the day: "The front is still holding; deeper enemy incursions have been contained. Send us soldiers; send us ammunition." His optimism and sense of accomplishment were shared by many officers. General Heinrici, who spent the day traveling from headquarters to headquarters and visiting field positions, was more circumspect. Congratulated at one command post for the Ninth Army's gallant stand, he replied, "I have learned never to praise the day until twilight comes."

By dusk the general's caution seemed justified. The newly blooded 9th Parachute Division was on the verge of being overrun. After their early action, the young soldiers had been moved back, up the hills flanking the highway, and there, in newly dug foxholes and trenches and machine-gun pits, they repelled one heavy attack after another for four hours. Nevertheless, the Russians established themselves north of Seelow village and around the Seelow railroad station; when the fighting stopped for the night, 30 per cent of the men of the 9th Parachute Division were dead.

That night, Zhukov suffered through an altogether unpleasant radio-telephone conversation with Stalin. Zhukov had to report his failure to take any of the day's objectives, and word of the successes achieved by Konev west of the Neisse exacerbated Zhukov's humiliation. Stalin reproved Zhukov for committing the First Guards Tank Army in Chuikov's sector, and then asked Zhukov an insulting question: "Do you have any certainty that you will take Seelow Heights tomorrow?"

Zhukov later admitted that he had nearly lost his composure, but he managed to give Stalin the assurance he wanted. Then Stalin needled Zhukov with the suggestion that Konev's tank armies might be shifted north to attack Berlin. Zhukov agreed that the shift was feasible, but proposed an alternate strategy that he hoped would divert Stalin's attention from Konev's force. Stalin cut him short with a flat "Good-by" and hung up.

On the second day of the battle, Germans and Russians acted out their hatred for each other. Russians shot a number of Germans—civilians as well as captured soldiers—in cold blood, and not even strict recent orders prevented an epidemic of rapes in captured towns. Germans, too, committed atrocities. Near the town of Zechin, just east of Seelow Heights, an SS unit captured 16 Russians from one battalion of the Third Shock Army; the SS troops cut off the prisoners' genitals and then slowly strangled the men with piano wire. For this piece of work, the Soviet battalion would soon exact a conspicuous revenge.

As the action developed on April 17, the superiority of Soviet manpower and matériel began to tell along Seelow Heights. Zhukov committed an army that he had held in reserve, the Forty-seventh, and harried the commanders of his stalled armies until they got their outfits moving. He concentrated most of his armor around Seelow village and at the town of Wriezen near the northern end of the heights; in both sectors, the 56th Panzer Corps, a six-division reserve shared by the Ninth Army and the Third Panzer Army, had to send up units on the double to stop a breakthrough. At Seelow, in fact, the highway to Berlin lay wide open for a while after the men of the 9th Parachute Division fled when their artillery ran out of ammunition.

To the Germans, there now seemed to be Russians everywhere. "They keep coming at us in hordes, in wave after wave, with no regard for loss of life," a division commander reported by phone to Ninth Army headquarters. "My men are fighting until they run out of ammunition. Then they are wiped out or completely overrun. How long this can continue I don't know."

Scanning the situation reports, Heinrici knew that he had to counterattack. He was facing local defeat on a front riddled with gaps and was hard put to find reinforcements to plug them. Looking at one of his trouble spots, he saw a way to solve a tactical problem and gain needed manpower at the same time. About 20 miles south of Seelow Heights, at Frankfurt an der Oder, Soviet units of Zhukov's Sixty-ninth Army had crossed the river to the north and the south of the city. Sooner or later the Soviets were bound to cut it off. Frankfurt was garrisoned by a motley force of about 30,000 troops under Colonel Ernst Bieler; if Heinrici could withdraw those men, he would not only save them but also might use them in a counterattack that would let Germany regain the initiative and strengthen its defenses.

Heinrici's idea was sound—but it had one major flaw: Frankfurt had been designated a fortress by the Führer himself. The designation meant that the city had to be defended "to the last man and to the last drop of blood"—a phrase Hitler particularly fancied. Asserting that a last-ditch defense would tie up disproportionately great numbers of enemy soldiers, the Führer had sent tens of thousands of German troops to their deaths in an effort to hold dozens of cities and towns and thousands of acres of terrain. The theory had rarely held up, but Hitler had seldom downgraded the defense status of a designated fortress in order to save the men holding it.

Nevertheless, Heinrici telephoned the *Führerbunker* and asked Hitler to release Bieler's force for a counterattack. Hitler instantly dismissed the request. Holding Frankfurt was extremely important, he said; Heinrici would have to find troops elsewhere.

The point at which Heinrici had wanted to counterattack was to the south, where Konev had now achieved an enormous breakthrough; the First Ukrainian Army Group had shattered the joint between Army Group Vistula and Field Marshal Schörner's Army Group Center in Czechoslovakia. So far, that breakthrough was more dangerous to the Germans than Zhukov's penetrations in the north, because if Konev's tank armies could cross the Spree River they would find only handfuls of defenders between them and Berlin.

Konev, to his regret, was still bound for the Elbe, not Berlin, but he continued to make rapid progress on the 17th of April. By morning, both of his tank armies had completed their crossing of the Neisse and were moving to the Spree along with his spearhead armies, the Thirteenth and the Fifth Guards.

The vanguards of Konev's tank armies reached the Spree before noon; by then the army group had virtually destroyed four German divisions. The commander of the Third Guards Tank Army, General Pavel S. Rybalko, decided to ford the river rather than wait for pontoon bridges to be built. Scouts found a shallows south of Spremberg, and the tanks began splashing across at once. The Fourth Guards Tank Army, under the command of General Dmitri D. Lelyushenko, hit the Spree farther south and also began fording the river. Within three hours, sizable advance units of both armies were on the far side.

All these good things Konev reported with relish to Stalin that night. Toward the end of his report, Stalin interrupted and said, "Things are pretty hard with Zhukov. He is still hammering at the defenses." Then he challenged Konev: Would it be possible to pull Zhukov's armor from his front, send it to Konev and slam it into Berlin from the south?

The suggestion was wholly impractical: To disengage two tank armies from battle and move them to another front fully 50 miles away would halt the offensive for days. Furthermore, if Konev used Zhukov's armor, Konev probably would lose control of his front to his rival. Konev made haste to reply: "Comrade Stalin, that would take a lot of time and would greatly complicate the situation. There is no need to transfer tank forces from the First Belorussian Army Group. Things are going well with us. We have sufficient forces and are in a position to turn both our tank armies toward Berlin." Konev went on to explain that his armies could move on the city along the highway through Zossen, the headquarters of the German General Staff, about 20 miles south of Berlin.

Then Stalin gave the word Konev wanted to hear: "Very good. I agree. Turn your tanks toward Berlin."

Now there was a race between Konev and Zhukov for the capital. In high spirits, Konev ordered his two tank-army commanders to turn toward Berlin, taking care to envelop its western limits in order to cut the city off. Konev's instructions for the movement, as he recounted them in his memoirs, were a blueprint for blitzkrieg: "Bravely ahead, don't look back; don't fight the Hitlerites at the strong points; don't, under any circumstances, attack them frontally. Outflank them, maneuver, take care of your equipment and always remember that you must have reserve strength for the final mission—to fight for Berlin.''

Following these orders, the tanks would leave a number of combat-worthy enemy divisions and bypassed strong points behind them, to be eliminated later by their mixed armies. Rybalko's and Lelyushenko's men, having gotten their equipment across the Spree, labored all night to swing every tank and truck in a massive pivot toward Berlin. Both tank armies started moving north at dawn. On April 18, Rybalko's army traveled 19 miles against light resistance, and Lelyushenko's army sped 28 miles, meeting even less.

As Konev was unrolling his thrust on the left, Zhukov was still struggling to wind up the battle at Seelow Heights. His armor drove through for 10 or 12 miles southwest of Seelow and west of Wriezen, but in neither sector did the defenses collapse or did the tanks make a breakthrough. Zhukov was still raging, making rash and panicky moves; he threw rear-area supply and service troops into combat, and gave orders to shoot any soldier who failed to advance. "We have a lion on our hands," said General Popel.

Zhukov's frantic fumbling came as a surprise to German officers, who had expected his thousands of tanks to make quick work of the defenses. Hitler and his fellow occupants of the Führerbunker were jubilant and, noted a Naval liaison officer, "the voices of hope were loud."

That was April 18. German hopes went aglimmering on the following day: Zhukov broke through. His units in the Seelow area, including Chuikov's Eighth Guards Army and the First Guards Tank Army, bludgeoned their way as far as Müncheberg, 20 miles due east of the Berlin city limits. The shape of the disaster threatening the Reich was plain to see: Zhukov's northern force was now in a position to sweep west around Berlin and link up with Konev's tank units pushing in that direction from the southeast; if that happened the city would be surrounded.

Konev's tanks kept coming fast. The force of General Lelyushenko covered more than 30 miles on April 19, and General Rybalko's army logged about 22 miles. (Konev was not satisfied, for he had learned that Zhukov was finally picking up speed. "Comrade Rybalko," he radioed, "you are moving like a snail.")

With threats looming everywhere, Heinrici tried again to get Hitler to release Bieler's men from the Frankfurt fortress.

Heinrici's call to the Führerbunker was answered by Lieut. General Hans Krebs, Chief of Staff of the Army. An urbane officer with little experience as a commander, Krebs had replaced General Guderian three weeks earlier, after the veteran tank expert had been relieved for arguing with Hitler. Krebs would never be accused of such an offense; critics on the staff called him a "nodding donkey"—a yes man.

When Heinrici explained that he wanted the Frankfurt force released, Krebs was so horrified by the request that he would not even relay it to the Führer. "Hitler would never agree to that!" he exclaimed. "Hold all positions!" Then he hung up the phone.

On April 20, Lelyushenko's Fourth Guards Tank Army covered 29 miles against stiffening resistance. His army swerved west, swallowed up the huge German munitions depot at Jüterbog and reached the town of Luckenwalde, about 22 miles south of Berlin. Rybalko's Third Guards Tank Army, which had easier going farther to the east, traveled 38 miles that day.

Once Rybalko moved north past Baruth, only one enemy unit was in place to challenge his progress to Zossen. This was a 250-man mechanized squadron based at Zossen for the security of the German General Staff; it was commanded by a lieutenant named Kränkel. General Krebs decided that it was better to attack than to be attacked; he sent Kränkel south to confront Rybalko's tank army.

For a while it seemed that Kränkel's squadron had disappeared without a trace. But around dawn on April 21, Captain Gerhardt Boldt, an officer attached to the General Staff's small Berlin office, was awakened by a ringing telephone. It was Kränkel, calling from south of the capital. "About forty Russian tanks have passed us," he said, and reported that motorized infantry accompanied the tanks. "I shall attack at seven o'clock." Two hours later Kränkel called again with the predictable news: "My attack has failed with heavy losses. My reconnoitering tanks report more enemy tanks advancing north."

This moved even Krebs to beg Hitler to let him abandon and destroy Zossen before it was too late. Permission was finally granted, but so late that when the office personnel at Zossen fled from enemy tanks, they left communications lines operative and maps on the walls. Kränkel himself showed up at the Führerbunker in Berlin, exhausted and

A German artillery crew mans an antiaircraft gun converted to antitank duty against Russian bridgeheads across the Oder. Such guns, used to fill the gaps in the German Army's depleted arsenal, proved highly effective. But with little heavy transport available to move them, many had to be left behind as the Germans abandoned their positions.

caked with mud, to report that his squadron had been whittled down to about 35 men and a few vehicles.

As Rybalko's drive was taking Zossen and approaching within 20 miles of Berlin, Zhukov came still closer to the city on April 20. His Second Guards Tank Army captured Bernau, just 10 miles northeast of Berlin, and headed toward Oranienburg, 19 miles north of the capital. Meanwhile the left flank of Zhukov's force managed to drive an armored column southwest to Fürstenwalde, behind the lines of the German Ninth Army, 20 miles east of Berlin.

This thrust, together with Rybalko's slashing march north, threatened to trap a major portion of Busse's army. Heinrici asked Krebs to get Hitler's permission for the Ninth Army to withdraw to a position closer to Berlin. This time Krebs relayed the request to the Führer, who thought about it off and on for most of the day and finally instructed Heinrici to tell Busse to hold all positions but somehow protect his flanks. Though Busse realized that his army would have to fall back to avoid being cut off, he welcomed the standfast order for one reason that did him credit: He did not want to withdraw and leave Bieler's force to be completely cut off and subsequently chewed up in the Frankfurt fortress.

Heinrici also received dolorous news from the 100,000-man Third Panzer Army. To the north, beyond Zhukov's breakthrough, Marshal Rokossovsky's Second Belorussian Group now joined the offensive and hacked out numerous bridgeheads on the west bank of the Oder between Stettin and Schwedt. These were the first steps toward a breakout by Rokossovsky that was aimed at helping to encircle Berlin and at occupying the north German plain. Opposite Rokossovsky, the Third Panzer Army was commanded by General Manteuffel.

Manteuffel's army was a sorry collection of either battered or inexperienced divisions; a fair number of its units had been drained off by Heinrici to oppose Zhukov's grinding advances. Rokossovsky would require two or three days to develop his bridgeheads and build up strength for his breakout, but after that interval Manteuffel could not be expected to hold the German line for more than a few days.

Amid these incipient disasters, Adolf Hitler celebrated his 56th birthday. The Allied air forces also celebrated, sending more than 1,000 planes to pulverize Berlin's rubble. On this day of self-congratulation for the National Socialist overlord, his chief vassals came to pay their respects. Hitler welcomed them all cordially—even Speer, who recently had been out of favor for expressing opposition to the Führer's scorched-earth policy.

Reich Marshal Göring showed up bluff and hearty, but not in his customary sartorial splendor. in place of the flamboyant costume of white linen, pastel-blue silk or iridescent gray cloth that Göring had sported in the heyday of the

Third Reich, he wore a simple olive-drab uniform—looking like an American general, as one guest at the birthday party whispered to Speer, implying that Göring was already abandoning Hitler to seek a haven with the enemy. Göring had come to the party from Karinhall, his estate 50 miles northwest of Berlin, where he had filled 24 trucks with art treasures and other stolen valuables, and then blown up the mansion. Göring had long been out of favor with the Führer because of the failure of the Luftwaffe, but on this day Hitler seemed to hold no grudge.

Another guest, Reichsführer-SS Himmler, had also fallen in Hitler's esteem—the result of his brief, disastrous stint as the commanding general of Army Group Vistula during the Soviet drive across Poland in January. The Reichsführer-SS was now conspiring to commit treason on a grand scale. With the connivance of SS Brigadier General Walter Schellenberg, his young chief of foreign intelligence, Himmler—having talked with a Swedish representative of the World Jewish Congress—had said he would release token numbers of Jews from the concentration camp at Ravensbrück to be smuggled into neutral countries. Himmler's gesture was intended to redeem his noisome reputation in the West so that he could negotiate a separate German peace with the United States and Great Britain.

Himmler and Schellenberg exhibited a remarkable capacity for self-delusion. They believed that the Western Allies, who had insisted on the unconditional surrender of the Reich throughout the War and who were now on the verge of absolute victory, would sit down with Himmler, a man who had cold-bloodedly sent millions of people to their deaths, and negotiate a surrender that betrayed their ally, the Soviet Union.

Grand Admiral Dönitz came down from his headquarters at Plön, near the Baltic, to be with Hitler on his birthday. A Nazi by disposition though not by formal affiliation, Dönitz was one hierarch whose star had recently been in the ascendant. He had earned his post as commander in chief of the Navy with superb work as a U-boat leader. Hitler himself had given planes and tanks higher priority than submarines, so he did not blame Dönitz when it became clear that German U-boats did not possess the technology to defeat the Allies' radar, convoys and aircraft carriers.

Dönitz was efficient and ruthless—a man after Hitler's own heart, and all the more so because he was not the leader of the failed Army or Luftwaffe. In appreciation, Hitler on April 20 reaffirmed a previous appointment of Dönitz as commander of all northern German territories in the event that the Soviet Union and the United States joined hands, thus splitting the Reich from east to west. Field Marshal Kesselring, known as a devoted Hitler man, was to command the southern territories.

On the subject of command, the top Nazis repeatedly urged Hitler to leave Berlin and run the War from the Berghof, his estate near Berchtesgaden in the Bavarian Alps. There, deep inside a mountain called the Obersalzberg, lay a communications center second in size and quality only to the one at Zossen. Much of the government had already departed for the Obersalzberg, and the Nazi hierarchy had assumed that the Führer would follow. But Hitler procrastinated. "I am not being indecisive," he announced. "You know that I sometimes delay a decision, but when I make it nothing can shake me from it. I shall decide later what I shall do."

He might not have that luxury, Göring told Hitler; only a single overland escape route lay open, and it might close at any moment. Hitler replied with bombast: "How can I call on the troops to undertake the decisive battle if I myself withdraw to safety? I shall leave to fate whether I die in the capital or fly to the Obersalzberg at the last moment!"

The Nazis attended the regular midafternoon situation conference, and then the birthday assemblage began to disperse. Göring shook hands with the Führer, muttering that he had urgent work to do supervising affairs at the Obersalzberg; Hitler gazed at him absent-mindedly and answered with a few indifferent words. "I was standing only a few feet from the two," wrote Speer, "and had a sense of being present at a historic moment: The leadership of the Reich was splitting asunder."

Dönitz left to set up new northern command headquarters at Flensburg, just south of the Danish border. Himmler repaired to his castle headquarters at Ziethen near Berlin, then went on before dawn to keep two secret appointments arranged for him by Schellenberg. The first meeting was at the estate of Felix Kersten, Himmler's masseur, with Norbert Masur, a Swede who represented the World Jewish Congress. Himmler promised to smuggle out 1,000 Jewish women from Ravensbrück—but said he would need to label them as Poles instead of Jews to make it easier for Masur to keep secret their arrival in Sweden. Masur did not object.

Later Himmler breakfasted with the Swedish diplomat Count Folke Bernadotte, who Himmler hoped would agree to serve as an intermediary between himself and the American authorities. They met at the sanatorium of Dr. Karl Gebhardt, Himmler's physician, who in his spare time conducted medical experiments on concentration-camp inmates. To impress Bernadotte with his good will, Himmler spoke of his conversation with Masur, and topped his prebreakfast offer by asserting that he was willing to release *all* of the women in Ravensbrück. Nevertheless, Bernadotte was not persuaded to act as intermediary.

One of the last to leave after Hitler's birthday party was Albert Speer; he stayed on to remonstrate with Goebbels. As the *Gauleiter*, or Nazi district leader, of Berlin, Goebbels had certain municipal-defense responsibilities, and Speer had heard that Goebbels planned to blow up the capital's hundred-odd bridges to obstruct the Russians' advance. Speer implored Goebbels not to go through with the plan; the destruction of the bridges, he said, would cut off food deliveries into the city and starve nearly everyone who survived the battle.

After a lengthy discussion, Goebbels agreed to destroy bridges only if and when they became strategic objectives in the course of battle—a concession that General Krebs tattled to Hitler. Probably out of deference to Goebbels, the Führer accepted this decision. At this juncture, Hitler held Goebbels in such high regard as an articulate, long-time keeper of the Nazi faith that he asked Goebbels and his family to move into the bunker for the ordeal that lay ahead.

By April 21, Soviet soldiers standing atop rises or tall buildings sighted their goal, Berlin, in the distance, wreathed in smoke from the previous night's American bombing raid. (Later, a number of units claimed the honor of seeing Berlin first, firing on it first, setting foot in it first. The claims were never settled.)

One of the first outfits to see Berlin was the battalion of the Third Shock Army that had lost 16 men captured, mutilated and killed near the town of Zechin. The men got their view of the city from a hill about nine miles to the northeast as they approached Berlin's outer defense line, which followed the 75-mile autobahn that encircled the capital. Here the battalion commander, Captain Stepan Neustroyev, was entrusted with the division's Soviet flag: Every division to enter Berlin would vie for the honor of hoisting the banner to the top of the Reichstag as a symbol of Russia's final victory, even though the building had not been used since its partial destruction by fire in 1933. The division commander said, "I don't want to see any other flag on the Reichstag, Stepan." Neustroyev answered with a grin, "I understand, Comrade General. I'll do my best to avoid being court-martialed."

Not far away, an artillery battery of the 266th Division of the Fifth Shock Army became one of the first to bombard Berlin. "Before us lay a huge city," wrote Sergeant Nikolai Vasilyev. "A feeling of joy and exultation swept over us. This was the last enemy position, and the hour of retribution had come at last. We did not even notice a car draw up. Our army commander, General Berzarin, alighted from it. He issued an order to our commanding officer; 'Target: The Nazis in Berlin. Open fire!'" The battery fired shells on which messages had been inscribed: "For Stalingrad," "For the Ukraine," "For the orphans and widows" and "For the tears shed by mothers."

These rounds may have been the first to land in central Berlin. Shells came hurtling toward Hermannplatz at exactly 11:30 a.m. Shoppers waiting in line at Karstadt's department store heard the shells too late. Moments later the square was littered with the dead and wounded.

The thudding of artillery near the Reich Chancellery shocked and puzzled Hitler. At first he thought that the Russians had built a railroad bridge across the Oder and were firing a railroad siege gun with a range of perhaps 50 miles. A Luftwaffe officer explained to him that there was no such railroad bridge, and Hitler fell silent.

Deluded as he was, Hitler assumed one of his traditional roles—that of military miracle worker. He presented his commanders with a three-phase plan for reconstructing the broken front and ensuring the salvation of the Third Reich.

The first phase was already under way, Hitler explained. One hundred twenty miles southeast of Berlin, units of Field Marshal Schörner's Fourth Panzer Army were counterattacking around Görlitz and making modest headway. Although Schörner himself made no such claims, Hitler asserted that the panzer units' counterattack would close up the hole that Konev had ripped in the line—a hole that was now about 40 miles wide.

As the second phase, Hitler ordered the Ninth Army to face west, away from the Oder, turn its back on Zhukov, and prepare to repel the armies that Konev was pouring north toward Berlin by attacking their flank. The Führer did not specify how this about-face was to be accomplished. (The movement was never initiated.)

Finally the centerpiece of Hitler's scheme was presented—a counterattack he had planned for SS General Felix Steiner. Steiner was one of those hard-driving, dramatic leaders who could do no wrong in Hitler's eyes. A former regular Army officer who had volunteered before the War for the nascent Nazi army called the Waffen-SS, Steiner had served with dash on both the Eastern and Western Fronts—most recently as commander of the Eleventh SS Panzer Army in Pomerania. When Steiner and the remnants of his army returned from Pomerania, they were in General Manteuffel's Third Panzer Army as part of Army Group Vistula, stationed north of Berlin.

But Army Group commander Heinrici, critically short of troops in the face of the Soviet offensive, had been unable to leave Steiner's units intact within the Third Panzer Army while the front-line forces that were assembled opposite Berlin were being ground down. As early as April 16, Heinrici detached the 18th Panzer Grenadier Division from Steiner's army and sent it to bolster Seelow Heights. Two days later, Heinrici ordered Steiner to dispatch the 11th SS Panzer Grenadier Division south to defend Berlin, and to send the tough SS Brigade "Nederland," another Steiner unit, farther south to contest Konev's breakthrough. By April 21, as Steiner later said, exaggerating only slightly, "I was a general without any troops."

At this point, Hitler ordered Steiner to attack through the northern flank of Zhukov's fast-moving force in order to consolidate the German front along the Oder. The Führer was startled to learn that Steiner had virtually no combat troops, but Hitler quickly fixed everything—to his own satisfaction, at least. For Operational Group Steiner, he ticked off three divisions and some odds and ends, including Hitler Youth and Luftwaffe ground crewmen. The Führer was so satisfied with these arrangements that he told Steiner, "You'll see, the Russians will yet suffer the greatest and bloodiest defeat in their history at the gates of Berlin."

Hitler expected Steiner to attack at once, but the divisions just handed him were scattered all over Greater Berlin. They would have to be first gathered, probably rearmed and then deployed, and Steiner would have to do all of this difficult and time-consuming work without assured sources of transportation or supply. He had only a directive from the Führer

to intimidate uncooperative functionaries: "Officers who do not accept this order without reservation are to be arrested and shot immediately." The order also included a threatening note for Steiner: "I make you yourself responsible with your head for the execution of this order."

In self-defense, Steiner telephoned Heinrici and told him that the attack simply could not be executed as ordered. Heinrici was exasperated, but there was little he could do to reassure Steiner. Heinrici had worries of his own. Despite Hitler's paper solutions, the situation was deteriorating very fast for the Ninth Army, and Heinrici was still denied permission to withdraw his troops. Heinrici was certain that the Ninth Army would be surrounded and lost if it was not pulled back that very night, and on April 21 he called General Krebs to express his concern.

Heinrici went on to say that there simply were not enough troops available to rebuild a solid line on the Oder, and for this reason it was essential to draw the Ninth Army closer to the city, where the available manpower could be concentrated on a shorter line. "Actually," he concluded, "what I should do is go to the Führer and say, 'My Führer, I request you to relieve me of my command. Then I can do my duty as a Volkssturm member and fight the enemy.' "

Krebs replied, "Do you really want me to pass this on to the Führer?"

"I demand it," Heinrici said. "My chief of staff and my operations officer are my witnesses."

A few minutes later, Krebs called back. The Führer's orders, he said, were for the Ninth Army to stand and fight.

The next morning, April 22, Hitler sat poking through piles of reports and asking for news of Steiner's attack. He learned that Zhukov had driven 30 miles beyond Oranienburg, completely outflanking Berlin to the north and beginning to swing southward. Konev's vanguard had fought to a point five miles south of the capital, Hitler was told, and Konev's guns as well as Zhukov's were shelling Berlin. But Hitler could not find out how Steiner was faring; General Krebs repeatedly said there was nothing definite to report.

Hitler tried to get information from General Eckardt Christian, the Luftwaffe liaison officer, who should have known Steiner's whereabouts because he had been ordered to send surplus Luftwaffe ground crewmen to Steiner. The general knew nothing, however, and telephoned the Luftwaffe chief of staff, General Karl Koller, who also knew nothing but said he would call around. Almost as if he had guessed what Hitler wanted to hear, Koller reported back that Steiner was practically ready to attack. Then others seemed to take the cue. Army headquarters announced that Steiner had attacked, and when Himmler was asked what he knew, he said he was positive that Steiner had attacked.

The facts of the matter were otherwise. Steiner had rounded up barely 10,000 men, most of them unarmed, and was busy deploying them along the Finow Canal northeast of Berlin. There, within cannon range—if only Steiner's men had had artillery—Zhukov's infantry was streaming southwest toward the capital, and Zhukov's armor was rumbling due west to outflank the city from the north. Steiner had no idea when, if at all, he would be able to attack.

Hitler, not satisfied with the reports that he was getting and harboring deep suspicions, opened his midafternoon situation conference without a shred of hard information about Steiner's attack. Field Marshal Keitel and General Jodl briefed Hitler about practically everything else—telling him, in particular, that Zhukov's northern column was swinging southwest past Oranienburg and would probably link up around Potsdam with Konev's spearhead within a week. Trembling with anger, Hitler demanded to know of Steiner's attack. Krebs finally confessed that the attack had not started, that Steiner's group was still getting organized.

The Führer flew into a frenzy. This was no mere tantrum of the sort his associates saw regularly; it was so violent that it frightened the most hardened witnesses of Hitler's rages. Out of control, his eyes bulging, his face purple, Hitler screamed that all the world had lied to him and betrayed him and deserted him, that now even his own SS had failed him, that the Third Reich was bankrupt. "The War is lost!" he cried—the first time he had made this admission without qualification. It was finished, cried the Führer; he would stay in Berlin and shoot himself when the Russians came. And then he collapsed into a slack-jawed, glassy-eyed silence, even more frightening to see than his rage had been.

The officers circled around Hitler, talking to him, murmuring solace and encouragement, trying to call him back to life. They told him all was not lost. Schörner's army, they said, was still strong in Czechoslovakia; so was Field Mar-

Weary German prisoners of war, some of the half million whom the Russians claimed to have captured during the final battles between the Oder River and Berlin, pause on their long march eastward to prison in the Soviet Union. The topmost road sign points to Berlin, 26 miles behind them. They faced a bleak future: Of the nearly 3.5 million Soviet-held prisoners, nearly half died in captivity, and some 50,000, designated "war criminals," were imprisoned until 1956.

shal Kesselring's force in Austria and southern Germany. The Führer, they urged, should go to the Obersalzberg and continue the War from there. Hitler came out of his trance. He told the generals that they might and indeed should leave Berlin, but declared, "I shall defend the city to the end. Either I win this battle for the Reich's capital or I shall fall as a symbol of the Reich."

For three hours the overheated conference went on. One at a time, the officers excused themselves to telephone the news of Hitler's breakdown to their headquarters. The Naval liaison officer, Rear Admiral Hans-Erich Voss, reported to Admiral Dönitz in Plön. SS Major General Hermann Fegelein, Himmler's liaison officer and brother-in-law of Hitler's mistress Eva Braun, gushed out the story. Himmler was so upset that he telephoned Hitler twice to urge him to keep up the good fight and to promise him some SS troops for the battle. Then, inspired by Hitler's breakdown to make a play for the succession, Himmler sped by motorcade to another meeting with Count Bernadotte. They met on the evening of April 23 at the Swedish Consulate in the Baltic port of Lübeck, and this time Bernadotte agreed—albeit pessimistically—to pass Himmler's written petition to his government for transmission to the Allies.

The Hitler meeting addressed other issues besides the immediate Berlin battle situation—and all of these subjects were of historic import. At one point the generals, apparently realizing that Hitler seemed to be washing his hands of all military decisions except those pertinent to the fight for Berlin, implored him not to abandon them. "You can't leave the Wehrmacht in the lurch," pleaded Keitel. "It is simply impossible, after you have been directing and leading us for so long, that you should suddenly send your staff away and expect them to lead themselves."

Who would give them their orders? someone asked. Not I, Hitler replied; they should ask Reich Marshal Göring. No one would fight for Göring, Keitel remarked; Hitler pointed out, "There's not much fighting left to be done, and when it comes to negotiating, the Reich Marshal can certainly do that better than I."

That remark was a most significant cue for the events that followed—a melodramatic sequence that eventually led to the undoing of Hermann Göring. In the heat of the moment,

Luftwaffe General Christian concluded that Hitler was stepping down as Führer so that Göring could negotiate a peace. As Göring's Luftwaffe subordinate, Christian felt a great need to discuss this development with his immediate superior, General Koller; but Christian was unwilling to entrust his important news to the telephone. He hurried across Berlin to Luftwaffe headquarters at Krampnitz near Potsdam and there told Koller in person.

Koller decided to take the news to Göring personally and for that purpose requisitioned a fighter plane, flew to Munich and then motored to the Obersalzberg. When informed, Göring was thrilled by the prospect of his rise to Führer. He knew that in June 1941, Hitler had signed an order appointing the Reich Marshal his successor. Nonetheless, Göring cautiously sought legal advice from the State Secretary, Hans Heinrich Lammers. Had the Führer, Göring asked the lawyer, issued any decree that superseded the order of June 1941? Lammers answered, No. Could Göring legally succeed the Führer while Hitler was still alive? Nothing specifically prevented it, Lammers said.

With the aid of Lammers and others, Göring concocted a telegram to Hitler designed to confirm and authenticate his new position. The message was a masterpiece of tact.

My Führer!
    In view of your decision to remain in the fortress of Berlin, do you agree that I take over at once the total leadership of the Reich, with full freedom of action at home and abroad as your deputy? If no reply is received by 10 o'clock tonight, I shall take it for granted that you have lost your freedom of action, and I shall act for the best interests of our country and our people. You know what I feel for you in this gravest hour of my life. Words fail me to express myself. May God protect you and speed you quickly here in spite of everything.

                                Your loyal
                                Hermann Göring

When the telegram arrived at the Führerbunker, it fell into the hands of one of Göring's great enemies, Hitler's chief Nazi Party executive, Martin Bormann. Bormann was widely and cordially disliked; General Guderian called him the "sinister guttersnipe." Bormann quickly convinced Hitler that Göring had issued an ultimatum in setting the 10 p.m. deadline for a reply. Before long, Bormann had Hitler believing that Göring was trying to oust him from the post of Führer. Hitler accepted Bormann's interpretation without much argument and dictated a telegram to SS headquarters at the Obersalzberg, ordering the arrest of Göring, Lammers and Koller for high treason. In consideration of their previous service, he spared their lives; Hitler told Goebbels merely to announce in the press that ill health had forced Göring to resign all of his offices—even that of Reich Master of the Hunt, an office he had held since the 1930s and that made him responsible for German game conservation.

The momentous April 22 meeting in the *Führerbunker* had a far more important consequence than Göring's tragicomic grasp at the Nazi succession. The most vital issue was a bold proposal by General Jodl calculated to renew the Führer's interest in the War: Late in the April 22 conference, Jodl suggested that the German Twelfth Army, which was facing west against the Americans and guarding a 120-mile stretch of the Elbe River southwest of Berlin, turn around and attack Konev's advance from the rear, slice through the Russian lines and enter the capital.

The plan would, of course, open the way for the Americans to advance in their own turn, but Jodl had good reason to think that that risk was minimal. Recently, under mysterious circumstances, the Armed Forces High Command had acquired a copy of the Allied plan for the occupation of Germany. The plan, which ran to 70 typescript pages and included maps, showed that all of the territory between the Oder and the Elbe (save for a tripartite administration of Berlin) was to be in the Soviet occupation zone. Jodl deduced that the British and the Americans were unlikely to mount a new offensive to capture an area that they would subsequently have to turn over to the Russians. There appeared to be sufficient confirmation of his conclusion in the fact that the U.S. Ninth Army had reached the Elbe fully 11 days earlier, but since then had made no effort to cross the river in strength.

Whether the Twelfth could do anything to help out in Berlin was another matter. The army, organized in early April, was sketchily trained and poorly equipped, with only a token complement of armor. Its main assets were spirited, high-caliber personnel, including many officer candidates, and a commander, Lieut. General Walter Wenck, whose skill on the Eastern Front three years before had made him, at 42, the youngest general in the German Army.

In better times, Jodl never would have considered an army as unreliable as Wenck's for a combat assignment, much less for such a critical one. But now the Twelfth presented a hope, if only a wan hope. Keitel supported the proposal; indeed he was so eager to do something constructive that he insisted on personally bringing the new orders to Wenck. Hitler embraced the plan, became his usual animated self while discussing the details, and added a wrinkle: Reviving his earlier impulse to turn the Ninth Army in its tracks and send it west, Hitler ordered a joint attack by the Ninth and the Twelfth, with Berlin the goal, as Jodl had suggested. Hitler also became as solicitous as a *Hausfrau* about Keitel's journey. He ordered a picnic lunch—sandwiches, chocolate and brandy—put up and insisted that the field marshal consume an entire bowl of hot pea soup before his departure.

It was past midnight when Keitel located Wenck's command post in a gamekeeper's lodge in Wiesenberg Forest about 60 miles southwest of Berlin. On his arrival, Keitel blurted out, "We must rescue the Führer!" He went on to outline the plan for the relief of Berlin. The Twelfth and Ninth Armies were to attack toward each other and, upon joining ranks south of Berlin, smash their way into the capital. Already, in the absence of orders of any sort, Wenck had taken the first step in the plan: Noting the inactivity of the Americans, he had turned the army away from the Elbe to face the oncoming Russians—had in fact beaten off a Soviet tank attack near Belzig on April 21. But Wenck thought that entering Berlin was too ambitious a goal for his army, and after Keitel left to return to the capital, Wenck sat down with his chief of staff, Colonel Günther Reichhelm, and roughed out a scheme of his own.

His army, Wenck decided, must make a last battle, and nothing the soldiers of the Twelfth could do would be more valuable than to rescue their beleaguered comrades of the Ninth Army. As soon as possible, the Twelfth Army would attack southeastward and open a corridor through the Soviet lines. Busse's men would escape through the corridor, reach the Elbe and, along with the Twelfth Army survivors and any refugees that they could save, surrender to the American troops.

Wenck and Reichhelm had no illusions about the attack: It would take several days to mount, for they were fighting off Russians all the time; it would cost them many lives, and it might well fail. Meanwhile, the generals in Berlin saw the planned assault through their rosiest glasses. Krebs telephoned Heinrici and told him that Wenck's thrust would quickly relieve Soviet pressure on the capital. Heinrici pointed out that Wenck's two corps were centered well to the west of the capital and could not cover the ground overnight. But the news did not sound unpromising: Heinrici even had some hope that the plan would work.

Later that night, Krebs again called Heinrici to start coordinating Wenck's attack with Busse's. He told Heinrici that Hitler, now suddenly sanguine about the prospects, had finally authorized Busse to pull back the Ninth Army to a line running north from the vicinity of Cottbus, the northern shoulder of Konev's breakthrough area. The Führer also said that General Bieler could leave the Frankfurt fortress. While withdrawing, Busse was to free one division forthwith to start his attack westward to meet the Twelfth Army.

An alert commander, Marshal Konev had already considered the possibility that the German Twelfth Army might try to attack through his lines toward the Ninth Army. To block any such adventure, he placed one corps in a strong defensive position around Baruth, on a highway that either the Twelfth Army or the Ninth Army would have to take in order to reach the other. Two of Konev's armies were probing westward toward the Elbe to find Wenck's forces—or the Americans. They encountered what Konev called "furious attacks," which made it appear likely that Wenck was trying to organize some sort of counteroffensive.

For the moment, however, the German Ninth Army was of much greater concern than the Twelfth to Konev. He and Zhukov had received orders from Moscow to complete the encirclement of the Ninth Army by April 24 at the latest, and six Soviet armies—three from each marshal's command—were closing in on Busse's men from all directions. Once the Ninth was cut off from Berlin and forced to fight on without resupply or reinforcement, it would soon be worn down—of that the two marshals were certain.

Hitler made the job a little easier for the Russians. On the afternoon of April 23 he ordered the 56th Panzer Corps, which was protecting Busse's northern flank, to pull back into Berlin and to defend the eastern and southeastern approaches to the city.

The Ninth Army was finally cut off on April 24 by the first of several strategic linkups. At 6 a.m., men of Chuikov's Eighth Guards Army, hooking toward Berlin from the east, met up with a northbound unit of Rybalko's Third Guards Tank Army near Schönefeld airfield on the southeastern edge of the capital. Chuikov reported the juncture with Konev's Army Group to Zhukov's headquarters and quickly received a puzzling return call from Zhukov himself. The marshal demanded to know—insisted that Chuikov dispatch responsible investigators to find out—the exact identity of the Konev unit that his men had met and the exact time when it penetrated the outermost city limits of Berlin. Chuikov guessed that Zhukov was preparing to refute any claim by Konev that the First Ukrainian Group had beaten the First Belorussian Group into the capital.

Eight Soviet armies were now converging on Berlin, entering the capital at several points along its 56 miles of city limits. It was all brutal slogging now; the easy gains of the past few days had come to an end. "The closer to Berlin," Konev wrote, "the denser the enemy defenses became, and the enemy infantry were supported by more and more artillery, tanks and *Panzerfäuste*." In the midst of all this violence, civilians huddled in cellars and shelters, making the best of it—not always successfully.

Konev, driving toward Berlin on a broad front from the south, had a special problem: the Teltow Canal, which cut across the south side of the city. Roughly 150 feet wide and nine feet deep, its bridges blown or heavily mined, its high walls studded with pillboxes and lined with strong stone houses, the canal made a formidable defense line. One 7.5 mile stretch was defended by 15,000 German troops, 250 guns and mortars, 130 tanks and other armored vehicles, more than 500 machine guns and many *Panzerfäuste*. Konev's men could not avoid storming the canal, but once they had cleared it, they would encounter only one more coordinated defense line—around the center of the city.

General Rybalko was the field commander in charge of the assault on the canal. He spent all of April 23 in preparation, bringing up nearly 3,000 artillery pieces, heavy mortars and self-propelled guns, and concentrating them on his main penetration area, a sector less than three miles wide. The guns totaled about 1,000 muzzles per mile.

Rybalko's artillery opened up at 6:20 a.m. on April 24, and assault parties soon began crossing the canal in collapsible boats. Some parties were wiped out or driven back by German counterattacks, but by 1 p.m. Soviet engineers had completed the first pontoon bridge and tanks were rumbling across. The battle was won then and there, although the fighting raged all night long and would continue for days in some places.

To Rybalko's right, most of the Eighth Guards Army came in from the east without having to cross the Teltow Canal. In the vicinity of Tempelhof airfield, Chuikov's men crashed into an enemy that had been fighting them more or less steadily since their drive past Seelow seven days earlier: the Müncheberg Panzer Division. This unit, comprising men and vehicles from the tank training center at Müncheberg, was one of the hastily assembled, makeshift outfits now prevalent in the Wehrmacht; they were never given a proper identifying number, much less a fair complement of men and equipment. The Münchebergs had been savaged again and again, but they stood their ground on April 24. One of their officers wrote in his journal for the day:

"Russian artillery is firing without letup. The Russians burn their way into the houses with flame throwers. The screams of the women and children are horrible. Three o'clock in the afternoon and we have barely a dozen tanks and around 30 armored personnel carriers. We constantly get orders from the Chancellery to send tanks to some other danger spot in town, and they never come back."

The German defenses in the area crumbled as the afternoon wore on. The officer's staccato diary entry continued: "Our artillery retreats to new positions. They have very little ammunition. The howling and explosions of the Stalin Organs, the screaming of the wounded, the roaring of motors, and the rattle of machine guns. Dead women in the streets, killed trying to get water. 8 p.m.: Russian tanks carrying infantry are driving on the airport. Heavy fighting."

On the north side of Berlin, three of Zhukov's armies were breaking into the city. In the van of the Third Shock Army, Captain Neustroyev and his battalion were slowed down by heavy fighting in the Moabit district, and it seemed unlikely that they would be the first to plant the Soviet flag on the Reichstag. But they had just received an assist from Moscow. Stalin had redrawn the boundary between the

Russian women, clutching their belongings, are liberated from a forced-labor camp near Berlin by Soviet troops in late April, 1945. More than half of the three million slave laborers imported from Russia by the Reich were women—conscripted for farm and factory work, and as servants, under Hitler's order "to relieve the German housewife."

First Belorussian Group and the First Ukrainian Group with his usual favoritism for Zhukov, placing the center of the city—with the Reichstag, the *Führerbunker* and the government buildings—on Zhukov's side of the line along with the northern districts.

North Berlin was also the target of the only two real counterattacks that the Germans were able to mount until Wenck and Busse were ready to begin their southern assault. Both northern offensives were made by units of the Third Panzer Army, which as late as April 24 was still containing the Second Belorussian Group, led by Rokossovsky, in its Oder bridgeheads.

The commander of both attacks was the harried Steiner. When Steiner had complained that he lacked enough men for the job, he was reinforced with another large contingent of Hitler Youth. But Steiner sent the boys home, saying, "Their commitment would have been irresponsible." Steiner's failure to attack in spite of the most urgent exhortations had prompted Hitler to announce on April 23 that he did not want the man to command any troops, ever again, under any circumstances.

Steiner was relieved of his command and replaced by Lieut. General Rudolph Holste, commander of the 12th Corps in Wenck's army. But Holste wanted to stay with his own outfit, so he and Steiner agreed to ignore the ordered change in command.

Steiner actually did attack late on April 23, aiming to link up with the 56th Panzer Corps. Moreover, his men gained a little ground southward past Eberswalde. But just at that moment the 56th Panzer Corps was pulled back into Berlin. Steiner's group was left dangling in the middle of nowhere. Heinrici called off the attack and asked Steiner to try again 25 miles to the west, with the objective of recapturing the town of Oranienburg.

Steiner did move west, did attack again on April 25, and once again scored small gains. This time, Keitel and Jodl, at Hitler's headquarters, called off the attack to keep Steiner from being trapped. Hitler had inevitably learned that his once adored and now despised Felix Steiner had been left in command. Captain Gerhardt Boldt, Kreb's aide-de-camp who had now been assigned to the *Führerbunker* staff, reported that Hitler did not lose his temper, as everyone ex-pected. Instead the Führer remarked wearily, "I told you so, under Steiner's command the whole attack was bound to come to nothing."

As the battle for Berlin began to develop, control of the western approaches to the city remained in doubt. The northernmost spearheads of Zhukov's drive west, the Second Guards Tank Army and the Forty-seventh Army, had veered southwest from Oranienburg as early as April 21, and since then had been pushing south through the western suburbs of Berlin toward a meeting with Konev's Fourth Guards Tank Army. But the linkup, which would seal all Berlin inside a giant Soviet trap, was valiantly opposed by a force that consisted chiefly of teen-age Hitler Youth, mixed with some elderly *Volkssturm* troops. This motley outfit had been rushed into the Spandau sector of West Berlin and held the bridges over the Havel River for two days against the best Soviet forces, keeping open one last escape route to the northwest and the possibility of contact with the Western Allies.

On April 22, Konev's northbound armor was working its way into Potsdam, 25 miles short of Zhukov's southbound spearhead. On April 23, the gap was narrowed to 16 miles. By nightfall on the 24th, there were unconfirmed rumors of a linkup; perhaps patrols did meet briefly. Finally, at noon on April 25, the point tanks of Konev's VI Guards Mechanized Corps met at Ketzin, on the Mittelland Canal, with armored units of the 328th Division of Zhukov's Forty-seventh Army. At the same time Konev closed a smaller ring of Soviet steel around Potsdam.

By then, the last and most celebrated linkup—between Russians and Americans—had been in the making for two days. Three Soviet corps from two of Konev's armies had reached the Elbe on April 23. They were probing gingerly for the American troops and sending radio messages, which American operators answered with alacrity, begging for specific information. But the Russians would not reveal their units' locations because the Germans were listening in and making occasional sarcastic interruptions, such as: "Americans, quit your worrying, you'll meet up with your hoodlum Russian friends."

The mechanics of the Soviet-American linkup—scheduled to take place on the Elbe-Mulde line—had long worried both commands. The Americans considered that the area between the Elbe and the Mulde Rivers offered particularly dangerous possibilities of accidental clashes between Soviet and American troops; for an extra measure of safety, the U.S. First Army prohibited its patrols from moving more than five miles east of the Mulde.

But early on April 25, impatience got the better of Lieutenant Albert Kotzebue of the 69th Division, part of the U.S. First Army. Determined to make the linkup himself, Kotzebue took a large jeep patrol well beyond the five-mile limit, came upon a lone Soviet horseman in a small village and followed his eloquent hand signals to the town of Strehla on the Elbe. There, at 1:30 p.m., the Americans met a group of Soviet soldiers under the command of Lieut. Colonel Alexander Gardiev of the 175th Rifle Regiment, Fifth Guards Army. It was a subdued encounter, and it was ended abruptly by a Soviet public-relations officer who expected the arrival of some very senior officers and wanted to delay the celebration until they got there.

Kotzebue radioed word of the meeting to his regimental commander, who received the news at 3:30 p.m. Unfortunately Kotzebue sent the wrong map coordinates, and a small plane dispatched by the division commander to inspect the site was not welcomed—in fact it was driven off by Soviet antiaircraft fire. U.S. headquarters knew very little about the meeting, but they did know that Kotzebue had disobediently gone far beyond the five-mile limit; he had advanced against orders, and his superiors were in no great rush to credit him with the linkup. They waited for further information, and by then it was too late for Kotzebue.

The official honors fell to 2nd Lieutenant William D. Robertson, an intelligence officer of the same 69th Division, who was not even looking for Russians. With a patrol of three enlisted men, Robertson on April 25 set out from the town of Wurzen in a truck to search for Allied prisoners of war. Halfway between the Mulde and the Elbe, the little party ran into some released British POWs who said there were plenty of American and Russian prisoners in a camp near Torgau on the Elbe.

Robertson and his men reached Torgau in the middle of the afternoon and found two Americans; both had been released from the camp by the Germans, who were eager to surrender. Then the Americans heard small-arms fire from across the Elbe, presumably from Soviet troops in a fight with German holdouts.

To alert the Russians to their presence—and identify themselves—the GIs stopped at a pharmacy, picked up colored inks, improvised an American flag and ran it up on the turret of a riverside castle. The Russians paid no attention to the flag and even shot at Robertson. Then he remembered that there might be Russians back at the POW camp. He sent men to fetch someone who could communicate with the trigger-happy Allies across the river; when a Russian POW arrived, he shouted at his compatriots, who stopped firing and began crossing the river on the twisted girders of a wrecked highway bridge.

Robertson started crawling out on the bridge and at midstream came face to face with the Russian who was in the lead. They grinned and pounded each other with a joy that needed no words.

Late that night, while the Soviet-American linkup was being celebrated throughout the Allied world, a German official picked up the news from a neutral radio station and brought word to Hitler and his attending generals. The official said the radio report had also mentioned a dispute between local Soviet and U.S. commanders over the sectors of the Torgau area that each was supposed to occupy under Allied agreements.

The Führer had just learned that Rokossovsky's armies had burst out of their Oder bridgeheads and were racing west, that Wenck was at last starting his counterattack but was getting nowhere, that Busse's army was also attacking but was weakening fast, and that Berlin was surrounded. However, as Captain Boldt remembered the scene, the mere mention of an inter-Allied disagreement electrified Hitler. He sat back with his eyes shining and said triumphantly, "Gentlemen, here again is striking evidence of the disunity of our enemies. Would not the German people and posterity brand me a criminal if I were to make peace today when there is still the possibility of our enemies falling out tomorrow? Is it not possible that on any day, even at any hour, war will break out between the Bolsheviks and the Anglo-Saxons over Germany, their prize?"

ENCOUNTER ON THE ELBE

ssians, including women bearing bouquets, greet American GIs at the Elbe River about 75 miles south of Berlin, as the two armies meet on April 25, 1945.

A MOMENTOUS LINKUP OF GREAT ARMIES

In the final week of April 1945, the Allies were poised expectantly for a historic linkup of armies—a meeting that at home would be synonymous with final victory. Yet Western Allied commanders, largely ignorant of Soviet dispositions and strengths, feared an inadvertent clash as the great hosts came together. In 1939, during the Wehrmacht's sweep through Poland and the simultaneous Russian invasion of that country, German troops moving east had collided with Soviet units marching west; both sides had suffered casualties in the ensuing conflict.

Six years later, Americans of the 69th Division, part of the U.S. First Army, occupied positions along the Mulde River about 70 miles southwest of Berlin. They seemed the likeliest to run into the Russians. In an effort to maintain strict control, Major General Emil F. Reinhardt, commander of the 69th, ordered his patrols to venture no more than five miles beyond the Mulde.

The incident that everyone feared happened in spite of the order. The meeting between Americans and Russians came about partly because two young officers of the U.S. 69th Division led their patrols 20 miles farther east than they had been authorized to go—in fact the patrol commanders ventured all the way to the Elbe. As the units began to encounter Soviet forces, some shooting occurred; when one of the patrol leaders raised an improvised American flag to identify himself as an ally, he drew fire from a wary Soviet outfit.

No one was hurt in the skirmish, and once the fact of a linkup had been established, both armies turned the occasion into a memorable one. Men celebrated with exchanges of food—canned American rations for Russian black bread and onions—and with toast after toast from a seemingly endless supply of Russian vodka. In all the fraternal hubbub, the faltering toast of one Soviet lieutenant summed up the emotion on both sides: "You must pardon, I don't speak the right English, but we are very happy, so we drink a toast. My dear, quiet please. Today is the most happy day of our life. Long live our two great armies."

Attempting to coordinate a meeting of allies, a U.S. Army jeep patrol in Germany uses an interpreter (foreground) to contact the Russians by radio.

Leaders of the Allied divisions that first met on the Elbe, General Emil Reinhardt and General Vladimir Rusakov lead the way to an impromptu celebration.

A Russian soldier offers a cigar to a U.S. infantryman. He got an American cigarette in return—a symbolic exchange photographed all along the Elbe.

THE EXUBERANT MEETING OF IVAN AND JOE

Soviet and American troops along the Elbe flung themselves at each other like long-lost comrades-in-arms. With the Russians shouting out "tovarisch" ("comrade") and "Amerikanets," and the GIs singing "The Volga Boatman" (the only Russian tune they knew), the victorious fighting men embraced and saluted, exchanged small presents—and took stock.

Americans found the Russian military style astounding. For example, many Red Army troops wore no helmets into combat, but they fought wearing all their medals. Soviet horse-drawn artillery and supply wagons struck the heavily motorized Americans as antiquated. But the quality of Russian automatic small arms was impressive. Throughout the first day of their encounter, Soviet soldiers and U.S. GIs swapped medals for insignia, took hundreds of photographs posing together, and spent hours boasting over whose weapons were the best.

An American (left) receives the traditional Russian greeting: a bone-bruising bear hug.

A GI examines a Soviet submachine gun while another breaks down his pistol for a curious Russian.

Aiming his .30-caliber carbine, a helmeted American private prepares to demonstrate his marksmanship on a target pointed out by a Red Army soldier.

At a party celebrating the meeting of Soviet and American forces, a young Red Army officer (right, center) offers a speech to solidarity among the Allies.

Toasting each other with captured German wine, Soviet and American celebrants raise their glasses.

HEARTY TOASTS TO SOLIDARITY

In the first days after the Russian-American linkup, both sides of the Elbe River erupted in celebrations. On the east bank, each Soviet officer entertained his counterpart in the U.S. Army, from regimental commanders right up to the top. On the west bank, American commanders returned Russian hospitality with lavish dinners.

Impromptu feasting marked the festivities in the lower ranks. The Russians piled tables with ham, cheese and sausages. Bottles of German wine and brandy stood alongside vodka. The Americans brought with them eggs, chocolate and K rations, which—to their amusement—the Soviets loved. The air rang with toasts—to Roosevelt, to Truman, to Stalin and to Churchill. For the Americans, a delightful bonus was the Russian women soldiers, who became their first dancing partners in months.

The unaccustomed revelry caused many guests to fall asleep on the grass. Others kept on enthusiastically celebrating: The Americans found themselves scrambling for cover as the Russians, like cowboys on a Saturday night, joyously fired their weapons in the air.

Red Army women, whose presence at the front surprised the Americans, serve at a buffet table.

American and Russian officers dance with Red Army women beneath photographs of Stalin and Roosevelt and a banner saluting the U.S. First Army.

Arm in arm, American and Soviet soldiers march down a German street, symbolizing the union of allies who had fought for almost four years on separate fro

3

As the Russians closed in on Berlin during the second half of April 1945, the Western Allies were pursuing a strategy of immobility. Since crossing the Rhine on March 22, Anglo-American armies under General Eisenhower had cut Germany in two and reached the Elbe River. Eisenhower—no longer interested in Berlin as an objective and constrained by international agreements establishing postwar zones of occupation—proposed to stop there and, as he summed it up for the Combined Chiefs of Staff, "clean up my flanks."

Indeed, the smashing drive through Germany's midsection had left the Western Allies little else to do. The two American armies that executed the drive, the First and the Ninth, had quickly spread out along the Elbe and the Mulde, manning a line that wriggled some 180 miles south from Wittenberge to the neighborhood of Chemnitz. By the 19th of April the First and the Ninth had captured Leipzig and Magdeburg respectively. Their sector of the front was now so secure that several divisions could be spared to assist the more heavily engaged Allied commands to the north and south. Now the burden would fall upon the British-Canadian Twenty-first Army Group in northern Germany and Holland, the U.S. Third Army and the American-French Sixth Army Group in southern Germany, and the Anglo-American Fifth Army Group in northern Italy.

Everywhere in the West, the shooting war persisted only sporadically. The Germans, their country bisected and their units skeletonized by attrition, were no longer capable of a coordinated defense—a fact Hitler acknowledged by dividing Germany's split Western Front into independent northern and southern commands. On the firing line, the typical German defense was local and spontaneous—a hot little skirmish at a roadblock or river crossing, followed by a retreat. Field Marshal Albert Kesselring, recently the German commander in chief of the Western Front and now the head of the new southern command, later wrote with rueful pride that his troops "marched, broke away, fought, were overrun, outflanked, battered and exhausted, only to regroup, fight and march again." It was, Kesselring said, "an immense effort of endurance, for all its limitations, out of all proportion to what it did or could achieve."

The Germans' conspicuous weakness was underscored by anti-Nazi insurgency that began to surface among segments of the civilian populations. Nevertheless the Allies

MARKING TIME IN THE WEST

were cautious, and not without reason. The British and Americans, leery of incurring heavy losses with the end of the War in sight, were understandably reluctant to engage in battles that might prove meaningless. Moreover, the Americans had recently learned that the Germans were still capable of stiff resistance: A large part of the U.S. Seventh Army had been forced to fight hard for four days to capture Nuremberg, which finally fell on April 20. The Allies also were haunted by the memory of Hitler's unexpected 1944 offensive in the Ardennes, and they were determined to avoid another costly, embarrassing surprise.

They looked for such a booby trap in the so-called national redoubt, said to be a fortified area located in the mountains of southern Germany or western Austria. Allen Dulles and his OSS colleagues in Switzerland had suggested that Hitler's Alpine estate at Berchtesgaden on the Obersalzberg would make a convenient command post for a last-ditch defense of the surrounding area, and might be the headquarters of a redoubt. It was partly to prevent a German influx into the area that Dulles kept pressing for a general surrender in northern Italy. The experts of Eisenhower's Joint Intelligence Committee compounded the alarm by estimating that fully 100 German divisions were deployed within easy reach of the redoubt area—a calculation that was grossly exaggerated.

The Germans were aware of the Americans' suspicions and did all they could to confirm them. They spread stories of military movements and supply build-ups in the area, and they sent engineers there to explode dynamite charges as if for construction of heavy fortifications and underground factories. Eisenhower's intelligence analysts concluded that the reported installations could support 20 SS divisions for a year, and their opinion was echoed by General Omar Bradley of the U.S. Twelfth Army Group. As late as April 24, Bradley informed a group of Congressmen touring the war zones: "We may be fighting one month from now and it may even be a year."

There was no redoubt—so said common sense and the Third Army's General George Patton. And yet things stranger than a fortified area were being uncovered by the Allies as they moved ahead. Millions of dollars worth of bullion turned up in a salt mine at Merkers—the gold reserve of the Third Reich. Artworks appropriated from all over Nazi-

occupied Europe were found in the same place. Troops pushing eastward came across the ghastly charnel houses called Dachau and Buchenwald. And there were increasing evidences that Germany was flying apart as its central authority withered in Berlin: scattered uprisings against Nazi rule, high officers scrambling to make treasonous deals, weary civil officials seeking an end to the bloodshed. In this weird twilight of the War anything was possible, and the unexpected often lurked just beyond the next bend in the road.

On the Allies' northern flank, Field Marshal Sir Bernard Montgomery was proceeding with Eisenhower's latest plans for his Twenty-first Army Group. Montgomery had three principal assignments: clear the Germans out of the Netherlands, capture a first-class port such as Bremen or Hamburg in northern Germany for operations against German formations still in Denmark and Norway, and send a strong British force across the neck of the Jutland peninsula in Schleswig-Holstein to occupy Lübeck and Wismar. The Jutland thrust was a patently political maneuver designed to block the Russians' land approaches to Denmark and keep them bottled up in the Baltic. The Russians were bent on securing Lübeck and Wismar, and an undeclared race was on to see who could get there first.

Though these were reasonable objectives, Montgomery seemed to have lost his usual zest for battle when Eisenhower's shocking change of strategy in late March had canceled his drive toward Berlin. A severe, uncompromising autocrat whom Churchill aptly called "that Cromwellian figure," Montgomery was restless and discontented.

In Holland, as Montgomery had long since learned, a conclusive military solution was extremely hard to obtain—water always got in the way. By April 18, the Canadian First Army had driven north from Emmerich and Nijmegen to the Zuider Zee. On the 20th of April it reached the North Sea, bisecting the Germans' Netherlands command of General Johannes Blaskowitz and trapping the Germans against the sea near Amsterdam. While the Canadian II Corps fought its way eastward over swollen streams and through tough German remnants, the Canadian I Corps turned west to attack the trapped enemy and to bring food to the Dutch population, who were starving behind their lines. But Montgomery was fearful of a German threat to open the dikes and drown the Dutch if he attacked their so-called Grebbe Line near Amsterdam; he ordered the Canadians to hold up at Amersfoort.

At about this time, the Canadians received word that Dr. Arthur Seyss-Inquart, the Reich Commissioner of Holland and a man not noted previously for humanitarian instincts (he had instituted a regime of terror in occupied Poland in 1940) was eager to discuss a deal. He would spare the Dutch further suffering (and save the trapped German forces) in return for a cease-fire in the Netherlands. The message was passed to Montgomery, to London, and thence to Washington. The U.S. Joint Chiefs of Staff thought the Germans were unlikely to make good on their threat to open the dikes. They reminded the British of the lesson learned in the Dulles talks about surrender in Italy—that the Russians tended to respond angrily unless talks with the Germans dealt only with unconditional surrender and unless Soviet officers were present to monitor the negotiations. Eisenhower's opinion was solicited; he suggested bargaining with Seyss-Inquart with a Soviet guest in attendance. If that failed, it would be time to send in the Canadians to relieve the Dutch.

On April 28, an unofficial truce was declared at the town of Achterveld long enough for a few British and German officers to arrange a considerably larger meeting. Full-scale discussions convened two days later in a schoolhouse on the edge of town. Chief among those present were Seyss-Inquart and his staff; Eisenhower's Chief of Staff, General Walter Bedell Smith, and Chief of Intelligence Major General Kenneth Strong; Montgomery's Chief of Staff, General Francis de Guingand, and an aide; Prince Bernhard, commander in chief of Dutch forces fighting with the Allies; and a duly invited Soviet delegate, Major General Ivan Susloparov, the chief Russian liaison officer with Eisenhower's headquarters.

General Smith put the case to Seyss-Inquart in bold terms: Give up or suffer the consequences—which could, given the prospect of needless loss of civilian lives, involve trial for murder. The German flatly refused to surrender and negotiations seemed stalled. Then the Allies decided to make a move outside the bargaining process. While talks were going on, the RAF Bomber Command and the U.S. Eighth Air Force dropped 510 tons of foodstuffs and medicine to the long-suffering Dutch; thereafter 1,000 tons of supplies a day were delivered by truck without German objection. Hostilities in western Holland never resumed.

Meanwhile Montgomery's British Second Army, advancing northward three corps abreast toward the Elbe, was having its own problems. The British route to the Elbe basin was stream-cut and swampy; the Second Army's engineers had to build hundreds of bridges along the way, seriously delaying the transport of supplies. Eisenhower was so concerned about the Second Army's ability to beat the Russians to Jutland that he had repeatedly offered Montgomery transportation or whatever other American help seemed necessary.

Montgomery declined the offer, but he would have to manage his forces well to reach the objective in time. By April 20 the XXX Corps, on the Second Army's left flank, which would not be engaged in the urgent advance on the Jutland peninsula, had invested the battered port of Bremen. The corps commander, Lieut. General Brian G. Horrocks, felt no great compulsion to rush into a costly assault. Horrocks served the town fathers with an ultimatum: Surrender within 24 hours or be bombarded to smithereens. Then he waited for two days without receiving a satisfactory answer.

Squabbling had broken out inside Bremen. The commandant of the city, Major General Fritz Becker, had at his disposal 6,000 assorted Army, Navy and home guard troops, and he intended to fight. However, the city council wanted no part of a battle. The councilmen—mostly industrialists and shipping magnates—argued that the War was about to end no matter what they did here, and that it was time to start rebuilding instead of destroying the little that Allied bombers had so far missed. Still Becker refused to change his mind; when the council appealed to Gauleiter Paul Wegener, the Nazi official in nominal control of the Bremen area, Wegener refused to consider negotiations. He urged last-ditch resistance—then sneaked out of town.

On April 22, Horrocks at last called in RAF bombers and put his XXX Corps gunners to work. After more than 48 thunderous hours—and still no surrender—he sent his troops carefully into battle. The 3rd Division attacked the portion of Bremen that lies on the west bank of the Weser River, and the 43rd and 52nd Divisions, which had crossed the river upstream, delivered a right hook at eastern Bremen

The Mayor of Leipzig, Alfred Freyberg, and his wife and sister lie dead in his office after taking poison when U.S. troops entered the city. Most German officials ignored the warnings of Allied brutality churned out by their crumbling government and took their chances with their conquerors.

from the south. On April 24 the attackers fought their way into the city, and German resistance crumbled. It took three more days to mop up the last pockets of resistance but, as Montgomery wrote, "the chief impediment to progress lay in the debris caused by our own bombing."

During the XXX Corps's tussle for Bremen, the Second Army's other two corps had closed to the Elbe all along Montgomery's appointed 90 miles of front running northwest from Wittenberge to the North Sea. Montgomery proceeded with great deliberation. On the right, the VIII Corps, supposedly advancing apace with the U.S. Ninth Army, had a relatively easy cross-country journey but nevertheless reached the river six days after the Americans' spearhead. The XII Corps, in the middle of the British line, was later still; not until April 23 had it cleared the Germans from the west bank of the Elbe opposite Hamburg. Then days passed while the two corps methodically prepared for what might be a difficult multiple operation: a combat crossing of the Elbe, an assault north to capture Hamburg and a fight northeast across the base of Jutland to the Baltic.

By April 27 Eisenhower was convinced that Montgomery was not pushing his Second Army hard enough, and he became more than a little anxious. Large Soviet forces had broken through the Germans' Oder River line north of Berlin and were driving west toward Jutland against weak resistance. So the Supreme Commander—and Churchill as well—sent worried messages to Montgomery urging him to make haste. "I fear I got somewhat irritated," Montgomery later wrote, "and my replies possibly showed it!" He felt that he did not need to be told the drill: "So far as I was concerned the oncoming Russians were more dangerous than the stricken Germans."

Montgomery had meanwhile conceded that he might be able to use a little American combat help, and Eisenhower lent him three divisions under the command of Lieut. General Matthew Ridgway of the XVIII Airborne Corps. Though these divisions were scattered from the Ruhr to the middle Elbe, they assembled with such speed on the British front that Montgomery was inspired to move up his main river crossing from May 1 to April 29. According to the plan, the British VIII Corps was to cross first and establish a bridgehead from which the Americans would move eastward. But when Ridgway, strolling along the Elbe, drew no enemy fire, he concluded that the Germans were thoroughly dispirited and that he could make his own crossing without undue risk. Ridgway proposed the idea to the commander of the Second Army, Lieut. General Sir Miles Dempsey, and Dempsey concurred.

Before dawn on April 29 a detachment of British Commandos crossed the Elbe near Lauenburg against negligible resistance. In the American sector, six miles to the south at Bleckede, Ridgway chose Major General James M. Gavin, commander of the crack 82nd Airborne Division, to spearhead the assault. Gavin's paratroopers were highly disgruntled. They had prepared for what might have been one of the War's great exploits—an airdrop on Tempelhof airfield near the center of Berlin. But this plan had been canceled; instead they had been put on tedious Occupation duty near Cologne. Now they had been rushed across Germany to pull some British chestnuts out of the fire.

Gavin's assault force easily crossed the Elbe through an unseasonable snowfall at 1 a.m. on April 30. The Germans laid down a heavy bombardment to prevent engineers from bridging the river for tank and truck traffic. But all that day the paratroopers expanded their foothold, the engineers toiled under fire, and by nightfall the heavy equipment was rolling across the Elbe on a pontoon bridge 1,300 feet long.

The British and the Americans completed their build-ups on the east bank, then swiftly pushed their attacks across Schleswig-Holstein. To the north, the British 11th Armored Division rolled into Lübeck without firing a shot, trapping substantial German forces along the Danish border. The British 6th Airborne Division, part of Ridgway's corps, dashed 53 miles across the peninsula to Wismar. The rest of the corps formed a skirmish line that sealed off the peninsula against any possible Russian entry from the south. While Gavin's 82nd Airborne took Ludwigslust, supported by a combat command of the U.S. 7th Armored Division, the U.S. 8th Division drove 45 miles northeast across the neck of the peninsula to reach Schwerin between the coast and the Elbe on May 2. Two hours later, the British 6th Airborne Division met their first Russians at Wismar.

While the Schleswig-Holstein operation was under way, the British XII Corps units that had surrounded Hamburg braced themselves to storm the city—or to be attacked by a ragtag German force that had assembled to the northeast. Neither assault took place.

The city of Hamburg had become known in the collapsing Germany as a relatively safe haven; it was a magnet for important men who wished to abandon or scuttle the foundering Nazi ship of state. Prominent among the defectors was the Gauleiter of Hamburg, Karl Kaufmann, who was also the Reich Commissioner of Sea Transport. In Berlin in early April, Kaufmann had disagreed with Hitler's edict that Hamburg was an official fortress, to be defended to the death. Although he knew the Gestapo would henceforth be

watching him closely, Kaufmann contrived an elaborate conspiracy to surrender the entire North Sea coast to the British. This plan, which depended on the cooperation of Field Marshal Ernst Busch, the military chief of Admiral Karl Dönitz's new northern command, proved too ambitious. Kaufmann settled for arrangements to surrender Hamburg.

Through acquaintances in the shipping world—including members of the Ministry of Sea Transport and two German shipping experts living in Scandinavian capitals—Kaufmann was sending messages to British authorities. This network channeled word to the War Office in London to speed up the British advance on Hamburg. Kaufmann had little trouble rallying local sentiment for surrender, for Hamburg was among the Reich's most heavily bombed cities.

A separate attempt to surrender Hamburg was being made through the Danish Resistance movement by SS General Hans Prützmann. Prützmann had been titular head of the Werewolves, a guerrilla group recently created by Hitler to commit sabotage and murder in the Allies' rear areas. The Werewolves were not a formal organization; membership was open to anyone who considered himself a member. Only a few diehards and fanatical schoolboys did, and their successes were minor. Still, the idea of the Werewolves fascinated Propaganda Minister Joseph Goebbels. He quickly usurped Prützmann's role by setting up a station called Radio Werewolf and broadcasting his own rabble-rousing prose. Displaced from his Werewolves job, Prützmann discovered that his surrender efforts were superfluous. He drifted north to escape but was captured by the British, and committed suicide before he could be interrogated.

Hamburg also harbored Minister of Armaments and War Production Albert Speer, a close friend of Kaufmann. Speer had flown north after paying a last sentimental visit to Hitler on April 23, and in Hamburg he rendezvoused with Luftwaffe General Werner Baumbach. Baumbach was a tall, blond, handsome man who looked like a propaganda picture of the archetypal Nazi, but he had grown bitter toward Hitler for allowing the Luftwaffe to deteriorate. Baumbach was in charge of the government's headquarters planes and had access to a flying boat in northern Norway loaded with six months' supplies. He and Speer had a plan to fly to Greenland, where they would wait out the postwar chaos and consider what to do next. But at the last hour Speer decided to abandon any idea of flight abroad. Along with Baumbach, he went to Plön and attached himself to the northern command around Admiral Dönitz.

Last but not least of the Nazis in Hamburg eager to turn coat was Reichsführer-SS Heinrich Himmler, who had set up his headquarters in the city's fashionable Hotel Atlantic. In the last week of April, Himmler's subversive activities reached and passed the critical stage. His offer to surrender all Germany to the western Allies, made through Sweden's Count Bernadotte on April 23, was rejected two days later by President Harry S. Truman (Roosevelt's successor) and Churchill because it excluded the Soviet Union.

Himmler still believed he would be summoned to negotiate a surrender, but he had a fallback plan that included escaping south to Prague by plane. To prepare for this departure he called in General Baumbach on April 28 and said, "If I have to start negotiations I shall probably need some airplanes. Have you got some?" Baumbach promised he would look into it. He consulted with Speer, and the two decided to put Himmler on a plane and have him flown to an airfield already in Allied hands. Himmler, his intelligence system still functioning, found out about the plot to deliver him to the enemy. He confronted Baumbach, snarling: "When people fly in your planes they don't know where they're going to land!"

Along with his plans to turn traitor and flee, Himmler also nurtured grand dreams for continuing the War to the north in Schleswig-Holstein. As it turned out, however, he ended up—like Baumbach and Speer—simply sticking close to Dönitz and the rest of what was left of an organized Reich. He left the Hamburg area and headed north to Plön.

The fate of Hamburg ultimately depended on Major General Alwin Wolz, the stout, bespectacled commandant of the city. The British commander who had invested Hamburg, Major General L. O. Lyne of the 7th Armored Division, was convinced that Gauleiter Kaufmann meant to surrender. But he was by no means certain that Wolz would direct his miscellaneous forces to lay down their arms. So on April 29 General Lyne began his negotiations tentatively, sending Wolz an appeal "in the name of humanity" to surrender while there was still a Hamburg.

Wolz's reply was encouraging. Despite his orders to hold

British artillery batteries unleash a night bombardment as Field Marshal Montgomery's armies prepare to cross the Elbe for the final push in northern Germany. Aided by the Americans, the British were to drive northward to the Baltic coast at Lübeck and capture Hamburg.

Running wild in the last days of the War, looters in Hanover distribute food to a crowd composed of both slave laborers and hungry German civ

...ries to stop freed Russian laborers from stripping a German store.

British soldiers aid laborers who had been trapped in a burning building.

REVOLT OF THE SLAVE WORKERS

...e climax of the war in Europe, 7.5 ...n slave laborers were working in ...any. Over a period of five years they ...een rounded up from occupied na- ...with characteristic Nazi efficiency: ...ypical sweep, young men and wom- ...re snatched off the streets on the way ...from their jobs and shipped direct- ...he Reich.

...e shanghaied laborers manned Ger- ...munitions factories, harvested Ger- ...crops and became domestic drudges ...erman housewives. Many were sub- ...d to viciously degrading treatment— ...fed, existing without heat or ade-

quate sanitation in bombed-out barracks, in damp caves, and even in dog kennels.

For those who survived to be released by Allied troops, the first moments of freedom often proved to be more than they could manage. In Salzwedel, about 70 miles to the southeast of Hamburg, mobs of freed laborers roamed the streets looting, fighting among themselves for booty and wreaking vengeance on their former masters. In one incident, a mob pulled a wounded SS man to the pavement and trampled him to death, clawing and tearing at his flesh. Other acts of revenge were mindlessly destructive: One group of

workers seized tubs of marmalade and dumped their contents in the street.

In these circumstances, Allied soldiers often found themselves in the middle—either defending German lives and property from rampaging freed laborers, or protecting the workers from desperate Germans. In Osnabrück, a German policeman spied a group of laborers looting the cellar of a store; after waiting until most of the group had entered the basement, he set fire to the building. British troops who had taken the town rescued most of the looters, but despite their efforts *(above, right)* two women laborers died.

Hamburg, he said, "I am prepared, together with the authorized representative of Gauleiter Kaufmann, to discuss the eventual surrender of Hamburg and the far-reaching consequences arising therefrom."

The meetings between negotiators that ensued went even better. As a friendly touch, one Oxford-educated German wore a scarf with his college colors, and Wolz removed all doubt with his opening statement: "The principal point is the actual time General Lyne wishes to enter Hamburg."

More remarkable still, it developed that the German emissaries were empowered to agree to so much more than the mere surrender of Hamburg that it became necessary to involve Field Marshal Montgomery in the talks. For all practical purposes, the Allies' campaign on the northern flank had come to an end.

On the southern flank, a new phase of the War had begun on April 14, the same day Eisenhower sent the Combined Chiefs of Staff his strategic plan for the resolution of hostilities. As stipulated by the plan, the armies in the south paused to regroup. The Supreme Commander finally told his American generals of the portentous change he had revealed to the British more than two weeks earlier: The Western Allies were not going to take Berlin. For reasons known only to Eisenhower, he had not informed even General Bradley, his closest confidant and the Allied commander in the west with the most troops. (Bradley's Twelfth Army Group comprised the U.S. First, Third, Ninth and Fifteenth Armies—more than 1.3 million soldiers.) Presumably Eisenhower had withheld the announcement to postpone the letdown in morale it was sure to cause among his generals.

General Patton's reaction was rather mild for him, perhaps because his Third Army was too far south to take part even if there had been an operation against Berlin. A Patton aide later recounted that when Eisenhower told the general the news, Patton simply stared in disbelief and said, "Ike, I don't see how you figure that one. We had better take Berlin and quick, and on to the Oder." Later in the conversation, Eisenhower remarked that he did not understand why anyone would want to take the German capital with all the problems it entailed. At this Patton put his hands on Eisenhower's shoulders and said, "I think history will answer that question for you."

In the middle of April, Patton's army reached its eastern stop-line south of the First Army, across a Mulde River tributary at Chemnitz. Patton's advance across Germany had been a swift one, though not swift enough to suit Patton. As he drove east down the corridor between Frankfurt am Main and Kassel, he had been obliged by Army Group plans to hold up several times so that the First Army could draw abreast. Then, after his armor had broken past organized opposition and was steadily making 15 to 20 miles a day with minimal losses, Eisenhower and Bradley told him he was going too fast. To Patton the admonition seemed overcautious; earlier he had written in his diary, "When those two get together, they get timid."

Patton was badly in need of a new fight, and Bradley gave him the most belligerent assignment he could. The Third Army was to veer southeastward along Czechoslovakia's western border, aiming toward Linz, Austria. On the way, Patton was to seek and destroy the National Redoubt, or at least help disprove its existence. Then he was to link up with the Russians at or near Linz.

Patton was less than delighted by the mission. Both he and his brilliant intelligence chief, Colonel Oscar W. Koch, were convinced that the National Redoubt was a hallucination; as for the Russians, Patton wanted to beat rather than meet them. Bradley did mention informally a possibility that excited Patton—that future developments might give the Third Army the job of invading and liberating at least part of Czechoslovakia. But in a way this inducement increased Patton's frustration. As his patrols into Czechoslovakia discovered on April 17, he could reach Prague, the capital, in three days and take it in one or two more. But he would have to act within the next three weeks, by which time the Russians could be expected to reach and enter the city.

Patton glumly ordered his army to regroup, a tedious procedure, and flew off on a day's leave to Paris, where he heard about his promotion to four-star general. Returning to Germany, he visited Merkers, where a citizen's casual remark to a GI had led to the discovery of the Reich's gold reserve filling the huge chambers of a salt mine. He visited the Ohrdruf concentration camp near Wiesbaden and became violently ill at the hideous sights he saw there, but persevered and visited a place worse by far, Buchenwald. He wrote: "From the execution room in the Buchenwald

In front of the Hamburg city hall, Major General Alwin Wolz (saluting) surrenders Germany's second-largest city and most important port to British officers. As occupying troops made their way through the devastated streets of Hamburg, they were struck by how neatly the rubble of war had been swept aside. "Even in defeat," wrote one soldier, "the Germans were resolutely tidy."

setup there was an elevator, hand operated, which carried the corpses to an incinerator plant on the floor above. The slave in charge of this took great pride and kept rubbing his hand on the floor and then showing me how clean it was.''

The Third Army started south on April 19, and Patton followed on the 22nd, moving his headquarters from Hersfeld over the mountains to Erlangen. Patton's four big corps—his army was growing rapidly to a prodigious 540,000 men—made steady and uneventful progress; the XX Corps on the army's right crossed the Danube on April 26 and seized historic Regensburg—captured in 1809 by Napoleon. On the 27th the Third Army captured its 600,000th prisoner since commencing operations on the Continent in August of 1944. Patton chose that day to take a look at the fabled Danube and reportedly walked away from its muddy waters unimpressed.

Indeed, nothing stirred Patton these days. Near Ingolstadt, his III Corps bumped into a large German force with an elegant name from German mythology, *Division Nibelungen*, but only a few obsolete tanks and no artillery. Patton obliterated it and did not even mention the battle in his extensive

correspondence. As the April days ran out, the man who had said ''I love war and the responsibility and excitement'' was dreaming of beating the Russians to Prague and then asking for a transfer to the Pacific. He wrote lugubriously in his diary and in a letter home: ''There is nothing of interest happening,'' and ''I feel as low as whale tracks on the bottom of the ocean.''

Though Patton was only vaguely aware of it, the fate of Czechoslovakia was being worked out between Eisenhower and the Soviets. After several days of negotiations in late April, Eisenhower got Russian concurrence for an American advance to a line that ran through the towns of Budweis, Pilsen and Karlsbad. On May 4, Eisenhower passed word of the agreement to Bradley, who granted Patton permission to cross the Czechoslovakian border. Patton gave a whoop of joy. Suddenly, almost too late, the War was beginning to get exciting again.

The broad swath cut by Patton's enormous army on his southeasterly track ran from Chemnitz to Regensburg and reduced the front that was the responsibility of General Ja-

cob Devers' Sixth Army Group, which now covered a line running from Ingolstadt to Stuttgart. Devers was grateful; he seldom got such help from Eisenhower's headquarters because his group's far southern position was outside the main thrust of the campaign. Devers' shortened front meant that his two armies were headed almost due south, with the U.S. Seventh Army under Lieut. General Alexander Patch on the left, aiming for Salzburg and western Austria, and the French First Army of General Jean de Lattre de Tassigny on the right, following the northern shore of Lake Constance and the Swiss border.

Reflecting on this arrangement of forces, General Patch had mixed feelings. After the losses his army had just suffered in the battle for Nuremberg, Patton's presence on his left was a relief. But he was less content with the Frenchman on his right: General de Lattre deliberately poached on his territory at every opportunity.

De Lattre saw the matter differently. The United States had originally equipped his army; but to de Lattre, the Americans expected in return slavish obedience without any specific agreement or any French voice in the councils of war. The leader of the recognized Provisional Government of France, General Charles de Gaulle, had often told de Lattre in so many words that the Americans were trying to frustrate France's legitimate national aspirations; that once a tract of German territory had been captured it belonged to the captor and not to the Allies mutually; and that de Lattre must use his army for frankly political purposes, to restore French pride and glory. De Lattre, a romantic poet and prose stylist as well as a skillful tactician, declared grandly, "It was my duty to be rash because the nation's stake made it obligatory."

On April 18, de Lattre had triumphantly entered Patch's Seventh Army territory to seize the university town of Tübingen. In a joint operation four days later, units of Patch's army were supposed to invest Stuttgart from the north and east to prevent the escape of the German Nineteenth Army; meanwhile French troops were to approach from the Black Forest to the southwest and storm the city.

The French took Stuttgart on schedule, capturing 28,000 prisoners at a cost of 700 casualties. But in the aftermath of the victory, they slighted workaday details such as maintaining order in Stuttgart—which was beset by hordes of

Near the frontier of Austria—the first country to be gobbled up by the Third Reich and one of the last to be liberated—men of the U.S. 11th Armored Division watch shellbursts along a ridge harboring one of the few pockets of German resistance they encountered in the area.

liberated slave laborers—so that supplies could be safely and expeditiously shipped through the town to Patch's Seventh Army farther east. Such an orderly state of affairs was especially important because the roads in this southeastern part of Germany were few and relatively poor; any obstruction was regarded as intolerable. Devers ordered the French to turn the city over to the Americans, but when U.S. units arrived on April 24 to take over, de Lattre declined to depart. Patch appealed to Devers, who twice ordered de Lattre to be gone.

At this point de Gaulle instructed de Lattre, "I require you to maintain a French garrison at Stuttgart and to institute immediately a military government." If the Americans protested, de Lattre was told, "you will reply that the orders of your government are to hold and administer the territory conquered by our troops until the French zone of occupation has been fixed between the interested governments." In his orders to de Lattre, de Gaulle was, in fact, holding Stuttgart hostage until the Allies mapped out in detail the territory that at Yalta they had generally agreed France should administer after the War.

When Devers notified Eisenhower that his authority had twice been flouted, the Supreme Commander lodged an official protest with de Gaulle. Eisenhower's protest to a difficult ally—de Gaulle consistently undercut overall Allied interests to further unilateral French goals—was subdued in tone. He said he would not cut off supplies to de Lattre or do anything to impair the effectiveness of French-American cooperation; on the contrary, he would redraw maps and rewrite orders so that the French could stay in Stuttgart. But since French divisions could not be counted on to take orders from the Americans, Eisenhower questioned the wisdom of equipping any more of them.

The French bottleneck in Stuttgart not only interfered with the American supply system but also imperiled the secret mission of a small group of American scientists disguised as soldiers. The code name of their operation, *Alsos*, was a clue to their work. *Alsos* is the Greek word for a grove of trees—an erudite pun on the name of General Leslie R. Groves, director of the *Manhattan Project*, the top-secret, high-priority American effort to develop an atomic bomb. According to U.S. intelligence reports, Germany's nuclear-research program was based at Hechingen, 50 miles south of Stuttgart. The town was within the territory taken by the French but had not yet been occupied by their forces. The *Alsos* team had come to capture the German scientists, study their experiments and learn how close the enemy was to producing an atomic bomb—all without revealing anything about the project to the French.

The *Alsos* men, led by Colonel Boris T. Pash and escorted by a contingent of combat engineers—who not only could fight but also could dismantle and repair machines and other equipment—headed for Hechingen by a roundabout route and bluffed their way through the French lines. Entering Hechingen, they captured the German scientists in the town and found the research installation concealed in a cave. It was soon obvious to them that the Allies had no cause for concern about German nuclear research. The Germans were primarily interested in developing a nuclear engine for submarines, and they had not yet advanced far enough to set off a nuclear chain reaction.

In Stuttgart, de Lattre was dissatisfied with the redrawn interarmy boundary line that legitimized French possession of the city. He wanted to capture Ulm, about 50 miles east of Hechingen, in part because Napoleon had won a splendid victory there against Austria in 1805. The city was 44 miles inside American Seventh Army territory. De Lattre had his heart set as well on taking the town of Sigmaringen, about 30 miles southeast of Hechingen, also part of Patch's area; leading politicians of the collaborationist Vichy regime that had ruled France under German control had fled to Sigmaringen in 1944, and had set up a government-in-exile there. Since both Ulm and Sigmaringen were on the Danube, de Lattre dispatched an armored column with orders to take Sigmaringen first, then follow the river downstream to Ulm.

De Lattre's column took Sigmaringen without much trouble but found that the Vichyites had scattered. De Lattre was undismayed. "Bravo!" he cried as his tankers rushed on toward Ulm. "The Americans may dislodge us, but the French flag will have flown there."

On April 22, units of Patch's 10th Armored Division reached the western outskirts of Ulm, which was held intermittently by small units of retreating Germans. The Americans had no idea that de Lattre was trespassing again, and it was fortunate that the GIs and their peripatetic allies recognized each other quickly when the French column, two battalions strong, came rumbling up from the southwest the next day. According to de Lattre, the 10th Armored's commander, Major General William Morris Jr., was not at all upset by the French intrusion. "Among tankers," Morris said, "we always understand each other."

It was quite another story when word of the incident reached Sixth Army Group headquarters. General Devers, his patience sorely strained, dispatched an officer to de Lattre's headquarters with an order for a prompt French withdrawal to the French side of the boundary. General de Lattre ignored the order.

On April 24, the battle for Ulm was joined by a combat command of the 10th Armored Division, an infantry regiment of the U.S. 44th Division and the two uninvited battalions of de Lattre's army. The French were in the thick of the daylong fight. "In the evening," de Lattre wrote, "our tricolor rose above the citadel." Only then did de Lattre agree to go back to his own side of the boundary.

The capture of Sigmaringen and Ulm destroyed the western end of Field Marshal Kesselring's defensive line, which ran roughly east-west along the Danube inside southern Germany; his armies were powerless to prevent de Lattre and Patch from advancing southward. De Lattre pushed on to Lake Constance, then followed the north shore of the lake. In Friedrichshafen he captured the old Zeppelin Institution that had developed the dirigibles famous for bombing London during World War I, and continued uneventfully into the Vorarlberg region of extreme western Austria. The fighting on this leg of the march was on a minute, almost personal scale, as shown in de Lattre's description of the encounter of a French sergeant and a few of his men with a proud German colonel at Überlingen:

"When called upon to surrender, he refused and continued to aim his weapon. The scene dragged on, for our men felt reluctant to strike down this solitary man whose obstinacy was not without greatness. Finally, to put an end to the situation, the sergeant made up his mind to put a bullet through the colonel's arm. Then, with great dignity, the colonel threw his revolver down and stepped forward, declaring, 'Now that I am wounded, I can surrender.'"

On de Lattre's left, the U.S. Seventh Army thrust southward and southeastward three corps abreast, each corps taking an average of 1,000 prisoners a day. The commander of the VI Corps, holding the right flank of the Seventh Army, told his troops, "This is a pursuit, not an attack." The GIs hurried forward, riding everything that could move, including vehicles that had been abandoned by German units when they ran out of fuel. They negotiated plunging, twisting mountain roads, crossed deep gorges and climbed through high, narrow passes; in breathtaking settings they captured the Passion Play village of Oberammergau and the ski resort of Garmisch-Partenkirchen. And they found nothing to suggest the existence of a national redoubt on either side of the German-Austrian border—which two VI Corps divisions crossed on April 29.

In central Austria, however, U.S. troops once again came upon units of de Lattre's army trespassing on their territory. The Americans and the French jockeyed frantically to beat each other to vital passes across the Austrian Alps. The sole point of this race was to reach the Italian border first and shake hands with Allied troops coming north from Italy. Pushed beyond endurance by the French, Patch barred them from his roads, and the French took to the mountains; in a hair-raising sprint in the Landeck area, a French platoon donned skis and took a 20-mile shortcut through mountains two miles high.

The other two corps of the Seventh Army, pushing into Bavaria on their way to Austria, ran into anti-Nazi uprisings. The XV Corps on the left and the XXI Corps in the center were approaching Munich and Augsburg respectively when, on April 27, their forward elements were intercepted by Germans who pleaded that their cities be spared until insurgents could take over and negotiate a peaceful surrender. In Augsburg, the revolt was staged by half a dozen small groups that had never heard of one another, much less met to coordinate their efforts. Though some citizens flew white flags from their houses and some artillery crews muzzled their guns with white pillowcases, forces still loyal to Hitler held out until a rebel led a battalion of the U.S. 3rd Division to confront the command post of the city's commandant. Five minutes later, Augsburg surrendered.

Munich, Germany's third-largest city and birthplace of the Nazi Party, turned out to be fertile ground for insurgents. Their leader was a young Army captain named Ruppert

Gerngross who had returned wounded and embittered from the Russian front in 1941, and who had been placed in command of a unit of Army translators in Munich. Over the years, Captain Gerngross and like-minded linguists from his outfit had cautiously recruited anti-Nazis from the ranks of local lawyers, doctors, professors and civil servants; they also gained adherents among the managers of three large factories and even several small infantry and reserve tank units stationed there. The organization, which Gerngross called Freedom Action Bavaria (FAB), had developed an intricate plan to take over the key facilities in Munich as soon as Allied troops were close enough to distract the main forces loyal to the Nazis. Gerngross sent two men to General Patch's headquarters to convey the plan in detail; Gerngross expected Patch to declare Munich an open city after FAB had taken over.

At 2 a.m. on April 28, the FAB men went into action, wearing white arm bands to identify each other in the dark. Rebel teams seized an Army barracks, arrested Franz Ritter von Epp, an elderly general who ran the Munich area for the German government, and captured one of the city's two radio stations. Gerngross went on the air to appeal for popular support. By morning, many citizens thought the War was over; in place of the Nazi swastika they ran up the blue-and-white flag of the old independent kingdom of Bavaria.

But the promise of the rebellion soon faded. Gerngross and FAB had failed to neutralize the two most important men in Munich: Gauleiter Paul Giesler, the top Nazi Party official, and Lieut. General Siegfried Westphal, Chief of Staff of Field Marshal Kesselring's southern command. Giesler stamped into the radio station that the rebels had not taken, went on the air and denounced the "contemptible scoundrels" who had fomented the uprising. Confronted with uncompromising established authority, public opinion swung back to the Nazis, and General Westphal slowly regained control of Munich's modest garrison. A number of insurgents were taken prisoner and hanged or shot; Gerngross and three colleagues managed to escape in a stolen SS car.

The U.S. Seventh Army had a fight on its hands after all. Its units converged on Munich from all directions. The 42nd and 45th Infantry and 20th Armored Divisions of the XV Corps approached from the northwest and north. Along the way the infantry divisions found and liberated the Dachau concentration camp. In addition, General Patch borrowed the 3rd Division from the XXI Corps and sent it from Augsburg to help out, and reconnaissance troops from another XXI Corps outfit, the 12th Armored Division, swung around to attack Munich from the southwest.

The battle, joined on April 29 with a heavy artillery duel, was a disorderly affair. Gerngross' rebels had managed to prevent the authorities from destroying the bridges into the city, so the Americans had little trouble getting into town. But once there the GIs found themselves in an unpredictable struggle. In several neighborhoods they clashed with German troops who were still busy fighting insurgents. Soldiers of the 3rd and 42nd Divisions were greeted by a small, cheering crowd as they paraded into downtown Munich, but men of the 45th Division had a long, vicious, room-to-room fight before they extinguished resistance in an SS academy on the northern outskirts. Not until nightfall of April 30 was Munich completely pacified.

Southward from Munich and Augsburg, the XV and the XXI Corps had a walkover. Every day seemed to be wash day in the toylike Bavarian towns—white sheets hung from countless windows in sign of surrender. On the rare occasion when Germans offered resistance, a GI's machine-gun

French General Jean de Lattre de Tassigny (left), commander of the French First Army, checks a map with American Major General Frank W. Milburn in January 1945. Ostensibly operating as part of a U.S. army group, de Lattre often followed orders from Paris designed to enhance the glory of France rather than obeying Allied directives.

To spare their city unnecessary damage, Munich police officials show officers of the U.S. Seventh Army where German troops in the city are still holding out. Although an anti-Nazi take-over by splinter groups hoping to surrender Munich was overthrown by Hitler loyalists, the near coup hampered effective opposition to the Allies.

burst usually settled matters. The reconnaissance units of the armored divisions, equipped with speedy but thin-skinned jeeps and armored cars, raced far ahead of the slower, less vulnerable tanks. The XV Corps reached the Austrian border so quickly that General Devers arranged with General Bradley for the corps to spread out eastward and take on the assignment of capturing the Salzburg area instead of giving the task to Patton's army, some of whose infantry had been slowed by foul weather.

As the XV Corps slipped east, several of its units competed energetically with XXI Corps outfits for the honor of taking the Berghof, Hitler's eagle's-nest estate on the Obersalzberg. There were traffic jams down below in the town of Berchtesgaden; "Everybody and his brother is trying to get into the town," reported Seventh Army headquarters.

Men of the 3rd Division reached the Berghof first, followed by some French tankers, then by paratroopers of the 101st Airborne Division. They tore the place apart. When *Time* reporter Percy Knauth arrived, he prowled the rooms, ransacked and bullet torn, and found only one personal memento of the owner: a calling card imprinted with the name of Eva Braun. "All the complex, lavish luxury of the Obersalzberg was in ruins now," wrote Knauth. "Above us, as we stood on Hitler's doorstep, the empty picture window leered out over the torn trees and bomb craters like a great, gaping eye. A huge sheet of half-melted tin hung down from the wall. The trees and shrubbery were gone, the grass was gone, there was just torn, brown earth and splintered rocks, a mockery of beauty and of power."

Between them, Devers' army group and Patton's army had sealed off all the Alpine passes that might have given enemy units egress from Germany into Austria. They had detected no evidence of a national redoubt in southern Germany or in northwestern Austria. In addition, Patton's army had blocked the western escape routes of all German forces in Czechoslovakia. If a redoubt existed somewhere in western Austria, German troops to man it would have to come from Italy, an unlikely possibility.

By mid-April, the spring offensive of Field Marshal Sir Harold Alexander, Allied commander in Italy, had doomed the German forces in the area. German Army Group C had been driven into the Po River Valley, where the Allies' superiority in tanks and aircraft put the Germans at a severe disadvantage. Alexander's field commander, U.S. Lieut. General Mark Clark, had alternated attacks by the British Eighth

Army and the American Fifth Army, permitting the Allied air forces to concentrate their air-ground support. The Germans retreated across the Po into hilly country north of the river.

Meanwhile, Operation *Sunrise*—the surrender negotiations initiated by SS General Karl Wolff and nurtured by Allen Dulles of the OSS—seemed to be dead. Wolff had been unable to win over either General Heinrich-Gottfried von Vietinghoff, the commander of Army Group C, or his old superior, Field Marshal Kesselring. Vietinghoff's hesitance, together with the Russians' protests over their exclusion from the meetings, had prompted the American and British governments to terminate the talks. On April 21, Dulles received a coded cable from Washington: JOINT CHIEFS OF STAFF DIRECT THAT OSS BREAK OFF ALL CONTACT WITH GERMAN EMISSARIES AT ONCE.

Dulles was disconsolate. The cancellation came just at a time when a new political worry made a quick German surrender all the more desirable. With the Germans weakening, partisan groups were taking over territory all over northern Italy. The strongest groups were Communist, and the organization that coordinated the groups, the Committee of National Liberation, was Communist dominated. It was possible that the Germans would delay the Allies' advance just long enough for the partisans to establish a Communist government in the north. Dulles hated to see the surrender negotiations die.

Sunrise in fact refused to roll over. In a curious way it was Heinrich Himmler who gave it new life. He called Wolff to Berlin on April 16 to explain his oft-reported treasonous behavior—his meetings with Dulles were strongly suspected. For Wolff it was the beginning of two weeks of hectic and improbable escapades.

Wolff flew to Berlin and staged a life-or-death bluff. Putting on an air of sincerity and uprightness, he talked Himmler into allowing him to appeal his case to Hitler. Then when Wolff met the Führer he reminded him of a conversation they had once had about the value of secret access to enemy leaders. Wolff claimed credit for opening channels to Truman and Churchill through his talks with Dulles. After a thoughtful pause, Hitler said, "I accept your presentation. You're fantastically lucky." He sent Wolff back to Italy on April 18, telling him to keep talking to the Americans and stalling for time.

Upon arriving in Italy, Wolff renewed his work of persuasion with General von Vietinghoff. This time he made progress. Vietinghoff's reluctance had been partly political—he had not wanted to act without a strong lead from Field Marshal Kesselring—and partly soldierly, in an honorable tradi-

tion. To protect his men, he wanted to soften the Allied insistence on unconditional surrender. Now, depressed by the worsening military situation, Vietinghoff backed down—though still holding out for some points, such as Allied assurances that German soldiers would not be forced to labor or be imprisoned for long on foreign soil. Wolff continued to press him, day after day.

On April 23, Dulles received a phone call from Major Max Waibel, his confidant in the Swiss intelligence service, who imparted the surprising news that General Wolff and two other German officers were crossing the border in civilian clothes to surrender all German forces in Italy. "To say I was in a predicament would put it mildly," Dulles later remarked. Unwilling to refuse a sure surrender or to resume the forbidden talks on his own responsibility, he sent off appeals to Washington and to Field Marshal Alexander for permission to reopen *Sunrise*. While he awaited replies, Waibel accommodated the three Germans in his own home on Lake Lucerne.

No answer came the next day, and Wolff returned to Italy to allay the suspicions of his Nazi superiors. He left behind SS Major Eugen Wenner with written authority to surrender all SS troops in Italy. The other German, Army staff officer Lieut. Colonel Victor von Schweinitz, carried a similar document signed by Vietinghoff.

Wolff, delayed by partisan roadblocks en route to his headquarters, stopped for the night of April 25 at the Villa Locatelli, an SS installation at Cernobbio—just one mile inside the Italian border. Soon after his arrival, in walked Marshal Rodolfo Graziani, the military commander of the so-called Republic of Salò, Benito Mussolini's German-supported puppet government. Graziani revealed that the Duce was nearby, heading for the mountains north of Lake Como to make a last stand with a few Italian troops. Wolff quickly took advantage of the chance meeting and persuaded the distraught old marshal to write out and sign a document surrendering what was left of the Italian Army.

By the early hours of April 26, Wolff realized he was in deep trouble. Partisan groups, learning that Mussolini and other Fascists had been seen near Lake Como, had converged on the area overnight and had surrounded the Villa Locatelli. But they neglected to cut the telephone lines, and Wolff managed to reach Dulles' aide, Gero von Schulze Gaevernitz, with a call for help. That evening, an OSS agent posing as the American Consul from Lugano managed to talk the partisans into letting Wolff leave the villa in the agent's custody. Mussolini and his mistress, Clara Petacci, were not so lucky. They were captured by the partisans, who shot them to death two days later.

On April 27, Dulles and Field Marshal Alexander received authorization from their governments to continue with *Sunrise*. The next day, the two German plenipotentiaries (who had been left in Switzerland when Wolff returned to Italy) were flown to Alexander's headquarters at Caserta, near Naples. There on April 29, after the Germans' last objections had been aired and dismissed, an instrument of surrender, to take effect at noon on May 2, was signed—under the watchful eyes of a Soviet delegation led by Major General Aleksey P. Kislenko.

The war in Italy seemed over. But one final scene remained to be played out. Field Marshal Kesselring, who had shown some sympathy for the idea of capitulation, now decided to prevent a real surrender from taking place. He summoned General von Vietinghoff to his headquarters at Innsbruck, Austria—a town already threatened by General Devers' southward advance—and replaced him with an obscure general named Friedrich Schulz. Other high officers involved in the surrender plot were placed under arrest.

SS General Karl Wolff, returning to his Bolzano headquarters, went back to work to persuade Kesselring and Schulz to let the surrender occur. Schulz refused to yield without Kesselring's approval, but Kesselring was in the field and could not be reached. Kesselring himself phoned Wolff at 2 a.m. on May 2, and Wolff spent two hours haranguing the field marshal, apparently without success. But half an hour after Kesselring hung up, Wolff got a call from Schulz, who reported that Kesselring had just ordered that the cease-fire be observed.

Finally the war in Italy really *was* over. As the Germans of Army Group C laid down their weapons, units of the U.S. Fifth Army, which had fought all the way up the Italian boot, were hurrying north to link up with other Allied troops. At the Italian town of Vipiteno near the Brenner Pass, men of the 88th Infantry Division shook hands with GIs of the U.S. Seventh Army's 103rd Division, winners of the race southward through Austria.

A GI stands in the shattered 12-by-30-foot picture window that dominated the living room of the Berghof, Hitler's Bavarian retreat in the mountains near Berchtesgaden. Beneath the sprawling compound, which included villas for the top Nazis, an SS barracks and even a small airfield, the Americans found a network of tunnels that led to comfortable, bombproof apartments and stores of luxury goods.

DEATH STRUGGLE IN THE CAPITAL

A defiantly scrawled message, "Berlin shall remain German," greets Russian self-propelled guns as they rumble down a street of the embattled capital.

IN BERLIN, A STORM OF FIRE AND BLOOD

By April 21, 1945, eight Russian armies—one and a quarter million men—surrounded Berlin. Russian tanks had broken into the outer suburbs, and Russian guns rained shells on terrified civilians. Defending Berlin were some 75,000 German troops who were short of everything—tanks, guns, ammunition, fuel, food.

Had sane heads prevailed at this moment, Berlin might have surrendered, sparing tens of thousands of lives and the ravaging of the city itself. Instead, an irrational will to resist turned the city into a battleground. Adolf Hitler, in the unreal quiet of his underground bunker, believed a miracle might still deliver Germany from its enemies. Even those generals who knew the War was lost wanted to hold off the Red Army in order to surrender to the Americans.

If fear of Russian vengeance or belief in the Führer's miracle were not enough to keep the German troops fighting, SS executioners made up the difference. Roving the streets, they hanged or shot suspected deserters on the spot.

Every foot of Berlin was bloodily contested. The Russians, by their own estimate, inundated the city with 1.8 million shells—some 36,000 tons of metal. Then, before the acrid smoke had lifted, the infantry rushed headlong into the survivors' machine-gun and artillery fire. Inside buildings the Russians routed the tenacious defenders room by room, using grenades, flamethrowers, automatic weapons—and on occasion their bare hands.

Block after block the city was demolished. Fires raged out of control; the dead and dying littered the streets. Berlin's 1,750,000 inhabitants—most of them women and children—were caught in the cross fire, and thousands died alongside the soldiers.

As the ring of Soviet troops tightened on the inner city, the fighting grew even more desperate. Waves of Russians charged the last German positions and eventually overwhelmed them. The human price of these assaults was enormous. "Every step cost us lives," wrote Soviet General Vasily Chuikov. But in the primitive arithmetic of war, the Russians had more lives to spend than the Germans.

A grinning Russian (left) guards Germans captured in Berlin, including the city's last commandant, Lieut. General Helmuth Weidling (right).

Fire sparked by Russian shelling turns a Berlin street into a swirling inferno. ''There were so many fires,'' one Berliner wrote, ''that there was no night.''

A mobile Russian assault gun pounds a German-held building at close range, preparing the way for an attack by infantry.

Their city incinerated and collapsing around them, residents of Berlin race from cellar to cellar trying to keep one step ahead of the oncoming Russians.

artillery had softened up German defenses, but it was the foot soldiers who had to carry the fight against hundreds of stubbornly held German redoubt

Russian infantrymen take up positions behind a wall of debris to return German fire from the buildings in the background.

A Soviet rifleman dashes across a Berlin street behind a tank column. At left is a Russian horse-drawn supply wagon

disabled tank provides cover for a Russian soldier. Early in the fighting Soviet tanks were unprotected by infantry, and hundreds were knocked out.

Soviet heavy tank halts on a Berlin street in the midst of battle while members of its crew carry off a wounded comrade to search for medical aid.

Backed by a tank, members of a Russian assault squad cautiously move in on the remains of a building that may still shelter armed German troop

ushed from his hiding place in a cellar, a German soldier is taken prisoner by a Russian wielding a submachine gu

4

All day long on April 26, Adolf Hitler in his *Führerbunker* was fed tempting tidbits of good news:

Field Marshal Ferdinand Schörner's Army Group Center, according to reports from the field, was gaining ground in its drive northward to reestablish contact with General Theodor Busse's Ninth Army, surrounded southeast of Berlin.

Busse, it was said, was making dramatic headway in his effort to break out of the Soviet trap and link up with General Wenck's Twelfth Army southwest of the encircled capital.

Wenck, diverted from the defense of the Elbe for a drive through Potsdam to relieve Berlin, was meeting with what the bunker generals called "gratifying successes."

Even General Felix Steiner's hapless 3rd SS Panzer Corps was said to have scored a small gain in its attempt to drive through to Berlin from the north.

All these reports emanated from areas where combat was actually going on, but otherwise they bore little relation to reality. Hitler warmed to each report as it came in, but their cumulative effect seemed to tax even his remarkable powers of self-deception; he seemed finally to have realized that fighting was going on inside Berlin itself, in the streets and in the subways—indeed, within a few thousand yards of his bunker. Thus, far from being encouraged, the Führer was in despair that evening—despair so black and so deep that it shook two dedicated Nazis who arrived at the bunker just before 7 p.m. They were General Robert Ritter von Greim, the Luftwaffe commander for the Munich area, and Hanna Reitsch, a woman test pilot who had an international reputation as an aviation pioneer.

Hitler had summoned General von Greim to Berlin by telegram, urgently and without explanation. Greim had left Munich the night before, taking his old friend Reitsch along as companion and copilot. They flew in stages to Gatow airfield, about 15 miles west of central Berlin, where they boarded a slow Fieseler-Storch reconnaissance plane that could land on the East-West Axis, a broad boulevard that passed a half mile west of the *Führerbunker*.

Greim flew over the city at treetop level, and from what he could see at that altitude, Berlin looked like hell's anteroom. Entire city blocks had been set ablaze by Sovet bombers and artillery, and here and there street fighting flared—a commotion of men running and white puffs of

LAST AGONIES OF THE REICH

gun smoke and black sprays of rubble from erupting mortar shells or *Panzerfäuste,* antitank grenade launchers. Above, Soviet and Luftwaffe pilots fought swirling dogfights. An artillery shell suddenly ripped open the underside of the low-flying Storch and smashed Greim's right foot. Amid a storm of shell splinters, Reitsch took the controls and landed safely on the East-West Axis not far from the Brandenburg Gate. There she commandeered a passing German Army vehicle that took her and her pain-racked friend to Hitler's door.

After Greim's wound had been treated by Dr. Ludwig Stumpfegger in the *Führerbunker* dispensary, the general received a visit from Hitler. The Führer declared bitterly that Hermann Göring had betrayed and deserted him; he then explained that Greim had been called to replace that cowardly scoundrel as commander in chief of the Luftwaffe with the rank of field marshal. With eyes half-closed, speaking in a strangely low voice, Hitler concluded, "In the name of the German people I give you my hand."

Greim was not dismayed that he had made his long, traumatic trip just to learn what Hitler might have told him in his telegram. Nor did the pain from his wound detract one whit from an honor even greater than promotion: Greim and Hanna Reitsch begged for—and Hitler granted them—permission to stay in the bunker and die with the Führer.

A little later that night, Hanna Reitsch learned that the death watch had already begun. Hitler called her to his private suite of four closet-sized rooms and said quietly, "Hanna, you belong to those who will die with me. Each of us has a vial of poison such as this"—and he handed her two small blue ampules of potassium cyanide, one for herself and one for Greim. "I do not want any one of us to fall to the Russians alive," Hitler went on, "nor do I wish our bodies to be found by them. Each person is responsible for destroying his body so that nothing recognizable remains. Eva and I will have our bodies burned. You will devise your own method. Will you please so inform Greim?"

Reitsch wept because the cause was lost and because the Führer realized with such tragic clarity that it was lost. She said through her sobbing, "My Führer, why do you stay? Why do you deprive Germany of your life? Save yourself, my Führer; that is the will of every German."

"No, Hanna. I must obey my own command and defend Berlin to the last."

For a few more days Hitler would move like a sleepwalker through his cramped concrete world, issuing orders that could not be obeyed, waiting until the time was right to die and he could become a figure of heroic legend. But late on the night of April 26, after Greim and Hanna Reitsch had agreed that they would destroy their bodies by pulling the pins on hand grenades just as they swallowed poison, both thought that the time to die was near. They heard, above the steady roar of the bunker's diesel-driven ventilation system, the explosion of artillery shells overhead, and they felt the shock waves through 16 feet of concrete and six of earth. The Russians were coming ever closer.

The fact was that most of the German successes reported to Hitler that day had been considerably exaggerated. For example, Schörner's advance had added little to the 15 miles he had gained in six days; it still left him 40 miles south of the Ninth Army pocket, and he would never get measurably closer. Ultimately, of course, none of the news was really good; it merely offered hope, and even the most sanguine expectations would prove hollow almost overnight.

The brightest hope was Wenck's Twelfth Army—about 70,000 young recruits with plenty of spirit but almost no armor. On the 26th, Wenck's 41st Panzer Corps was operating defensively well to the west of Berlin. The three divisions of Wenck's other corps, the 20th, were struggling to advance from the Belzig area, heading northeast toward Potsdam and east toward the road hub at Beelitz, a likely place for the projected linkup with the Ninth Army. The next day, elements of the 20th Corps managed to drive through thick woods in an effort to reach the town of Ferch, at the southern end of narrow Schwielow Lake, a few miles across the water from Potsdam.

Wenck realized that the 20th Corps lacked the strength to advance much farther; indeed, the question was, how long could the corps hold on in the Ferch area with its flanks exposed to Soviet counterattack? Nevertheless, the men of the 20th Corps tried to resume their advance during the next couple of days, and Wenck's headquarters radioed the High Command to send reinforcements. There were no troops available for such support. The only possibility was a weak two-division corps under Major General Hellmuth Reymann, which had been sent south from the capital to hold

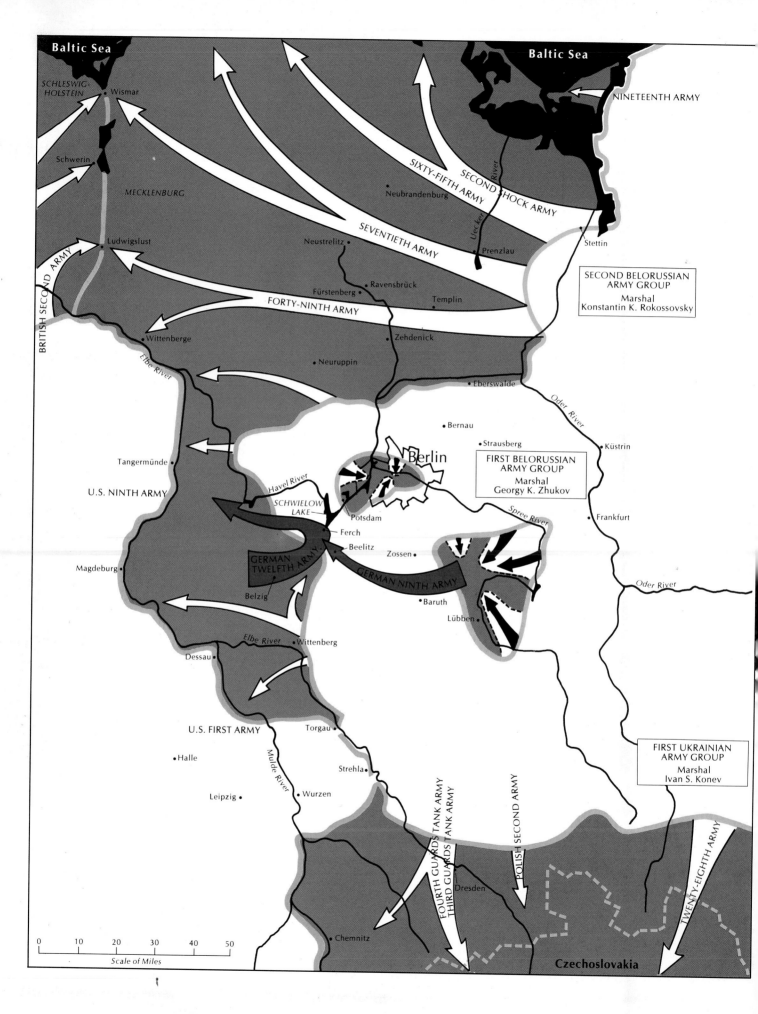

Baltic Sea

Baltic Sea

SCHLESWIG-HOLSTEIN

• Wismar

NINETEENTH ARMY

• Schwerin

MECKLENBURG

• Neubrandenburg

SIXTY-FIFTH ARMY

SECOND SHOCK ARMY

Uecker River

SEVENTIETH ARMY

• Ludwigslust

• Neustrelitz

• Prenzlau

• Stettin

SECOND BELORUSSIAN
ARMY GROUP
Marshal
Konstantin K. Rokossovsky

• Fürstenberg   • Ravensbrück

• Templin

FORTY-NINTH ARMY

BRITISH SECOND ARMY

• Wittenberge

• Zehdenick

Elbe River

• Neuruppin

• Eberswalde

Oder River

• Bernau

• Strausberg

• Küstrin

Berlin

FIRST BELORUSSIAN
ARMY GROUP
Marshal
Georgy K. Zhukov

• Tangermünde

U.S. NINTH ARMY

Havel River

SCHWIELOW
LAKE

• Potsdam

• Ferch

Spree River

• Frankfurt

GERMAN TWELFTH ARMY

• Beelitz

• Zossen

GERMAN NINTH ARMY

Oder River

• Magdeburg

• Belzig

• Baruth

• Lübben

Elbe River   • Wittenberg

• Dessau

U.S. FIRST ARMY

• Torgau

• Halle

• Strehla

FIRST UKRAINIAN
ARMY GROUP
Marshal
Ivan S. Konev

Mulde River

• Leipzig   • Wurzen

FOURTH GUARDS TANK ARMY

THIRD GUARDS TANK ARMY

POLISH SECOND ARMY

TWENTY-EIGHTH ARMY

• Dresden

| 0 | 10 | 20 | 30 | 40 | 50 |

Scale of Miles

• Chemnitz

Czechoslovakia

open a corridor to the city for the Twelfth Army, and it was being strangled in a Soviet noose north of Potsdam.

Meanwhile, General Busse and his Ninth Army were fighting with pathetic bravery for the dimmest sort of victory: to reach Wenck's units and, withdrawing with them to the Elbe, to surrender to the Americans. Busse had been surrounded since April 24 and had been under constant attack by at least five Soviet armies and their air support. Busse's strength was hard to estimate. On April 26, he still had perhaps one half of the 235,000 men who had borne the brunt of the assault by Marshal Zhukov's First Belorussian Army Group and Marshal Konev's First Ukrainian Army Group. Busse also had a corps of German Army Group Center's Fourth Panzer Army, which had been shattered by Konev's breakthrough on April 16, plus about 30,000 survivors who had escaped from Frankfurt an der Oder. The whole came to about 200,000 men.

This force had the impossible task of defending an ever-changing perimeter up to 75 miles long, and every time Busse's commanders shifted units to meet a new Soviet thrust, the troops were impeded by tens of thousands of refugee German civilians moving on the roads, pulling carts and wagons piled with their belongings. Yet the Ninth Army managed to hold its line and, in a major effort to join up with Wenck, shifted the majority of its remaining armor to the west, facing the towns of Baruth and Zossen on the highway between Berlin and Dresden. From there, though woefully short of supplies, Busse attacked on April 26.

That day, Busse's men fought their way several miles west and seized the Baruth-Zossen section of the highway. Some of the bloodiest fighting of the War seesawed back and forth in the Baruth area. Marshal Konev, revisiting Baruth nearly two decades later, wrote: "I still saw traces of the carnage in the neighboring villages. Rusty helmets and equipment were scattered in the woods, while the waters of one of the lakes, which had been filled with corpses during the fighting, could not yet be used." These scenes, Konev said, reflected "the courage of desperation and the gloomy determination of the doomed."

In reaching Zossen, Busse had advanced to within 23 miles of Wenck's position at Beelitz. But the Ninth Army was terribly weakened by the effort, as Busse reported by radio to Berlin and to Wenck. On April 28 he renewed his attack—and calamity struck. His armored spearhead was lopped off by the Russians and destroyed. Busse radioed news of the disaster and added that he could not guarantee resistance much longer. "Particularly wearing," the message emphasized, "is the shocking misery of the civilians pressed together within Ninth Army pocket."

In response to that news and his own worsening position, Wenck on April 29 radioed headquarters to the effect that an attack on Berlin was no longer possible, "especially since reinforcement through Ninth Army cannot be counted on." The chief of the OKW, Field Marshal Keitel, authorized Wenck to quit the drive—"if the Commanding General, Twelfth Army, despite the high historical and moral responsibility he carries, considers continuing the attack toward Berlin not executable."

The Twelfth Army halted in place. But the Ninth Army kept fighting, kept suffering heavy casualties—and kept making ground toward the west. On April 30, Busse's vanguard advanced to within one mile of Wenck's outposts at Beelitz. The next morning, Busse's very last tank broke through the Russians. Within hours, the pitiful remnants of the Ninth Army staggered into Wenck's line, followed by the civilian refugees. About one seventh of Busse's army— some 30,000 men—had survived. These troops, together with 70,000 of Wenck's men, eventually managed to surrender to the U.S. Ninth Army.

During the German Ninth Army's slow death in the south, the Third Panzer Army—the other half of General Gotthard Heinrici's Army Group Vistula—was fighting its last battle up north near Stettin. It lost with apparent suddenness. The enemy on the lower Oder, Marshal Konstantin K. Rokossovsky's Second Belorussian Army Group, had joined the Berlin offensive four days after the initial onslaught and then spent five relatively quiet days building up strength on the river's marshy west bank. But by April 27, just two days after Rokossovsky burst out of his bridgehead, the doom of the Third Panzer Army had been tactically sealed.

The Third Panzer was, as its commanding general Hasso von Manteuffel described it, "an army of ghosts" with no armor and practically no artillery. There was never a chance that it could withstand the April 25 assault by three Soviet armies, three tank corps, a mechanized corps and a cavalry

The climactic stage of the battle for Germany (fought in the light-red areas) lasted from April 25 through May 6, 1945. Soviet forces in the north broke through and swept across the German plain against resistance that disintegrated almost with their approach. British troops met these Russians near the Baltic on May 2. In the Berlin area, Soviet units pushed west to the Elbe and south into Czechoslovakia. Meanwhile, troops of the German Ninth and Twelfth Armies (dark red) fought to join forces, then turned west to surrender to the Americans along the Elbe.

corps. This array had broken a hole through the Third Panzer Army on a 30-mile front south of Stettin and headed west for a key road hub at Prenzlau on the Uecker River. Manteuffel and Heinrici both realized that if the Russians got through Prenzlau they could easily fan out in all directions on the network of roads—there would be nothing but a few small units to oppose them.

The two German generals also realized that Berlin and the War were lost, and they had no intention of losing any more lives than they could help. So, risking Hitler's wrath, they disobeyed his command to hold at all costs, and ordered the Third Panzer Army to fall back from the remnants of the Oder River line to the hills and lakes along the Uecker, about 20 miles to the rear. If Manteuffel's "ghosts" manned the new Uecker line swiftly enough, they might be able to hold for a while and prepare for the next phase of their retreat—toward the British and Americans along the Elbe.

Heinrici ventured along other subversive but soldierly avenues. It was obvious that General Steiner and his 3rd SS Panzer Corps, fitfully fighting southward from the Oranienburg area, were not going to break through the massive Soviet cordon north of Berlin. Instead, Heinrici proposed to turn Steiner's corps around and use it up north to strengthen the Third Panzer Army, to which it nominally belonged. The proposition horrified Field Marshal Keitel and his operations chief, General Alfred Jodl; these two, whose oft-moved headquarters were now at Neuruppin, in Third Panzer Army territory 40 miles northwest of Berlin, thought only of rescuing the Führer—who did not wish to be rescued.

By the 27th the fighting in the north was all but over. Late that night, Heinrici, in his headquarters at Birkenhain, a country estate 35 miles north of Berlin, received a phone call from Manteuffel announcing the demise of the Third Panzer Army: Half of the men had simply stopped fighting and were fleeing westward. Perhaps they knew that if they did not hurry, the fast-moving Soviet columns would swoop in ahead of them, cut them off, and prevent them from surrendering to the Western Allies.

Field Marshal Keitel was incensed by the Third Panzer Army's miserable performance, and the next morning he set off to the north to stiffen the soldiers' spines with his own presence. En route, to his further indignation, he discovered at the town of Zehdenick on the Havel River that one of Manteuffel's outfits was 20 miles west of the place it was supposed to be. Later and still worse, Keitel learned that Heinrici and Manteuffel had decided that the two SS divisions borrowed from Steiner were too far north to attack the Russians in Berlin from Templin as Keitel had ordered. Instead they had put the borrowed divisions into position around Neubrandenburg and Neustrelitz to defend against Rokossovsky—so far from Berlin that Keitel could never use them to extricate the Führer. The situation was too much for Keitel. In a rage, he summoned Heinrici and Manteuffel to conference at a crossroads near Fürstenberg. Manteuffel's staff officers expected the worst—arrest and possible summary execution of their chiefs—and three of them loitered nearby armed with submachine guns.

Keitel immediately began shouting at Heinrici, accusing him of deliberately disobeying direct commands. "The Führer ordered you to hold! He ordered you not to move! Yet you! You ordered the retreat!"

Heinrici, in his usual quiet manner, explained that the Third Panzer Army, with its available personnel and equipment, could not hold along the Oder, and that unless he got ample reinforcements he was going to have to continue retreating—he simply would not sacrifice lives in a defense that stood no chance of success.

"There are no reserves left!" Keitel cried, smiting his gloved palm with his field marshal's baton. Then to Manteuffel: "You will hold your positions. You will turn your army around here and now!"

"As long as I am in command," Heinrici said, "I will not issue that order to Manteuffel."

With his face turning purple, Keitel raved on about insubordination, cowardice, sabotage and treason. He said that the Third Panzer Army would be standing firm even now if General Heinrici had not been so weak, if Heinrici had executed enough men for deserting in the face of the enemy.

"If you want these men sent to the rear to be shot," Heinrici retorted, pointing to columns of retreating soldiers, "why don't you do it?"

Baffled, Keitel got into his car and left. In the late evening, after Heinrici had ordered further withdrawals—which he duly reported—Keitel relieved him of his command.

On April 28, the German retreat in the north became a

panic, and Soviet armored columns traveled as far and as fast as the clogged roads would permit, facing little more than uncoordinated local opposition. In many a town, the approach of the Russians set off a general exodus. Captain Francis Sampson, a U.S. Army chaplain who was one of 21,000 Allied prisoners of war in a camp outside Neubrandenburg, heard the woomph, woomph of Soviet artillery coming closer. Then, he wrote, "Russian planes flew over the city and dropped thousands of leaflets designed to terrify the German civilians; this they did very effectively. One of the pamphlets simply stated 'Rokossovsky is at your gates.'" The reputation of Rokossovsky's armies for butchery and plunder as they had rolled westward through East Prussia and Pomerania earlier in 1945 virtually cleared Neubrandenburg of its citizens.

"About midnight, April 28," Sampson's account went on, "the Russian tanks started coming in. The roar was terrific. The German opposition was almost totally ineffectual. The Russian infantry riding on the tanks (about 15 or 20 to a tank) seemed to be wild men; with 'squeeze boxes' and banjos strapped to their backs, and firing rifles and Tommy guns in every direction, they looked more like the old Mexican revolutionaries out on a spree than the army of one of the great powers of the world." Within an hour after the Russians' arrival, Sampson concluded, "Neubrandenburg was a sea of flames which rose higher and higher as the night passed. It burned all the next day."

Ultimately, 155,000 men of Manteuffel's Third Panzer Army managed to surrender to the British and Americans in Schleswig-Holstein. Along the lower Elbe, the German Twenty-first Army surrendered a total of 140,000 men.

In Berlin itself, the choice was not fight or flight. A soldier caught in the iron ring of eight converging Soviet armies fought or surrendered or deserted in place. These were the options for some 75,000 German defenders—antiaircraft crews and engineers in the regular garrison, combat units tossed into the city by the tide of battle (including some extremely tough SS units), elderly home guardsmen, Hitler Youth and police. The defenders stood not the slightest chance of success. No matter how well they fought or how many sacrificed their lives, they could only delay what was essentially a gigantic Soviet mopping-up operation.

The man now in command of the city's doomed defense had taken the job with no illusions about his prospects. Lieut. General Helmuth Weidling was a rough-hewn soldier who had joined the Army in 1911 and had risen from the ranks. As recently as April 21, Weidling had been condemned to death for deserting his men in battle. The battered 56th Panzer Corps he commanded in eastern Berlin had been out of touch with headquarters for several hours, and Weidling was reported seen west of Berlin. The report was false; once communication was resumed, Weidling reported in person to the Chancellery and angrily established his innocence. On April 24 Weidling was informed that he was to serve as commandant of Berlin, the third man Hitler had appointed to the post in as many days. As a German officer, Weidling was unable to turn down the command, but he stated candidly that he would prefer to be shot.

Weidling soon discovered that the situation was even worse than he thought: He was weak in manpower and supplies, his defenses were inadequate and his authority was limited. Instead of the 22 full-strength divisions called for in the defense plan for Berlin, he had—or would presently acquire—no more than five nominal divisions. All had been greatly reduced by attrition, and two of them were such pathetic fragments that they had to be combined to make an outfit of useful size. Weidling had few reserves, and only Hitler Youth to distribute as replacements. Weidling and his men needed more of almost everything—food, medical supplies, tanks, artillery, artillery shells and small-arms ammunition of all calibers. The shortage of ammunition was particularly acute.

Berlin's defense installations were makeshift. They consisted chiefly of three rings of crude roadblocks and trenchworks in parks and city squares. By April 26, the two outer defense lines had been broken in the north, east and south; only the innermost line, ringing the government quarter and the Tiergarten—the one-square-mile park and zoo in Berlin's center—was intact. Guns on its two huge concrete flak towers, designed to concentrate antiaircraft fire on Allied bombers, could not be lowered to fire at ground attackers.

The plight of Berlin's civilian population was nothing less than desperate. All of the services that supported urban life had broken down. The municipal power plants had been knocked out by enemy bombardment—or possibly sabotaged by Nazi zealots executing Hitler's scorched-earth policy. Without electricity to work the pumping stations, city water stopped flowing and sanitary conditions deteriorated alarmingly. Deliveries of food from the countryside had stopped. Civilians had quickly bought up the stocks in the stores; shopkeepers who had been charging exorbitant black-market prices had been glad to sell out their last wares for what they were offered—before the Russians took everything for nothing. By April 27, many Berliners were eating horsemeat: Horses pulled many a civilian wagon as fuel supplies shrank almost to the vanishing point; heavy bombing—and, later, gunfire—killed many of the animals, and people began butchering the dead animals for food.

Even for families who had sufficient food, hot meals were a rarity as stove-gas service stopped. Public transportation shut down and Berliners stayed close to home, living in their cellars and air-raid shelters when their districts came under attack. The main telegraph offices closed down—the last message received came from Tokyo and said GOOD LUCK TO YOU ALL. One by one, the newspapers — including the regular Nazi Party mouthpiece, *Völkischer Beobachter*—ceased publishing, though Goebbels started an emergency newssheet. Inspired by the heraldic figure of a

fierce beast in Berlin's coat of arms, he called it *Der Panzerbär (The Armored Bear).*

Life in a war zone filled with fire, flying metal and falling masonry was a matter of trauma and death; corpses went unburied, lying where they fell. Wounded civilians often lay in agony for a day or more, waiting even longer than the soldiers for treatment by overworked and exhausted surgeons. Supplies of anesthetics and painkillers dwindled fast.

And Soviet troops were everywhere. As conquerors, the Russians were unpredictable. They were capable of great kindness—especially to children—and great cruelty. For example, a Soviet soldier might, at risk of his own life, rescue an infant from a burning apartment or shoot the baby's parents for some imagined offense. The Russians were endlessly fascinated and baffled by such wonders of city life as water faucets and light bulbs, which some unscrewed to take home, believing that the bulbs themselves held light and would work anywhere.

The Russians were also primitive in their insistence on the spoils of war. They made much use of two catch phrases in pidgin German. One was *"Uri, uri!"* a Russified corruption of the German word *Uhr*—a demand for "Watches, watches!" The other phrase was a terrifying prelude to rape: *"Frau, komm"*—"Woman, come." Soviet soldiers raped females of all ages and nearly all conditions, excluding only those who seemed to have a disease that the Russians identified as scarlet fever—a misconception that caused many resourceful women to daub their faces with lipstick. Some women were raped two or three dozen times; a few others, kept under lock and key for the exclusive benefit of a particular unit, could not guess how many times they were raped. In a survey ordered by a postwar mayor of Berlin, researchers tabulated 90,000 rape victims who sooner or later had sought medical treatment. There was no way to estimate how many women died at the hands of rapists, or were driven to suicide by the experience.

The Soviet officers cared little about their troops' conduct so long as it did not interfere with their combat performance. Though the battle for the capital had long since been won strategically on the Oder and the Neisse, the generals were still in a hurry; Stalin wanted Berlin to cap the May Day celebration in Moscow, a traditional Communist holiday,

Elderly women emerge from a Berlin shelter during a lull in the bombing. Most civilians fled underground when the climactic attack by Soviet aircraft began, emerging only for supplies. Food was so scarce that at least one ration line held fast while being strafed by Russian planes.

and the days of April were fast running out. The men in charge kept passing pressure down through the chain of command—and paying a high price for speed. Losses were especially heavy among the tank units, even though crewmen had improvised clever defenses; tanks bristled with bedsprings and other metal shielding devices that detonated *Panzerfaust* grenades before they could explode directly on the tank hulls.

To all appearances, the Soviet armies were now making up the time they had lost reaching the capital. They overran Berlin's districts and suburbs at a swift rate as they closed in on the complex of government buildings at the center of the city that was their ultimate objective. They took the Zehlendorf and Dahlem districts in southern Berlin on April 26. The next day they captured Spandau in western Berlin and Neukölln in southern Berlin; Gatow in the southwest, Berlin's last airfield, also fell. By nightfall on the 27th, the Russians had squeezed the German defenders into an area nine and a half miles long from east to west and one to three miles wide, and by the 28th, fighting had started in the Charlottenburg and Wilmersdorf sections, respectively just to the west and the south of the Tiergarten.

The symbolic victory prize was the Reichstag, the former legislative house whose immense fire-gutted shell sprawled about a quarter of a mile north of the *Führerbunker*. After a 1933 fire had left the Reichstag in partial ruins, the Nazis (who publicly blamed Communist agents for setting the fire) had abandoned the building and allowed it to crumble—a symbol of German vulnerability to the Red menace. Now, in a supreme irony, the Soviet guardians of the Marxist faith so hateful to the Nazis had chosen the Reichstag as their own talisman of German defeat.

To prevent a wild scramble to capture the Reichstag and to keep order elsewhere, Stalin redrew the boundary separating Marshal Zhukov's armies from Marshal Konev's. As usual, the dictator favored Zhukov, placing the government quarter in his territory and restricting Konev to the southwestern quadrant of the capital. This still left a lively competition among three of Zhukov's armies: General Chuikov's Eighth Guards, coming up from the south, and the Third and Fifth Shock Armies, pushing down from the north.

Chuikov's forces pressed ahead from the area of the Tempelhof airfield, driving before them a German outfit they had been fighting all the way from the Oder: the Müncheberg Panzer Division. The division had been whittled down to 3,500 men and about 42 armored vehicles, and it could not hold the Russians back. Henceforth the Münchebergs would be forced to move often. In their desperate rearguard clashes, they would suffer as much as any other outfit—and keep up the vain Berlin battle longest of all.

The Münchebergs gave ground grudgingly. "Heavy street fighting," wrote a Müncheberg officer in a staccato diary entry—one of many that he managed to scribble during the battle. "Many civilian casualties. Dying animals. Skirmishes in the subway tunnels, through which the Russians are trying to get back of our lines." The division retreated northwestward across the Landwehr Canal, which formed the southern defense perimeter of the government quarter and the Tiergarten.

Late on April 27, Chuikov's force reached the canal on a broad front. The canal was a wide, deep waterway with high concrete banks, and all its approaches were thickly mined and swept by heavy machine-gun fire. Some units attempted to force the canal on the run, but they failed. Chuikov called a halt to regroup and bring up supplies. His decision was an eminently reasonable one, but it gave the Third

Trying to do business as usual, a uniformed ticket seller for the Nazi Party's welfare lottery warms his hands against a chill breeze. To the last days of the War, the lottery continued to raise funds that provided assistance for the needy on Germany's home front.

Shock Army, moving in from the north, an edge in the race to capture the Reichstag.

On April 28, the 150th Division of the Third Shock Army drew up along the Spree River, which framed the government quarter and the Tiergarten inside a bend in the north. The 3rd Battalion of the 756th Infantry Regiment had been awarded the Soviet flag of the 150th Division and thus became the division's official champion in the Reichstag assault; around noon, after fighting through northern Berlin for a week, this unit reached the Spree River at the Moltke Bridge, the westernmost of two spans in the river bend. The commanding officer of the 3rd Battalion, Captain Stepan Neustroyev, chose a platoon to attempt an assault crossing.

While German and Soviet artillery dueled along the Spree, men of the 3rd Battalion raced across the bridge. Then they fanned out along the far bank, heaving grenades through the windows of buildings to silence enemy machine guns. More and more Soviet units swarmed across the Moltke Bridge. That night elements of the 150th Division cleared the last Germans out of the smaller riverside buildings and brought artillery across the Spree to help them take their next objectives: the Ministry of the Interior, a huge building near the bridge that housed the headquarters of Hitler's internal security force, the Gestapo; the Kroll Opera House, which had served in place of the ruined Reichstag building as a forum for Germany's rubber-stamp parliament; and, across the 300-yard expanse of the Königsplatz, the Reichstag itself.

Captain Neustroyev was depressed to find that his casualties for the day were heavy. But his superior, the colonel in command of the 756th Regiment, laid a comforting hand on his shoulder. "Keep your chin up, Stepan," said the colonel. "The end is near."

The captain would have been more certain of that had he been able to witness the action to the south that morning, when the Eighth Guards Army started its assault across the Landwehr Canal. Chuikov's division commanders launched many small attacks in places of their own choice. Some groups of soldiers swam the canal and, working their way inland, attacked the enemy from the rear. The heaviest fighting was for the hump-backed bridge on the Potsdamer Strasse—the most convenient means of getting Soviet tanks into the Tiergarten and the government quarter. Slowly the

Germans were driven back by the sheer weight of Soviet numbers and Soviet artillery.

Chuikov's advance drove the Müncheberg Panzer Division to positions only a half mile south of the *Führerbunker*. Division officers set up their command post in a crowded subway tunnel under the Anhalter Railroad Station. "The station looks like an armed camp," wrote the Müncheberg diarist. "Women and children huddling in niches and corners and listening for the sounds of battle. Suddenly water splashes into our command post. Screams, cries, curses in the tunnel. People are fighting around the ladders that run through the air shafts up to the street. Water comes rushing through the tunnels. The crowds get panicky, stumble and fall over rails and ties. Children and wounded are deserted, people are trampled to death. The water covers them. It rises three feet or more, then slowly goes down."

The flood had been caused, on orders given in Hitler's name, by SS men who blew a hole in the wall between a subway tunnel and the Landwehr Canal; they intended to prevent the Russians from advancing through the tunnels but gave no thought to the countless civilians who used the subways as refuge.

On the afternoon of April 27, the Münchebergs retreated

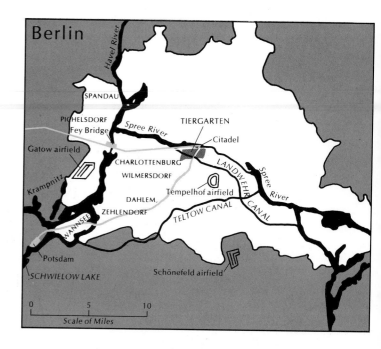

Most of Berlin's 340 square miles (above) became a battleground. The city's main defensive features were the Spree River and the Teltow and Landwehr Canals; the major prize was the government-building complex called the Citadel and located north and east of the Tiergarten, the park shown in light red above and in the large-scale map at right. Attacking south across the Moltke Bridge, the Russians drove to the Reichstag and the Brandenburg Gate. They fought to within a block of the Führerbunker, Hitler's last refuge (dark red), not realizing it was there.

to within a block or so of the *Führerbunker*. Now they were fighting in the huge Potsdamer Platz, which the division's diarist described: "A waste of ruins. Masses of damaged vehicles, half-smashed ambulances with the wounded still in them. Dead people everywhere, many of them frightfully cut up by tanks and trucks."

That day, men of the division had repeated run-ins with Nazi zealots who roamed the city court-martialing—or simply shooting or hanging without the formality of a hearing—anyone whom they suspected of desertion, shirking or defeatism. "Most of them are very young SS officers," wrote the Müncheberg diarist. "Hardly a medal or decoration on them. Blind and fanatical." General Werner Mummert, the commander of the Müncheberg Panzer Division until he was promoted to General Weidling's old post as commanding officer of the 56th Panzer Corps, was enraged by the flying court-martial squads. "A division made up of the largest number of men with some of the highest decorations," he declared, "does not deserve to be persecuted by such babies." Mummert decided, added the diarist, "to shoot down any court-martial that takes action in our sector."

The men that day, the diary reports, had "no rest, no relief, no regular food, hardly any bread. We get water from the tunnels and filter it. At night we try to reach the Propaganda Ministry for news about Wenck. Violent shelling in the center of town.

"We cannot hold our position. Around four o'clock in the morning we retreat through the subway tunnels."

While the Münchebergs were dying in job lots near the *Führerbunker,* Hitler became certain on April 28 that the time had come for him to die. Until then, nothing had changed appreciably in the bunker during the two days since General von Greim and Hanna Reitsch had flown in. Hitler continued holding his four situation conferences daily. Now from all quarters the news was bad.

There were a few minor interruptions. In one of these, some troops of the Führer's personal bodyguard brought in a member of the Hitler Youth who had been singled out for decoration. Captain Gerhardt Boldt, who was in charge of updating the Berlin battle map, wrote that "the little boy, in a severe state of shock and looking as if he had not slept for days, had put a Russian tank out of action. With a great show of emotion, Hitler pinned an Iron Cross on his puny chest, on a mud-spattered coat several sizes too large. Then Hitler ran his hand slowly over the boy's head and sent

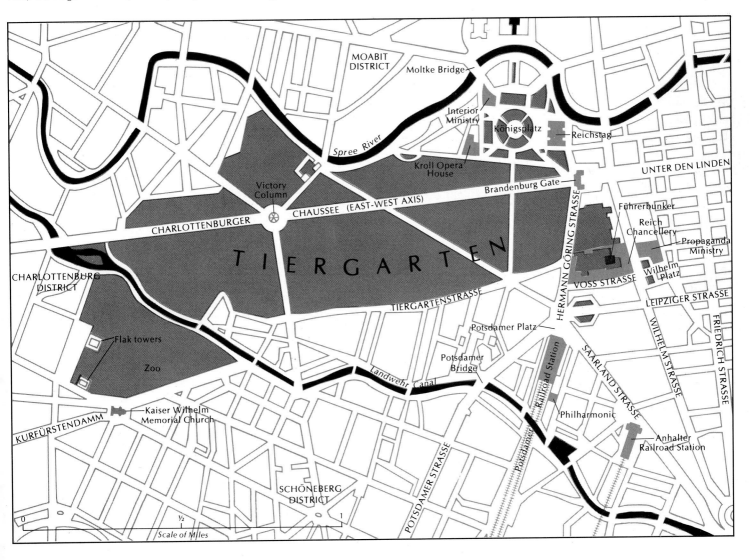

him back into the hopeless battle in the streets of Berlin."

Another interruption came when Hitler discovered that the senior SS liaison officer, Major General Hermann Fegelein, was unaccountably absent. Fegelein had solidified his rapid rise by marrying Eva Braun's sister Gretl, but in Hitler's mind he was by no means above suspicion. A detachment of SS men marched to the general's house in the Charlottenburg section, found him there dressed in civilian clothes as if about to flee—at any rate, to shed his reponsibilities as an SS officer—and brought him back under arrest. Fegelein was questioned and stripped of his rank and that seemed to be the end of the matter—until the hour of death arrived for both him and Hitler.

The death knell began sounding at about 9 p.m. on the 28th. One of Goebbels' aides arrived through the underground passageway from the Ministry of Propaganda with the text of a news bulletin, picked up from the BBC, that Reichsführer-SS Heinrich Himmler, in Lübeck, had offered to surrender Germany to the Western Allies. To all present, this was the ultimate betrayal. Hitler, wallowing in what Captain Boldt described as "a helpless paroxysm of rage, full of hate and contempt," called Himmler's act "the most shameful betrayal in human history." The Führer had lived comfortably through Göring's rather diffident and aboveboard reach for power. Hanna Reitsch was sure Hitler could not outlive Himmler's more devious treason, and so were others. Everyone, she said, looked again to his poison.

First, however, the Führer had some unfinished business to conclude. He had Fegelein interrogated closely by a master of the art, Gestapo chief Heinrich Müller. It is not known in detail what Müller found out, but it was quite clear to all that Fegelein was privy to Himmler's most secret plans. Fegelein was taken out and shot.

Hitler, still spewing vituperation, went to Greim and revoked his promise that Greim and Hanna Reitsch might die with him. Instead, the two old friends were to fly to Plön immediately and see to it that the despicable traitor Himmler received his just deserts. And while Greim was at it, he was to make sure that what remained of the Luftwaffe supported the foundering German counterattacks. With the woman pilot helping him, Greim dutifully hobbled off on crutches to the East-West Axis, where a light observation plane had managed to land; the Storch that had brought them had been destroyed by enemy shelling. Hanna Reitsch flew Greim to his destination, where he duly ordered the remnants of the Luftwaffe into the Berlin battle. He also confronted Himmler, who later admitted that Greim had "reproved" him. Some two weeks later, still immobilized by his painful foot wound, Greim made use of the cyanide capsule his Führer had given him. Hanna Reitsch, though drawn to the idea of suicide, survived to undergo capture and interrogation by American intelligence.

Soon after the two fliers departed the *Führerbunker*, Hitler paid off his debt to the person who he had prophesied would be the only one to remain perfectly loyal to him: Eva Braun. If she had ever dared to raise the subject of marriage, he had waved it away on the ground that the Führer had no time for domesticity; rather than seem merely human to the German people, he had maintained a relationship with Eva so discreet that it was known only to a few members of his staff and inner circle. But Eva's longing for respectability was no secret to Hitler, and now he gave it to her, if only for the few hours left to them.

A minor city official named Walter Wagner—who had worked with Joseph Goebbels in Goebbels' capacity as Berlin Gauleiter—was discovered fighting in a home-guard unit and was pressed into service late in the evening to preside at the Nazi marriage ceremony. Hitler, presented with the marriage license, filled it out but offered no information about his parents; he attested that he was of pure Aryan blood (the Nazi ideal), with no hereditary disease. The bride started to sign her maiden name but crossed it out and wrote "Eva Hitler, née Braun." They agreed aloud, before Goebbels and party chief Martin Bormann, that they were man and wife, and that constituted their wedding ceremony.

The death of her brother-in-law Hermann Fegelein just a couple of hours earlier apparently did nothing to impair Frau Hitler's happiness; she wore a black taffeta dress, Hitler's favorite, but the tears in her eyes, said Gerda Christian—one of Hitler's two private secretaries—were "tears of radiant joy." Wagner, his marrying function at an end, was sent on his way; he died, a victim of gunshot wounds, on his way back to his combat post.

Champagne flowed at the wedding reception, attended by a dozen or so *Führerbunker* inmates. But shortly it was

An officer gives instructions to a wounded member of the Hitler Youth, one of many 15- and 16-year-olds who volunteered for the defense of Berlin. Hastily trained with rifles and Panzerfäuste, they were flung into the Red Army's path—and were killed by the thousands.

back to business for the Führer. He closeted himself with Gertrud Junge, his other private secretary, and dictated his will and his political testament.

The will was a simple document. It explained that Hitler and his wife were committing suicide "to escape the shame of overthrow or capitulation." It left the Führer's personal possessions to the Nazi Party, or, "if this no longer exists," to the German state. Hitler added clairvoyantly, "If the state, too, is destroyed, there is no need for any further instructions on my part."

In the political testament Hitler set out to shape the future from beyond the grave. He appointed a successor government led by Grand Admiral Dönitz as President; Goebbels was to succeed Hitler in the post of Reich Chancellor; Bormann kept his post as party chief. The traitors Himmler and Göring were roundly damned and expelled from the party, while the inconstant Albert Speer received lesser punishment—omission from the Cabinet—but no condemnation.

Hitler enjoined the new government to continue the War by every means, and also to continue the Führer's personal war against all his enemies. By way of explaining the seriousness of these obligations, he recapitulated the principle to which he had dedicated his life: hatred of Jews. The ex-

traordinary document concluded with a ringing statement of Hitler's cardinal principle for good government: unrelenting persecution of "the universal poisoner of all nations, international Jewry."

Joseph Goebbels witnessed Hitler's signature to both documents, then sat down to disavow his new post as Reich Chancellor in an appendix to the Führer's political testament. He declared that he would not leave the bunker to serve in the new government even though it meant disobeying Hitler for the first time. "In the delirium of treachery that surrounds the Führer," he wrote, "there must be someone at least to stay with him unconditionally until death." Goebbels' wife, Magda, who had a fanatical faith in Hitler, also was eager to share his fate. The couple's decision to commit suicide also doomed their six young children, who a week earlier had moved into the bunker with their parents.

On the morning of April 29, soon after awakening, Hitler was informed that Benito Mussolini, his forerunner as a totalitarian dictator, had been slain by partisans with his mistress, Clara Petacci, and that their corpses had been mutilated. The Führer thus felt vindicated in his determination to commit suicide so that his body would be properly disposed of before the Russians could get it.

In this atmosphere of impending self-immolation, Captain Boldt poignantly recalled his commanding officer's advice on assigning him to Hitler's household staff: "When that bunch turns on the gas taps, see to it that you get out of the bunker in time and die a decent soldier's death." Besides, Boldt reasoned, there was nothing left for him to do; the bunker's direct communications with the outside world had been disrupted, making it nearly impossible to collect information to update the Berlin battle map. For a while, he had done the job by calling acquaintances or random telephone numbers in all of the city's districts where fighting was going on and asking whether the Russians had arrived. Then the telephone service was knocked out, and Boldt used the bunker's short-wave radio. But just that morning, the Russians had shot down the balloon that held up the aerial.

Boldt made a proposal, voiced for him by the Army Chief of Staff, General Krebs, at the end of Hitler's noon conference, that he and two of the other *Führerbunker* adjutants be permitted to join General Wenck and guide the relief army into Berlin. Hitler agreed, and the three officers left at

1:30 p.m. They sought escape by a route leading through the Tiergarten and Charlottenburg sections to the Havel River, where they hoped to travel by water south to Wenck's army. As they hurried westward along the East-West Axis, to their right the battle for the Ministry of the Interior was still raging. It took the men so long to work their way through the Tiergarten and battle-torn Charlottenburg that they decided to spend the night in empty offices in the miraculously undamaged Olympic stadium near the Havel River; it was clearly too late to reach Wenck. Over the next few days, Boldt and one companion did make it through the Soviet lines; the third man was captured.

Two more fugitives—a colonel and his orderly—left the *Führerbunker* that night with further exhortations from Hitler for Dönitz and the group at Plön. By the time they had run the gantlet westward, the Ministry of the Interior had fallen to the Soviet attackers. But, traveling by night and hiding by day, the pair also got through.

The loss of the Interior Ministry and other depressing military developments inside the capital were reported by General Weidling, the Berlin commandant, at Hitler's 10 p.m. situation conference on April 29. Weidling said that Soviet forces would reach the *Führerbunker* by May 1 at the latest;

earlier, he had put it more vividly—"By morning the Russians will be able to spit in our windows." Weidling offered to assemble a strike force for use in an attempt to break out of the city. Hitler said no: Escape was possible for individuals and small groups only. In any case, the Führer would not flee like a common criminal.

After the 10 p.m. conference Hitler sent his last message to OKW headquarters at Neuruppin, posing useless questions about the whereabouts of Wenck, the timing of his next attack, the location of the Ninth Army and where it was to break through into the city. Field Marshal Keitel answered quickly and did not mince words. He said that all relief attacks had been stopped cold and were doomed.

Hitler went to sleep to steel his nerves for his last day on earth. He slept about one hour and rose with the sun.

Berlin at sunrise on April 30 was a suitably apocalyptic setting for the last act in the drama of Hitler's life. A thousand fires, burning out of control for days, seemed to have consumed the city in flame, and the heavy mists rising from the Spree River and the canals were dyed blood red. The sulfurous air was thick with clouds of hot ash and rust-colored stone dust raised by constant shelling and collapsing build-

Soviet tanks and guns jam the roadway near the Moltke Bridge over the Spree River on April 29. During the previous day, units of the Third Shock Army

ngs. In the worst areas people emerged white-faced and ghostlike from the murk holding wet handkerchiefs over their faces to help them breathe.

There were other bizarre touches. A lion had been seen running along the Albrechtstrasse, and a zebra was said to have grazed in a cemetery; the animals' cages in the Tiergarten had been blown open by shellbursts. Through shell holes in the streets, civilian corpses could be seen lying several layers deep in the subways. The boom of cannon and the rattle of rifles were counterpointed by screams—of raped women, of the wounded, of children, and of German soldiers undergoing amputation without anesthesia.

The cannon's roar rose to a crescendo at 10 a.m. This was the artillery preparation for the climactic assault on the Reichstag. Captain Stepan Neustroyev, peering through the gun smoke across the Königsplatz, did not like what he saw. The huge square was honeycombed with trenches and tank traps. Beyond, the windows of the Reichstag had been bricked up, leaving ports for machine guns, and the ornate stonework on the roof sheltered additional machine-gun nests. The great stone pile and its approaches were defended by an estimated 6,000 to 7,000 troops, most of them SS.

The Soviet corps command designated a single division,

the 150th, for the storming of the Reichstag, with another to help mop up after the defense was broken. This decision cut down the number of Neustroyev's rivals for the honor of raising the flag atop the Reichstag, though Neustroyev's 500-man battalion was just one of three from the 150th that would attack abreast in the first wave. That left plenty of room for friendly competition—but it also gave the battalion its chance to gain a full measure of revenge for the brutality the Germans had inflicted on 16 of its members near the town of Zechin.

The assault began shortly after 10 a.m. Neustroyev's battalion charged on the left flank with his second and third companies leading the way and the first company, his best, advancing behind them. The attack was met with a terrific machine-gun broadside from the Reichstag and by German artillery from the Tiergarten. Neustroyev's front line had to hit the dirt after advancing to the edge of an antitank ditch.

As the Soviet gunners went to work again to soften up the defenders, Neustroyev called back Sergeant Ilya Syanov, who the day before had inherited the leadership of the first company when its commissioned officer was wounded. Syanov, a cocky little fellow, grinned when he heard his new orders; he was to have the honor of leading the bat-

med the heavily defended bridge, the only one intact over the Spree, and established a bridgehead just 600 yards from their ultimate goal—the Reichstag.

talion's charge into the enemy machine guns. "Let's hope I live to enjoy it, Comrade Captain," he said. "But I'll do my best. I'm a party member, you know." Then with a wave, he started back to his outfit.

Under cover of heavy fire from shrieking Katyusha rocket launchers, self-propelled guns and howitzers, Sergeant Syanov and his men plunged through the water-filled anti-tank ditch and dodged forward from shell hole to shell hole. Joined by Neustroyev's other two companies, they overran a line of enemy trenches. Syanov was nicked by shell fragments in the arms and chest but he kept going.

Then the sergeant and some riflemen reached the granite stairway and giant columns of the Reichstag's main entrance. Two mortar teams arrived and set up their 82mm weapons on the broad porch facing the bricked-up front door. With the mortar tubes depressed as far as possible, they fired and blasted a four-foot-wide hole in the doorway. Late in the afternoon, Syanov led the way into the cavernous gloom inside the Reichstag.

After a quiet morning with old associates, the Führer joined his two secretaries and his cook for a vegetarian lunch of spaghetti and tossed salad. He and Eva often lunched this way, but today she did not come, possibly because Hitler, with his old-fashioned attitudes toward marriage, thought it beneath her new status as the legitimate mistress of the house. Of course, as master he did as he pleased.

Whatever kept Eva away, it was certainly not depression. She spent the early afternoon cheerfully giving away possessions to a succession of Führerbunker inmates. To secretary Gertrud Junge she gave a silver-fox wrap, saying almost gaily, "Trudl, sweetheart, here's a present for next winter and your life after the War. And when you put it on, always remember me and give my very best to our native Bavaria—Bavaria the beautiful."

Shortly before 3:30 p.m., the Hitlers shook hands all around and retired to the Führer's rooms. Staff members waited in the corridor, immobilized by awful anticipation. They waited interminable minutes for the sound of the fatal pistol shot. It never came; the suite was soundproof. Later, nearly all of them believed they had heard the shot.

Finally, Hitler's valet pushed open the door. A gust of acrid odor drifted out—the bitter-almond smell of cyanide and the cordite stink of gunpowder. Still everyone hung back. Hitler's valet, who had opened the door, was afraid to enter. Then, with Bormann leading, a group of four, including Goebbels and the valet, pushed into the room.

Eva Hitler was curled up on the sofa in a comfortable position, dead of cyanide poisoning. Hitler was slumped at the other end of the sofa; he had died by putting a bullet through his brain. But to be sure he had bitten into a cyanide capsule the instant before squeezing the trigger.

Now a few men lurched into purposeful movement. They carried the bodies up the bunker's emergency stairway and deposited them in a nearby shell hole in the garden. They filled the shallow shell hole with gasoline from cans that had been delivered by Hitler's chauffeur. Two officers struck matches but a hot breeze blew them out. The valet ignited a twist of paper with his pocket lighter and handed it to Hitler's SS aide, who tossed it at the shell hole. The bodies were enveloped in a sheet of flame.

The mourners gave the stiff-armed Nazi salute, went downstairs and immediately indulged in a practice Hitler had always forbidden indoors—smoking. SS men would go out periodically to feed more fuel to the funeral pyre. After a while, deeming the shell hole too shallow to serve as a proper grave, the SS detail moved the corpses to a larger, deeper shell hole and covered them with earth.

While the others enjoyed their release from pent-up tension, Martin Bormann went to work to preserve his power. To remove one threat, he had already sent instructions to the SS command at the Obersalzberg, telling them to liquidate Hermann Göring as soon as Berlin and the Führer fell; but the SS guard did not accept Bormann's authority. They were holding Göring under house arrest in his castle near the Bavarian border and they turned him over to Luftwaffe men in the area. He was still living there three days later when American troops caught up with him.

Now Bormann fired off a message to inform Dönitz of the admiral's appointment as Hitler's successor in lieu of Göring, and that written authority was en route. He made no mention of Hitler's death—news that could inspire a coup by the turncoat Himmler. Bormann intended to disclose that news only after reaching the admiral's side and securing his own position as the real power behind the new government. Bormann and most of the other denizens of the bunker

Lieut. General Hans Krebs (right), the last Army Chief of Staff in the Third Reich, stands outside the Berlin headquarters of Soviet General Vasily Chuikov on May 1. Krebs had just tried, and failed, to arrange an exclusive cease-fire with the Russians—leaving out the Western Allies. The arrangement would have left a reorganized Nazi government in place.

had already planned a breakout attempt for the next day.

Bormann had also concocted an utterly fantastic scheme that seemed to him safer and potentially more productive than a furtive trip to Plön, which was now relegated to backup status. The plan amounted to a hedge against every risk Bormann could think of—the Russians and Himmler in particular—and a protected route to power for himself through a new German government to be guaranteed by the Russians. He proposed to Goebbels, whom he recognized as the senior official in Berlin, that someone make contact with the local Soviet commander and offer to surrender the entire Reich exclusively to the Russians—who, the cynical Bormann figured, would surely welcome the chance to leave the Western Allies out in the cold.

The German plenipotentiary would then explain that only the legal German government, in Plön, could validate the surrender, and therefore the Russians must either grant Berlin emissaries (i.e., Bormann) safe conduct to Plön to get official agreement, or permit the Plön government to move to Berlin (out of Himmler's reach, since the ex-Reichsführer would hardly dare enter the capital without knowledge of Hitler's death). Goebbels, bent on suicide and with no real interest in the matter, agreed readily. As their emissary, Bor-

mann and Goebbels chose General Krebs, who had served as military attaché in Moscow and spoke Russian. Word of Krebs's imminent arrival was conveyed by radio and messenger to the headquarters of Soviet General Chuikov.

To keep both his power play and his plan for a breakout alive as long as possible, Bormann sent a second, temporizing message to Dönitz. This one mentioned the Führer's testament and indicated that it was now in effect—but did not state that Hitler was dead. Bormann would say nothing more until he knew the results of Krebs's mission.

Meanwhile the battle for the Reichstag ground slowly toward its inevitable end. Outside, German forces repeatedly counterattacked to regain the line of trenches; each time they were repelled with heavy losses. Inside, Captain Neustroyev's 3rd Battalion and the other units that had joined it were locked in savage fights for each room and corridor.

Once Sergeant Syanov and his vanguard had managed to win control of the lobby and the rooms to either side, Neustroyev moved his command post there and tried to run an orderly battle. It was impossible. Reports and commands could not be heard; the eruption of hand grenades and the juddering of submachine guns blended into an incessant

earsplitting roar in the vast echoing spaces of the Reichstag.

Sergeant Syanov's men fought their way up the broad stairs to the second floor. It was a hand-to-hand struggle, Russians and Germans splitting skulls with rifle butts and disemboweling their enemies. In the rooms along the hall on the second floor, knots of men engaged in grenade-throwing battles, starting fires in the sofas and satin armchairs that still furnished the rooms, and occasionally catching fire themselves and then running about beating their clothing to put out the flames. Rooms were won and lost over and over again during the afternoon and into the dark.

After nightfall, the regimental commander joined Neustroyev in the lobby. Sensing victory, they sent to the rear for the flag awarded to the 3rd Battalion by the division's war council. "Send it with reliable men," the colonel ordered.

Soon the banner was on its way in the hands of two experienced scouts, Mikhail Yegorov and Meliton Kantaria, both of whom had fought in a partisan band during the German occupation of western Russia. They arrived with the flag a half hour later and were told to plant it on the roof among the ornamental statuary; the route to the roof ran via the third floor. Gunfire from holdout Germans marked their progress up the stairs, along the second-floor corridor and back again. Gasping for breath, they said that the stairs to the third floor seemed to be smashed and they could not find another route in the dark. Led by a lieutenant and guarded by a squad with submachine guns, they retraced their steps and crawled on hands and knees up the wrecked stairs. From there they made it easily onto the roof.

Yegorov and Kantaria crept to the eaves and found, in the lurid red glare of the burning city, a life-sized copper statue—the allegorical figure of Germania—with a gash in its base that looked like the right size to hold the flagstaff. "This is as good a place as any," said Kantaria.

At 10:50 on the night of April 30, Yegorov wedged the flagpole into the gash, and a great cheer rose from the Soviet soldiers mopping up on the ground.

To the Soviet forces, the flag raising signaled victory at the Reichstag, which in turn meant victory in Berlin. Both claims were premature. The fighting continued all night, and it was not until 6 a.m. on May 1 that the bulk of the German troops in the Reichstag surrendered. By then, Stalin surely knew that he was not going to get Berlin for May Day.

General Chuikov, established in a forward command post just across the Landwehr Canal from the *Führerbunker*, got word at 3:50 a.m. on May 1 that the German General Krebs had arrived to parley under a white flag.

Without preamble, Krebs declared, "I shall speak of exceptionally secret matters. You are the first foreigner to whom I give the information that on April 30 Hitler passed from us of his own will, ending his life by suicide."

"We know this," Chuikov lied with a poker face. Thereupon Krebs, surprised and crestfallen, lost any chance he may have had of steering the conversation.

Bit by bit, Chuikov pulled information from Krebs. Clearly Krebs was not proposing a surrender, but requesting a cease-fire so that a new Nazi regime could be brought into the picture. The suggested deal implied Soviet recognition of Admiral Dönitz' government and betrayal of the principle of Germany's unconditional surrender to all the Allies, a cardinal goal of the anti-Axis alliance. These were areas of negotiation far beyond Chuikov's authority to conduct.

Chuikov shortly excused himself to phone Marshal Zhukov at his headquarters 15 miles to the east and passed on the gist of his conversation with Krebs. Zhukov told him to keep pressing Krebs for unconditional surrender; then he

Embittered Berliners watch a woman tear up a copy of Mein Kampf, Hitler's personal political manifesto. Even as Nazi power ebbed, such an act—shown here in a Soviet photograph—was punishable by death at the hands of roving squads of SS troops.

phoned Stalin with the news of Hitler's death. "So that's the end of the bastard," Stalin responded. "Too bad it was impossible to take him alive."

Chuikov continued to play Krebs like a game fish, past dawn and past noon. He did not get a surrender and Krebs got no concessions. Krebs returned to the *Führerbunker* at 1 p.m. and, in the certain knowledge that all was over for the Third Reich, made ready to commit suicide. The failure of Krebs's mission prompted Goebbels to disclose, in a message to Dönitz, that the Führer was dead.

Affairs at the *Führerbunker* were swiftly terminated. Some time after 5 p.m., Magda Goebbels fed a drugged candy treat to her six children, and while they slept she crushed cyanide capsules in their mouths. At about 8:30 p.m. Joseph Goebbels escorted Magda up the steps into the garden. They bit into cyanide capsules and died quickly. By arrangement, an SS aide fired shots into their heads for good measure. It was all over in a matter of seconds and the SS men began a perfunctory cremation.

Martin Bormann and the bunker crew, finding flight to Plön the only tolerable course now open to them, slept most of May 1 to prepare for the ordeal and departed early the next morning. Acting on reports that the hitherto safe escape route westward via the Tiergarten and Charlottenburg had been closed, they headed north across the Spree River and scattered. Only a few of them made good their escapes. (Bormann may have been one of them; but Arthur Axmann, chief of the Hitler Youth, later said he had seen Bormann's corpse near a bridge in western Berlin.)

In the bunker they left behind an SS switchboard operator and the diesel technician who tended the roaring ventilator system. The maintenance man, fearing to be found by the Russians with an SS man, sent him away. But the technician felt that he himself had an obligation to stay: Besides air-conditioning the bunker, his machinery condensed water for wounded soldiers who had taken refuge in the nearby Reich Chancellery, and he refused to abandon them.

At 7 a.m. that day, General Weidling made his way to Chuikov's command post. He came not to play Krebs's game but to surrender the city and stop the pointless slaughter. Quickly he signed a surrender protocol. Then he drafted an order to his troops, assuring them that their oath of personal loyalty to Hitler was no longer binding:

"On April 30, the Führer to whom we all swore allegiance left us in the lurch. On command of the Führer, you still believe that you must fight for Berlin, even though the lack of heavy weapons and ammunition, and the situation in general, make this battle appear senseless!

"Every hour longer that you go on fighting prolongs the terrible suffering of the Berlin population and of our wounded. In agreement with the high command of the Soviet forces, I demand that you stop the battle immediately."

Weidling made a recording of his order, and Soviet sound trucks broadcast it throughout the city. It caused more and more scattered units to surrender. The Müncheberg Division heard it, but fought on. The outfit's diary-keeping officer wrote: "Perhaps it is genuine, perhaps not."

Not that the Münchebergs had much left to fight with. The drubbing they had taken in the bunker area reduced them to five armored vehicles, four field guns and a few hundred disheveled men—"walking skeletons," the diarist called them. Even so, and with barely any ammunition left, they clung to the hope of surrendering to the Western Allies rather than to the Russians, and fighting in that forlorn cause they managed to reopen the western escape route used by the *Führerbunker* fugitives through the Tiergarten to the outskirts closest to the British and the Americans.

On May 3, the survivors broke through to the Havel River and attacked a bridge. As the Münchebergs struggled to cross, they came under heavy Soviet fire. "The dead are lying all over the bridge, and the wounded, with no one to pick them up. Civilians are trying to cross; they are shot down in rows. Our last armored cars are forcing their way across the bridge through piles of twisted human bodies. The bridge is flooded with blood."

The terrible slaughter would not end. "The rear guard falls apart. The command crumbles. Our losses are heavy." But the shattered remnant of the division made it across.

On May 4, the Müncheberg officer made his last entry. "Behind us, Berlin in flames. Russian tanks all around us, and the incessant clatter of machine guns. We meet columns of refugees drifting about lost. They weep and ask for help. We are at the end ourselves. The unit breaks up. We try to go on in small groups."

The Müncheberg Panzer Division had perished. At last the corpse of Berlin belonged to the Red Army.

A VAUNTED ARMY'S COLLAPSE

In early April, 1945, an American tank rolls past four Germans—one walking with the aid of canes—making their way west under white flags to surrender.

LOSING THE WILL TO CONTINUE THE FIGHT

The Army of the Third Reich by the spring of 1945 was a pale semblance of the invincible machine that once had stormed across Europe with its blitzkrieg. Chances were that the young German who had written in his diary, "It is a wonderful feeling, now, to be a German," as ranks of panzers rolled into Poland in 1939, lay among the thousands buried along the road from Moscow or the hedgerows of Normandy. The vaunted panzer armor had shrunk to mere handfuls of tanks. A continental empire had diminished to a corridor less than 100 miles wide, defended in large part by teenagers and old men. Their Führer had made his last military decision: to die in the ruins of Berlin.

Everywhere they turned, the remnants of the Wehrmacht felt the dragon's breath of the Allied armies. As news of Hitler's death spread during the first days of May, the German soldiers finally lost their will to fight. For many, escape seemed the only option, and their best hope of survival lay with the Western Allies. As the defeated armies straggled westward, British and American troops began to worry less about being shot at than about coping with all the Germans bent on getting out of the path of the Russians.

"The War is over," said Lieut. General Hasso von Manteuffel, commander of the Third Panzer Army. "The soldiers have spoken." The soldiers' decision was most evident in the withering of the Wehrmacht's once-formidable cohesion and discipline; troops in effect demobilized themselves, some of the men even collecting their families (right) to join them in their flight.

Manteuffel's men fled toward the British lines in the north; they were a portion of the nearly one million German troops who would be able to reach the western Allied lines from the Eastern Front. But the destiny of innumerable others lay in the opposite direction; such great numbers were captured by the Russians on the southeastern front alone that when these men marched away to Soviet prison camps, Marshal Konev later wrote, "the head of the column was nearly at Dresden while its tail was still somewhere near Prague"—a distance of 75 miles.

On a walkie-talkie, an American sergeant consults with headquarters about the handling of Germans surrendering to him on April 29, 1945.

Their children perched on their shoulders, their wives trailing behind, German soldiers seeking a haven for their families trudge toward the British lines.

A LAYING DOWN OF ARMS

The easiest end to the War came for those Germans within quick reach of the Western Allies. Active combat troops laid down their arms—as at Munich *(below)*—when fighting no longer made sense. Occupation troops in Scandinavia headed for British compounds in north Germany.

Trying to confine the roughly five million Germans who surrendered during the last months of the War was a challenge to the Allied high command: Near the Baltic Sea, the problem was solved by herding prisoners into coastal peninsulas and sealing them off with their backs to the sea.

On May 17, Germans occupying Denmark cheerfully give up their arms to a civilian in Copenhagen after receiving assurances that they would go to a British prison camp.

German prisoners captured after a sharp fight near Munich are forced to lie prone as GIs of the U.S. Seventh Army search their comrades for weapons.

Men of a Wehrmacht division march 10 abreast to U.S. prison compounds after surrendering in north Germany on April 27.

Boys of a Hitler Youth unit, like members of a school athletic team, gather for a picture after giving up to American troops near Kronach, in western Germ

DESPERATE DUTY FOR BRAVE CHILDREN

As the German war machine ran low on manpower, Arthur Axmann, national leader of the Hitler Youth—the Nazi Party's organization for young people—pledged his boys to the defense of Berlin. Axmann dispatched thousands of willing but ill-prepared youngsters—none of them over 16 and some as young as 12—to shore up the faltering Wehrmacht.

It was an impossible task. A proud Axmann reported to Lieut. General Helmuth Weidling, then in command of a panzer corps east of Berlin, that the Hitler Youth were to reinforce the rear guard facing Soviet tanks at Müncheberg, an eastern suburb. But Weidling saw the tragic waste and tore into Axmann: "You cannot sacrifice these children for a cause that is already lost." Axmann agreed to rescind the order.

Elsewhere, German youths did face Russian armor. Near the Tiergarten, Soviet tank columns came upon 400 youngsters armed with *Panzerfäuste*, antitank weapons. General Vasily I. Chuikov, the Russian commander, directed his men to find some way to disarm the boys, but it proved beyond doing; the young Germans rushed the tanks, the Russians opened fire, and many of the youths went down. General Chuikov later lamented, "Who could have sent young boys to certain death? Only a madman."

A more sensible view of leadership saved some lives. One 22-year-old, in command of two dozen unarmed teenagers in southern Germany, concealed them in the forest until he found a passing American outfit to surrender to.

Taken prisoner as the British neared Bremen, these two soldiers are only 14 years old.

Civilians once more, captured Hitler Youths watch their piled uniforms burn in a Kronach street. They were soon sent home to their families.

A BRIDGE TO CAPTIVITY

On May 4 the remnants of two German armies that had been fighting the Russians south of Berlin sent word to the U.S. Ninth Army on the west bank of the Elbe River, asking for a formal surrender and safe crossing for the thousands of refugees who had escaped with them before the Russian advance. But Allied agreements required Russian participation in any large-scale surrenders; technically, troops who had fought against the Russians were subject to their control, as were civilians fleeing from the agreed-upon Soviet occupation zone.

The American command did agree to take prisoner any individual soldiers who could cross the Elbe. The nearest bridge, at Tangermünde, was a wreck. Nevertheless, the next day large numbers of soldiers and refugees set out to make the perilous crossing, most of them picking their way over the ruined bridge. By the end of hostilities on the 7th of May, nearly 100,000 of the Germans had crossed the river and surrendered to the Americans.

German military and civilian refugees crowd the east bank of the Elbe River, waiting their turn to start across the remnants of the bridge at Tangermünde.

In midstream, German soldiers help civilians inch westward across the half-sunken ruins of the bridge.

On the riverbank near the bridge, wounded Germans wait to be ferried on barges across the Elbe.

More than 160,000 German soldiers fill one of the tent camps that were hastily thrown up to shelter the growing mass of prisoners behind American lines.

Stalin's men had fought to give him Berlin by May Day; they missed by minutes. Not long after midnight on May 2, radio operators of the Soviet Eighth Guards Army received a German message. "HELLO, HELLO," said the voice. "56TH PANZER CORPS CALLING. PLEASE CEASE FIRE AT 12:50 A.M. WE WILL SEND TRUCE EMISSARIES TO THE POTSDAMER BRIDGE."

Wholesale surrender of German troops began at daybreak. By evening 135,000 had been taken prisoner; some of them, particularly the officers, would not see home again for many years. Others never would.

Berlin's civilians fared little better. Thousands of families streamed across the bridges to Spandau in the western suburbs to escape the city, but many more stayed in their homes—or what was left of them—hoping for the best. Though the shooting had stopped, the situation was grim: In most districts there was no electricity, telephone or transport, hardly any medical supplies and little food or water. People "eat grass and tree bark," a Russian official reported.

Berliners were sometimes surprised by the discipline, even the kindness, of frontline Red Army veterans. They did not act like barbarians but stopped to befriend children or share a glass of wine with adults. "I must tell you, however," a Soviet lieutenant warned the mother superior of a convent, "the men who are following us are pigs."

Though the lieutenant's comrades were no angels, he was right about many of those who arrived later to occupy the city. Women were raped by the tens of thousands; neither the very young nor the elderly were spared. Hundreds of Russians got drunk and roamed the streets. One band of soldiers raided a film-studio costume department and cavorted through the city wearing Napoleonic hats and 19th Century skirts and firing their weapons in the air.

Most soldiers seized spoils of war. Each enlisted man in the occupying force was allowed to ship home 33 pounds of loot per month (officers could send 66 pounds). Watches and cameras went toward home, but the booty also included clothing, bedding and household goods—almost anything portable that was not nailed down.

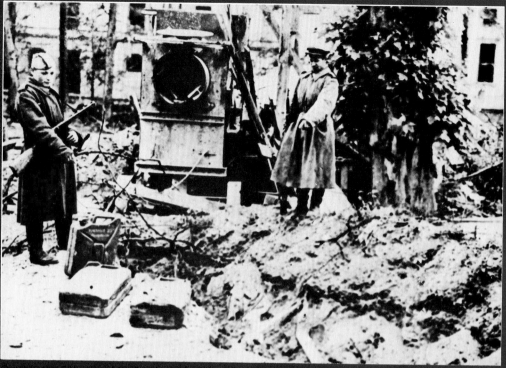

Outside the Führerbunker, Russians view the gasoline cans that mark Hitler's probable cremation site.

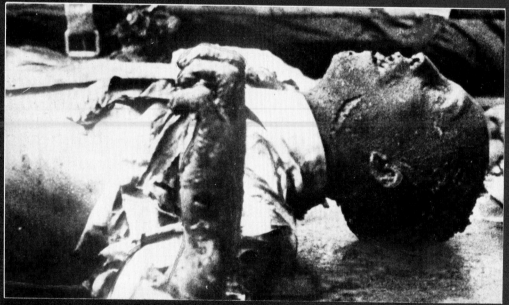

The burned remains of German Propaganda Minister Joseph Goebbels lie outside Hitler's bunker.

GRISLY MEMENTOS OF HITLER'S FINAL HOURS

The Russians found Hitler's bunker under the Reich Chancellery garden on the last day of the fighting. A search team came first upon the bodies of the Army Chief of Staff, Lieut. General Hans Krebs, and Hitler's adjutant, General Wilhelm Burgdorf. They had shot themselves while sitting at a long table littered with bottles and glasses. Then the search party found the burned remains of Joseph and Mag-da Goebbels and their six young children.

In a shallow grave outside, the searchers also discovered a badly charred body, at first identified as Hitler's. Later, the identity of the corpse became clouded by conflicting official reports, which contributed to wild tales that Hitler had escaped. Eventually the Russians confirmed finding the Führer's body; what they did with it remains a mystery.

5

Admiral Dönitz plays for time
Cyanide for Himmler
The choice: capitulation or chaos
Surrender at Rheims—and an encore in Berlin
"Who's going to take Prague?"
The Czechs' bloody revenge
A field marshal in peasant attire
The harsh fate of Russian renegades
Rancor among the victors
Hitler's prescient forecast

A VIOLENT EPILOGUE

As May began, the Allies increasingly turned their attention to the final challenge of the victorious war in Europe: establishing peace. They had long realized that the War might not end neatly with Germany's national capitulation: The Third Reich might disintegrate, leaving no central government or supreme command with the authority to satisfy the Allies' demand for an unconditional and simultaneous surrender on all fronts.

This requirement had arisen partly from Stalin's deep fear that if large German forces surrendered in the West while fighting continued in the East, Britain and the United States would make a separate peace with Germany and allow the Germans to continue the war against the U.S.S.R. The Allies had agreed in effect that German units engaged against Soviet forces were supposed to capitulate only to the Russians, and Germans opposing British or American armies were to surrender only to them.

As early as August 1944, the Combined Chiefs of Staff of the Western Allies had issued a set of guidelines for possible local surrenders by German units facing British and American forces. The document was based on three principles:

> Surrender, in general, was to be unconditional. Specifically, however, terms might be related to the immediate local military situation.
>
> The Germans were to receive absolutely no promises or commitments.
>
> Local surrender would be subordinate to any general surrender instrument agreed upon by the three major Allies, who were prepared, in time, to take over all Germany and install military governments in their respective occupation zones.

The guidelines were put to good use as German units one by one began to capitulate in the spring of 1945. Nevertheless, the Allies realized that a general surrender, presumably handled by a responsible German leader, would offer substantial benefits. In the process of surrendering, the leader could save lives, condemn sabotage, appeal for order and exact compliance from diehard Nazis; his presence could reduce tension and confusion during the turbulent period of transition—thereby speeding the pace of relief shipments, reconstruction work and the repatriation of prisoners of war, civilian refugees and other "displaced persons."

The question of who that national leader might be was crucial: The Allies would not accept surrender from Heinrich Himmler or any other personal henchman of Hitler; nor had they the time or inclination to seek out anti-Nazis to form a government of reconciliation. (In fact, by order of General Eisenhower, high-ranking Germans of all stripes were automatically suspect as war criminals and were subject to arrest.)

Ironically, Hitler himself, seeking a successor who would fight to the bitter end, supplied the Allies with a transitional German leader who suited their needs. Grand Admiral Dönitz, whose appointment as President of the Third Reich was announced by Radio Hamburg on the evening of May 1, was highly respected by both the German military and the German people. He had no political handicap, even though he was an unquestioned Hitler loyalist. As a military leader—chief of the Navy since 1943 and before that head of the fearsome submarine service—Dönitz had been so successful that any acknowledgment of national defeat he might make would presumably silence hardened Nazis.

A Dönitz statement would also preclude any repetition of the insistence of some Germans after World War I that the German Army had not really been vanquished—only betrayed by weak-kneed civilian leaders who sued for peace. Later on the night of May 1, Admiral Dönitz broadcast from his headquarters at Plön in northern Germany a proclamation of policy that, while it defied the Russians, was encouraging to the Western Allies.

From Allied statements and from captured documents outlining occupation zones, Dönitz knew the draconian surrender demands he was up against. He also saw where the real danger lay: "My first task," Dönitz said, "is to save German men and women from destruction by the advancing Bolshevik enemy. It is to serve this purpose alone that the military struggle continues. For as long as the British and the Americans continue to impede the accomplishment of this task, we must also continue to fight and defend ourselves against them."

Dönitz' words amounted to an appeal for a cease-fire in the West—a move that surprised and puzzled his close associates at Plön. After all, the admiral was famous for his fighting spirit, which had earned him the nickname The Lion in the U-boat service. Indeed, Dönitz was a military

man who did his duty. Until April 30, duty had taken the form of obedience to the Führer. Now, as the Reich's chief policy maker, his duty was to the German people.

Admiral Dönitz spent the first few days of his stewardship in almost constant conference with commanders and politicians from the scattered remnants of the Greater German Reich. He formed a government of ministers of his own choice; for example, he made an adviser of Albert Speer, who had been out of favor with Hitler at the time of the Führer's death, and he threatened to arrest on sight one obnoxious candidate recommended by Hitler: Martin Bormann.

Dönitz called in Himmler, who had been strutting about unoccupied northern Germany as if he were the new Führer. As SS chief, Himmler was at least theoretically in command of the police, the Waffen-SS and other miscellaneous troops. Dönitz could do nothing with confidence until he knew Himmler's intentions, since the SS chief might yet contest the validity of the admiral's appointment.

Escorted by six armed SS bodyguards, Himmler arrived at Dönitz' headquarters in Plön about midnight. Sullen and impatient, Himmler sat facing Dönitz across a desk on which the admiral had hidden a pistol under some papers.

"I handed Himmler the message containing my appointment," Dönitz later recalled. " 'Please read this,' I said. I watched him closely. As he read, an expression of astonishment, indeed of consternation, spread over his face. All hope seemed to collapse within him. He went very pale. Finally he stood up and bowed. 'Allow me,' he said, 'to become the second man in your state.' I replied that it was out of the question and that there was no way in which I could make any use of his services."

This calculated rebuff ended Himmler's notorious career. For a while he drifted aimlessly about northern Germany, asking associates whether he should commit suicide. Then he shaved off his mustache, so much like Hitler's, donned an eye patch, adopted the pseudonym Heinrich Hitzinger and went into hiding. A British dragnet finally caught him in mid-May, and when a doctor tried to investigate a little bulge in his cheek, Himmler bit into the bulge—a cyanide capsule—and swiftly expired.

After neutralizing Himmler, Dönitz fled north from Plön on May 2, one jump ahead of the advancing British, hoping to avoid capture as long as possible so that he could keep negotiating. He installed his government in a Naval training school at Mürwick, a suburb of the Baltic port of Flensburg on the German-Danish border, and began working out the tactics for his pro-Western, anti-Soviet surrender strategy.

The calculations began with a head count. General Jodl and his OKW operations staff—still functioning under Dönitz' direction—estimated that the Wehrmacht had 1.8 million fighting men still engaged somewhere on the Eastern Front. Since the Allies insisted that every German unit surrender to the force it had fought, nearly all the Germans in the East would have to submit to the Russians—if Dönitz capitulated at once. The admiral had to play for time.

Some of the numbers had to be written off. It was too late to help most of the 300,000 Germans trapped far behind Soviet lines in Latvia and East Prussia. Another 300,000 included recent casualties and prisoners who could not be accounted for, and survivors of the Berlin battles who were already struggling to reach the West. That left about 1.2 million troops who, with proper coordination and skillful rearguard action, still had a chance to fight their way westward and northwestward in order to surrender to the Americans and the British. Among them were 600,000 men of Army Group Center in Czechoslovakia, 430,000 of Army Group South in Austria and 180,000 of Army Group Southeast in Yugoslavia. In terms of numbers of men—and defensible positions, especially in the mountains ringing Prague—Czechoslovakia might provide the solid underpinning for Dönitz' delaying tactics.

For a firsthand report on the Czech situation, Dönitz summoned Lieut. General Oldwig von Natzmer, chief of staff of Field Marshal Schörner's Army Group Center, and Karl Hermann Frank, a vicious German native of the Czech Sudetenland who had tyrannized his country as head of the so-called Reich Protectorate of Bohemia and Moravia (two of Czechoslovakia's principal regions). After a hazardous flight from Prague across enemy-held Germany, the two men arrived in Flensburg on May 3 and immediately went into conference at Dönitz' headquarters.

General von Natzmer pronounced the military prospects grim. Army Group Center, with only 200,000 effective combat troops available, was bracing to withstand attack by more than two million Soviet soldiers who were slowly approaching from the north, east and south. It was Schörner's opinion, Natzmer said, that his armies would hold together for about two weeks.

Karl Frank reported increasing underground activity in Prague and predicted a large-scale revolt within a few days. But he proposed a scheme that might save Prague for the postwar West: Let him start turning over the Czech government to certain non-Communist politicians, and through them negotiate to surrender the capital to General Patton's U.S. Third Army, which had been loitering along the Czech-German border for two full weeks. Dönitz authorized Frank to test his proposal, and ordered Army Group Center to hold in place as long as possible, then to retreat westward and surrender to the Americans.

Having done the little he could to delay the Russians, Dönitz turned to the delicate matter of both delaying and propitiating the Western Allies. The admiral had set up a negotiating team led by his successor as commander in chief of the Navy, Admiral Hans-Georg von Friedeburg. He empowered Friedeburg to negotiate with British Field Marshal Sir Bernard L. Montgomery, the commander of the Twenty-first Army Group. Dönitz put strict limitations on Friedeburg's authority, carefully stipulating the surrender offers he could make and the order in which he should make them. Since every proposal that Dönitz authorized Friedeburg to make involved one exception or another to the Allies' terms of unconditional surrender, Dönitz did not expect an enthusiastic response. He was still stalling for time.

Friedeburg arranged to meet Field Marshal Montgomery on May 3 at the British advanced tactical headquarters on Lüneburger Heide, a large heath near the west bank of the Elbe, about 30 miles southeast of Hamburg. Friedeburg's first ploy was a proposal he knew was expressly forbidden by inter-Allied agreement: He offered to surrender to the British all the men of the German Third Panzer, Twelfth and Twenty-first Armies who had been fighting the Russians north of Berlin. With a show of propriety, Montgomery turned down the proposal. But while stressing his refusal to accept such a surrender "in a body," he said that the troops of the armies in question would be admitted as individual prisoners to the British lines. The Germans gave Montgomery to understand that they received and appreciated the

Hitler greets his eventual successor, Karl Dönitz, in a 1942 photograph. At the time Dönitz was commander of Germany's fearsome U-boats.

THE ADMIRAL HITLER TRUSTED

On April 30, 1945, Grand Admiral Karl Dönitz received a radio message stating that Hitler had named him the new leader of the Third Reich.

The move was unexpected: Dönitz was not part of the Nazi inner circle. But the choice was an indication of how much Hitler esteemed the stern commander in chief of the German Navy—and how few of his close associates he could still rely on. The Führer felt that both Hermann Göring and Heinrich Himmler had betrayed him; the senior generals of the Wehrmacht were discredited by their failures; Joseph Goebbels and Martin Bormann, though still loyal, were trapped with him in Berlin.

Admiral Dönitz, by contrast, had won the Führer's respect by the dramatic U-boat successes of 1939 to 1942, and he had never lost his standing with Hitler. Knowing nothing about submarine warfare himself, Hitler had always given Dönitz a far freer hand than he allowed other German military commanders, with whom he constantly interfered. The Führer's final expression of confidence in Dönitz, the leadership of the Reich, was an office that would exist only for days. But with it came a duty that Hitler could not face himself: to surrender and end Germany's agony.

signal: Any troops in northern Germany who could reach the British lines would be safe from the Russians.

Montgomery quickly demanded: "Will you surrender to me all German forces on my western and northern flanks, including all forces in Holland, Friesland with the Frisian Islands and Heligoland, Schleswig-Holstein and Denmark? If you will do this, I will accept it as a tactical battlefield surrender of enemy forces immediately opposing me." This was an acceptable move under the Allied agreements, but it was so sweeping as to frustrate Dönitz' aim of delaying the surrender process in order to give as many men as possible a chance to reach the Western Allies' lines. In any case, Montgomery's proposition exceeded Friedeburg's authorization, and he could not accept it.

At this point, Montgomery declared that it was time for lunch, and sent the Germans off to eat and reflect. "Friedeburg wept during lunch," Montgomery later wrote laconically, "and the others did not say much."

After lunch, Montgomery served up a brisk ultimatum: Dönitz must agree to his proposal by 6 p.m. the next day, May 4, or the British would resume the fighting, and would inflict heavy casualties.

Friedeburg hastened to Flensburg to discuss Montgomery's demands with Dönitz overnight. He flew back to British headquarters before the deadline with permission from Dönitz to surrender the territories in question, but Montgomery, who was holding a press conference, kept him waiting. At length the Germans were escorted into a tent full of journalists and photographers. There, as cameras clicked, Friedeburg signed a surrender drawn up by Montgomery in accordance with standing orders from the Combined Chiefs of Staff and approved by General Eisenhower. Montgomery was keenly aware of the importance of the moment. "Did you get that picture?" he called to the photographers. "Good. A historic picture—historic."

During the negotiations on Lüneburger Heide, a question had arisen about the surrender of German-occupied Norway. The issue was serious: Up to 100,000 Germans were in Norway, and their commander was a hardliner, Lieut. General Franz Böhme. "In Norway," he boasted, "we can accept any battle."

Montgomery referred the question of Norway to Eisen-

hower, who ruled that surrender negotiations concerning any further territories, including Norway, must be handled through his own headquarters. Accordingly, on May 5 Admiral Friedeburg and his team journeyed to the forward base of Supreme Headquarters, Allied Expeditionary Force (SHAEF), in the French cathedral town of Rheims, 85 miles northeast of Paris. By the time Friedeburg arrived, the Germans in Italy had surrendered to British Field Marshal Sir Harold Alexander, and with German Field Marshal Albert Kesselring trying to surrender his other armies in the west, it seemed likely that the Rheims negotiations would conclude all the piecemeal surrenders, including Norway, to the Western Allies.

At Rheims, Friedeburg discovered that the talks were to be conducted not by Eisenhower but by his chief of staff, Lieut. General Walter Bedell Smith; Eisenhower, deeply revolted by a recent visit to a Nazi concentration camp, refused to see the Germans until they had signed an instrument of surrender.

In Smith's office at SHAEF headquarters, Friedeburg also found that the chief of staff was not negotiating terms; he was dictating them. The German was shocked to learn that Eisenhower insisted not only on complete surrender in the West but also on simultaneous surrender to the Russians in the East—exactly what the Allies had demanded all along. Smith, intent on proving to the Germans that their position was hopeless, displayed battle maps and indicated Allied attacks, real and hypothetical, that were projected if they did not acquiesce.

Friedeburg once more found himself asked to make a decision that was beyond his authority. He relayed the terms of Eisenhower's ultimatum to Dönitz. Because of disrupted communications, the message went to Flensburg by a roundabout route, buying a little more time for the Germans in the East.

As the Germans inched painfully toward definitive capitulation, the Allies in Rheims realized they had a last-minute problem of their own. The difficulty lay with the instrument of surrender, which had been carefully drawn up in advance by the European Advisory Commission, the group of Allied diplomats who also had planned the occupation zones for Germany and Austria. The three Allied powers had approved the surrender document as early as July 1944;

Field Marshal Sir Bernard L. Montgomery (right center) reads surrender terms to a German delegation near Hamburg on May 4. Germans facing the camera are Rear Admiral Gerhard Wagner (left) and Admiral Hans-Georg von Friedeburg. The surrender that Montgomery accepted on behalf of the Allies encompassed all German forces in Denmark, northwest Germany, the Netherlands and Dunkirk, one of several French ports that were still held by German troops.

since then, the French had joined the EAC, but they had not been told that at Yalta in February 1945 the British, Americans and Russians had altered the surrender document. The change was a single word—"dismemberment"—added to the list of rights the victors would claim for themselves. From the German viewpoint, the change threatened the end of national identity. From the short-term Allied standpoint, the change created a document unrecognized by France.

There was one more hitch. The surrender document called for the signatures of both civilian and military authorities in Germany. The Allies did not recognize Dönitz as a civilian head of state, only as the military commander of German troops still under arms. What should be done, General Smith's staff asked, about the absence of a recognized German civilian authority?

Smith and Ambassador John G. Winant, the London-based U.S. representative on the EAC, discussed the two problems by telephone and decided, in effect, to start all over again. A new document entitled Act of Military Surrender could be written that would give the French a legally unencumbered document to sign, bypass the problem of

German civilian authority and accomplish the surrender with the least possible delay.

Within hours, as the Allies at Rheims awaited a response from Dönitz, the new document was drafted. It was chiefly the work of British Colonel John Counsell, an actor in civilian life. He borrowed much of the document's terminology from a report in Stars and Stripes, the U.S. military newspaper, detailing the terms of the German surrender in Italy on May 2. Two of the three major Allies quickly approved the draft. Only Moscow had not yet answered a request for instruction from its representative, Major General Ivan Susloparov, chief of the Soviet Military Mission in Paris.

Admiral von Friedeburg's message to Dönitz did not reach Flensburg until later on the morning of May 6. Reading the ultimatum, Dönitz decided it was still too early to accept a general capitulation. As many as 210,000 German troops evading the Russians had streamed into British and American lines in the past few days, but the escape of German forces in Yugoslavia, Austria and—especially—Czechoslovakia had barely begun. The admiral called on General Jodl, a strong opponent of general surrender and

the man most determined to resist Allied pressure, to fly to Rheims and continue to stall.

Dönitz authorized Jodl to surrender only to the Western Allies. If this position failed and the Allies renewed their threats of punitive air and ground attacks, Jodl was empowered to negotiate a general capitulation on all fronts, but only in slow stages. First would come a cease-fire during which German troops could move about freely—that is, flee westward and enter Allied lines. If, as a subsequent stage, Eisenhower insisted on a provision stopping all movement, such a freeze should be postponed as long as possible. Jodl's authority to conclude a surrender was contingent on final permission from Dönitz.

Jodl arrived at Rheims on the evening of May 6 and, with Admiral von Friedeburg, quickly opened a discussion with General Smith and British Major General Kenneth Strong, the German-speaking chief of SHAEF intelligence, who served as translator. Smith presented the instrument of surrender. Its five paragraphs called for the unconditional and simultaneous surrender at 11:01 p.m. on May 8 of all German land, sea and air forces on all fronts; it also required

the Germans to destroy no machinery or military equipment and to submit to all Allied orders and to accept punishment for any disobedience. It further noted that the purely military surrender would be superseded by any general instrument of surrender that might be imposed later.

Jodl began raising obstacles. He argued, among other points, that it would be impossible to cease operations by the time specified in the document; it would take the High Command longer than that merely to transmit orders to all fronts. He argued for a 48-hour postponement.

After an hour of discussion, Smith concluded that Jodl was stalling, and he reported his opinion to Eisenhower. Eisenhower sent Smith back with orders to tell the Germans to stop delaying. Smith told Jodl that the capitulation must be signed that day, that hostilities must cease by midnight two days later and that he had 30 minutes to think things over. Jodl sent Dönitz the message by radio and added, "I see no alternative—chaos or signature."

This time the ultimatum reached German headquarters swiftly, and Dönitz' kindest word for it was "sheer extortion." He later contended that Eisenhower had "no proper

appreciation of the new turn of events in world affairs that had now taken place," implying that America and Germany should have begun a joint resistance to Soviet ambitions in Europe. Dönitz spent two hours trying to avoid the inevitable a little longer. Then, just after midnight on May 7, he sent Jodl permission to sign the unconditional surrender.

Jodl and Friedeburg were escorted to the SHAEF war room, a recreation hall 30 feet square in the red brick boys' school that served as headquarters. There, nearly a dozen officers from four victorious nations awaited them, along with the press. General Smith stood blinking in the glare of news photographers' floodlights. Behind the lights, 17 correspondents took notes in dead silence.

With General Strong translating, Smith asked whether the Germans were ready to sign the instrument of capitulation. Jodl nodded. At precisely 2:41 a.m. he signed. Then, in order, General Smith signed for the Supreme Commander of the Allied Expeditionary Force; General Susloparov, though he still had not heard from Moscow, signed for the Soviet high command; and French Major General François Sevez signed as witness.

Rising, General Jodl asked to speak, and made a statement in German:

> General! With this signature the German people and German armed forces are, for better or worse, delivered into the victor's hands. In this War, which has lasted more than five years, both have achieved and suffered more than perhaps any other people in the world. In this hour I can only express the hope that the victor will treat them with generosity.

The German negotiators were at last taken to General Eisenhower. He asked them if they thoroughly understood the surrender terms and warned Jodl that he would be held accountable for any violations. Jodl saluted and departed.

Eisenhower then sent the Combined Chiefs of Staff a message of dazzling simplicity: "The mission of this Allied force was fulfilled at 0241, local time, May 7, 1945."

But the German capitulation was far from finished. Six hours after the ceremony in Rheims, Moscow's response arrived, commanding Susloparov not to sign any documents.

The message virtually accused General Eisenhower of settling with the Germans in order to allow them to continue fighting the Soviet Union. The Soviet response went on to insist that the surrender document must be signed later, in Berlin, and stipulated that only a Berlin signing would be recognized. General Susloparov was recalled to Moscow to receive "strict punishment"—a term that usually meant execution. (Fortunately for Susloparov, he had influential friends in Moscow; he was later informed that Stalin "did not hold any grudge against Susloparov for what he had done at Rheims.")

The Russians were upset for several reasons. Having learned that the new surrender document was not identical to the one approved by the European Advisory Council, the Russians informed SHAEF that their instrument of surrender would restore language from the original EAC document. In addition, they said, it appeared that the surrender excluded the Soviet Union. According to the Russians, German headquarters had issued orders to its armies near eastern fronts to cease all hostilities toward the British and the Americans, and to fight their way through Russian forces to reach the Western Allies' lines.

In reply, Eisenhower pointed out that the brief military surrender signed in France had been written to include the understanding that the Germans must sign a more general document later. Eisenhower declared himself ready to attend that final signing, which was being arranged for the following day in Berlin under the aegis of Marshal Zhukov.

Eisenhower was keen on attending the ceremony; he wanted to see Berlin, and to meet Zhukov. But members of his staff, and Prime Minister Churchill, convinced him that the event was merely a formal ratification of the Rheims surrender. Eisenhower appointed his deputy commander, British Air Chief Marshal Sir Arthur W. Tedder, to represent the Western Allies.

In the Berlin ceremony, the game of protocol was played to the hilt, punctuated by squabbling among the representatives of the Western Allies over who was to sign the instrument of surrender, in what capacity and in what order.

The bickering over the signing originated with Charles de Gaulle, provisional head of the French government, who had instructed his representative, General de Lattre de Tassigny, to sign as a witness, just as the French had done at

Rheims—as long as Eisenhower or his representative signed for the Western Allies as a group. However, if the document was to be signed by representatives of each of the Allies, de Lattre had a different set of instructions: He was to insist on equal treatment with the Americans and British. When de Lattre told Tedder about his orders, Tedder promised that after he had executed the principal signature for the Western Allies as a group, both de Lattre and the American representative, General Carl Spaatz, would sign the capitulation as witnesses.

The Russians had a different idea. They felt that since Tedder had been designated by Eisenhower to sign jointly for the British and the Americans, de Lattre, as witness, should be the only additional signatory from the West. The Americans rejected that arrangement. General Spaatz insisted on signing if de Lattre was allowed to sign. De Lattre was also adamant. At length, the Russians accepted Tedder's original plan: Tedder and Zhukov would sign as principals, and de Lattre and Spaatz would sign as witnesses. Ironically, when the moment arrived, neither de Lattre nor Spaatz had a pen, and each had to borrow one in order to sign.

Even the Germans managed to compound the rancor and confusion surrounding the sequence of surrender ceremonies. To demonstrate solidarity, the Allies tried to coordinate a simultaneous announcement of German surrender in Washington, London and Moscow on May 8. A news blackout had been imposed on all correspondents following the ceremony in Rheims. The ban was observed by everybody except the Associated Press, which, on May 7, monitored a radio broadcast from Dönitz' headquarters at Flensburg, prompted by the admiral's decision to accept Eisenhower's surrender terms. Dönitz wanted German troops to know how little time they had to escape to the West. The AP considered the broadcast an independent news event, and broke the biggest story of the year.

The news organizations that had abided by the ban were understandably angered by the unauthorized AP scoop—but no more so than the Russians. Uncertain until the last moment that the Germans were actually going to surrender to them, the Soviets insisted on waiting until they had German signatures on their own surrender documents before allowing announcement of the War's end; they requested a

Field Marshal Wilhelm Keitel proudly snaps a salute with his riding crop as he arrives at the site of the Berlin surrender ceremony, which was presided over by the Russians. Accompanying the field marshal are Luftwaffe General Hans Jürgen Stumpff (left) and Admiral von Friedeburg.

Signing the surrender document at 11:30 p.m. on May 8 is Field Marshal Keitel, as (from left) Soviet Marshal Georgy Zhukov, U.S. General Carl Spaatz and French General Jean de Lattre de Tassigny bear witness. The ceremony in Berlin satisfied the Russians, who regarded the Rheims surrender at Eisenhower's headquarters as only a preliminary.

delay of the formal joint Allied announcement from May 8 to May 9. But by the time Moscow's request was received, American and British plans for the proclamation of victory—and for attendant celebrations—were too far along to change. As a result, victory in Europe was proclaimed in Washington and London on May 8; in Moscow the statement was issued on May 9. Ever since, V-E Day has been celebrated a day later in the East than in the West.

For most of the British, French and American soldiers who had fought the Germans, the victory celebration was muted. Some had seen so much suffering and bloodshed that the news evoked less joy than a kind of exhausted relief. "We sat in silence," wrote an American private named Lester Atwell. "I searched for some feeling, waited for it to develop. There was hardly any sensation at all. A moment later I was aware of an inward caving in, followed by a sore-throat feeling when I thought of those who had been forced to give up their lives for this moment."

The good news raised skeptical thoughts in a few men. James Byrom, a British medic on duty in a hospital in northern Germany, stood at a window watching a magnificent sunset. He wrote: "Up from the British lines came brilliant flares, singly and in clusters, but without pattern or prodigality, as if one soldier in each platoon had been given an official colored hat and told to fling it in the air. But farther away, in the Russian lines, the glow of bonfires steadily lit up the sky. I could fancy that they were ghost fires, the fires of other historic triumphs, so strongly did I feel them as a symbol of the unreality of victory in relation to the recurring failure to keep the peace."

The Soviet troops, who had pursued the retreating Germans until the very end, celebrated wildly and alcoholically. At one of the victory parties attended by American officers, they toasted everyone over and over again with vodka: "Premier Stalin. The President of the United States. The Russian Army. The American Army. General Eisenhower. Premier Stalin. . . ."

The Soviets were by no means deceived by the German surrender. They knew that more than one million German troops were still either fighting them or fleeing in violation of the accord. They knew that Soviet forces in Czechoslova-

kia and Austria, and Tito's army in Yugoslavia, could not stand down until the Germans there were pacified and rounded up. The fact was that, although the war in Europe had officially ended, it was still going on.

Some of the War's ugliest episodes were taking place in and around Prague even as the Germans signed their various surrenders. The battle for Prague, fought from May 5 to May 9, was more than an anticlimax. It was also a prologue to the peacetime struggle between East and West that soon became known as the Cold War.

Until early May of 1945, Prague lay in a backwater of the rip tides that had been roiling Eastern Europe for months. The Soviet drive across Poland in January had brought three Soviet army groups within striking distance of the Czech capital, where they halted. The Fourth Ukrainian Army Group, commanded by General Andrei I. Yeremenko, had driven deep into Slovakia, to a line some 150 miles east of Prague; there it faced stiff resistance from the First Panzer Army, one of the three armies in Field Marshal Schörner's Army Group Center. Marshal Rodion I. Malinovsky's Second Ukrainian Army Group was driving west and north from Vienna; his forces had outflanked the 24th Panzer Corps on the right wing of the Army Group Center defense line and were fighting in the area around Brno, some 100 miles east and slightly south of the Czech capital.

The bulk of the third great Soviet force, Marshal Konev's First Ukrainian Army Group, had been heavily engaged in the assault on Berlin. Late in April, Konev received a phone call from Stalin who, in his usual manner, without greeting or preamble, demanded, "Who's going to take Prague?" Konev gave the right answer—he was.

In fact, only the southern elements of Konev's army group, which in April had engaged Schörner's battered Fourth Panzer Army in the Dresden area, were as close to Prague as Malinovsky's and Yeremenko's forces. Konev's troops now drove south from Berlin and southeast from Dresden on a broad front, with orders not only to envelop Prague but also to cut off Germans retreating through the capital in hope of surrendering to the Americans.

Konev disengaged his two tank armies from mopping-up operations in Berlin and rushed them south into position to spearhead his drive on Prague. Moscow reinforced his command with an army taken from Zhukov's First Belorussian Army Group. The Soviet high command issued formal orders on the first four days of May: About 1.7 million troops would be committed to the Prague offensive, equipped with 1,800 tanks and self-propelled guns, 30,000 field guns and mortars, and more than 2,900 combat aircraft. It would be an operation comparable in size to the Berlin offensive. The final assault would begin on May 7 and was expected to last as long as two weeks.

Converging on Prague, these huge forces drove before them hordes of refugees—including German residents of Czechoslovakia, freed slave laborers and concentration camp inmates. Hundreds of thousands of refugees fled west ahead of Malinovsky's armies. A U.S. officer who scouted near the Czech-Austrian border in a reconnaissance plane reported that the displaced persons—or DPs, as they were beginning to be called—"cover the landscape, crawling like ants along the roads, overflowing into the fields, camping hopelessly in the suburbs of rubbled cities, creating a problem to which no one has found a solution."

Prague itself was a refugee center. Its large population of resident Sudeten Germans now swelled with other German residents of Czechoslovakia, with Czechs fleeing the Russians, and with bureaucrats from Berlin whose government offices had been moved south before the Soviet onslaught.

The Red Army's approach had propelled large numbers of Czechs into purposeful motion in early May, many of them as part of the Soviet advance. As many as 30,000 belonged to the Czech I Army Corps attached to the Fourth Ukrainian Army Group; they were pushing slowly westward through wooded, mountainous terrain toward the city of Olomouc, 140 miles southeast of Prague. Other armed Czechs—members of many small partisan groups—were moving into position to attack and disrupt German garrisons in the country-wide insurrection that Karl Frank had predicted in his Flensburg conference with Admiral Dönitz.

Czech attitudes toward the oncoming Soviet armies were ambivalent, not least because the Russian troops were looting and committing wholesale rape as they advanced. The Czechs had long expected their liberation to come from the East and had no history of animosity toward the Russians. However, they were the most Westernized and democratically inclined of the Slavic peoples, and most of them did not relish the prospect of being pulled into the Soviet-Communist orbit after the War.

The Czechs' emotional struggle to decide between East and West was personified in the career of Eduard Beneš, the prewar President of the Czech Republic, who had returned to Czechoslovakia after years in exile; under Soviet sponsorship, he headed a "National Front," which represented the various Czech political parties but had Communists holding key leadership posts. In early April, Beneš' provisional government had been established in the liberated Slovakian town of Košice.

In spite of his gratitude to the Soviet Union, Beneš remained emotionally committed to the West. This he revealed in his reaction to a report on April 18 that the U.S. Third Army had invaded Czechoslovakia. Beneš, who hated to show feelings of any kind, cried, "Thank God! Thank God!" Then, his secretary recalled, "he rushed into the adjoining room to share the good news with his beloved wife. 'Haniçko, Haniçko, the Americans have just entered Czechoslovakia! Patton is across the border!'"

In reality, the American movement was simply a large patrol action. Patton had to wait for more than two critical weeks before General Eisenhower—urged to move forward by the British and advised to stay where he was by the Soviets—at last compromised and authorized the Third Army to join the move into Czechoslovakia. An agreement with the Russians allowed Patton to advance eastward as far as a line roughly drawn on the map through the towns of Karlsbad, Pilsen and Budweis.

To lead Patton's advance the U.S. V Corps, on the Czech border facing Pilsen, was transferred on May 4 from the First Army, under General Courtney H. Hodges, to Patton's Third Army. The corps commander, Major General C. Ralph Huebner, who had served with Patton in Sicily, sat down to dinner shortly after learning of his transfer and remarked to his staff, "Well, I'll give us about twelve hours before General Patton calls up and tells us to attack something."

The soup was still hot when Huebner's chief of staff called him to the telephone and said with a grin, "It's General Patton." Their conversation was reported thus:

"Hello, Huebner?"

"Hello, General. How are you?"

"Fine. I'm sure glad you're back with me again."

"Glad to be back, General."

"I want you to attack Pilsen in the morning."

"Yes, sir."

"Can you do it?"

"Yes, sir."

"Fine, move fast now. We haven't got much time left in this War. I'll be up to see you. Good-by."

General Huebner returned to his dinner. "Well, I missed that one," he told his staff. "Instead of twelve hours it was twelve minutes."

On May 5, Patton's massive forces lurched eastward across the Czech border. Ragtag German troops appeared, including remnants of the 11th Panzer Division; all were eager to surrender to the Americans. The V Corps halted just east of Pilsen, on the line agreed upon with the Russians. Patton, however, apparently found the U.S.-Soviet accord a less-than-compelling reason to halt; he asserted that "a nation as great as America should let other people worry about the complications." True to his convictions, Patton did not come to a complete stop; he sent units of the 4th Armored Division through Pilsen to reconnoiter the road toward Prague. He later claimed that the scouts went only five miles past Pilsen, stopping 45 miles from Prague. In fact, they went a great deal closer, but they would have no real impact on the struggle developing for the capital.

As Patton's army penetrated into Czechoslovakia, a far smaller unit was already in position to play an important role in the events in Prague. It was the 25,000-man 1st Division of the ROA—initials that stood for *Russkaya Osvoboditelnaya Armiya,* or Russian Liberation Army. The ROA was made up of Russians whom the Germans had recruited from prisoner-of-war camps and occupied areas of the Soviet Union to fight against the Red Army. Estimated to number close to one million, the Russians had fought in units that were scattered throughout the German Army during the last years of the War.

The leader of the ROA was Andrei A. Vlasov, formerly a Red Army lieutenant general and a bona fide Soviet hero, who had been persuaded by the Germans to join their cause after they captured him near Leningrad in 1942. He personally commanded only a small portion of the ROA—two divisions consisting of some 50,000 men, and a 4,000-man group designated as an air force, although it had no planes.

Tall (6 feet 5 inches), charismatic and intelligent, Vlasov had long since realized that in joining the Germans he had staked his life on a losing cause, and he assumed that he and his men would be treated harshly if the Red Army captured them. But he also believed, like the German officers who advised the ROA, that the collapse of the Third Reich would precipitate an early East-West confrontation, and he nurtured an illusion that the Western Allies would need an anti-Communist Russian army to fight against the Soviet Union. Vlasov did not know that he and his men had been doomed by an agreement at Yalta that committed the Allies to repatriate all prisoners of war and displaced persons. This accord applied to anyone who had been a Soviet citizen in 1939—whether or not he or she now desired to return to the Soviet Union.

Vlasov's 1st Division was under the field command of General Sergei Bunyachenko, a tough, hard-drinking soldier who shaved his head in the Red Army style. The division had been on the Oder front just before the Red Army launched its Berlin offensive. There, after German orders exposed his troops to a suicidal attack, Bunyachenko resolved never again to obey anyone but Vlasov. In mid-April he angrily pulled his division out of the line and headed south, ostensibly to join Army Group Center. Actually, he hoped to join the Americans advancing east or to form an alliance with insurgent groups in Czechoslovakia, who were loosely organized in bands both inside and outside the capital at Prague, roughly divided into Communist and nationalist factions.

By the end of April, Bunyachenko and his men had marched 300 miles and pitched camp at the town of Beroun, 18 miles southwest of Prague. In roughly the same period, the ROA's poorly equipped 2nd Division had evacuated its barracks at Münsingen in southwest Germany, moved by train into Austria on orders to join Army Group South at Linz, then marched north into Czechoslovakia toward Budweis, 75 miles from Prague.

Vlasov, meanwhile, detoured to Karlsbad to marry his German mistress. He then went on to Prague, where he opened negotiations with nationalist leaders of the Czech partisans. He proposed that the ROA and the partisans join forces,

After six years of German occupation, the jubilant townspeople of Moravska Ostrava, in central Czechoslovakia, welcome Russian armored units as liberators. The Czech industrial center had contributed heavy machinery and clothing to the German war effort.

seize the mountain-rimmed Bohemian basin surrounding the capital and hold this natural fortress until the Western Allies arrived. The partisans declined the offer, saying that the Western Allies had abandoned Czechoslovakia before and would do it again. Besides, they told Vlasov, the Czechs would not resist the Red Army because their leader, President Beneš, was working with the Russians.

Discouraged by the partisans' refusal, Vlasov was further depressed when he sent his deputy, General Vasily Malyshkin, to Nesselwang on the Austrian border to arrange with Lieut. General Alexander Patch of the U.S. Seventh Army for the ROA to go over to the Americans. Instead, Malyshkin was detained by Patch as a prisoner of war in all but name. Patch wanted no part of a partnership with Russians in German uniforms.

The Czech uprising against the Germans, which had started outside Prague, built slowly to a grisly apogee in the city. The revolt began when news of uprisings against the Germans in the Czech countryside reached the capital on the 1st of May. That night, several bridges on the outskirts of Prague were blown up by partisan units. During the next two days, Czech national flags and Communist red flags began to appear over villages and towns. Czech railroad workers walked off the job, abandoning trains full of German refugees from the east, and the railroad stoppage forced factories to suspend production.

On May 4, the Czechs held mass meetings in town squares. Shopkeepers began painting over their German-language signs, and that night Czech students tore down German street signs. The German commandant of Prague, General Rudolf Toussaint, declared a state of siege and set a curfew. But the Czechs paid no heed, and Toussaint, who had few troops of his own and who did not control the SS or the police, was powerless to enforce his edicts.

The next morning, Sunday, May 5, Prague was quiet for a while. The call to action came without fanfare, signaled by a news broadcast on a local radio station: Two announcers, who usually alternated reading in Czech and German, read the news in Czech only. According to a young Czech who had escaped from a German concentration camp in April and arrived in Prague on May 1, the violence began almost simultaneously. "A man named Svoboda," the escapee recounted, "disarmed the guard at the front entrance of the station and was killed for his trouble. He was probably th first casualty. The Germans tried to fight their way in and th announcers broadcast an appeal for all good men and tru to come to their aid. A lot of people did." Among the man volunteers were armed Czech policemen and Czech re serve officers, who were called naftalinky—mothballs—fo the smell given off from their long-stored uniforms.

"Toward 11 o'clock," recalled a Sudeten German minin executive who was in Prague on business, "the storm broke Barricades were thrown up, German houses were attacked and the first Germans were dragged out of their houses. A hour later I saw many battered and trampled Germans lyin in the streets." The atrocities would escalate.

Karl Frank, who returned that morning from his meetin with Admiral Dönitz, wanted to turn over the governmen to the Czechs, as Dönitz had authorized, but he was too late. The Czechs were already taking over by force of arms By nightfall on the 5th, the insurgents had taken over mos of the government buildings, the bridges and railroad sta tions, the two radio stations, the central telephone exchang and the main thoroughfares. The Soviet-controlled Bene

A Czech partisan marches a German prisoner down a Prague street during the uprising of May 1945. The Czechs exacted a brutal vengeance for their years under the Nazi boot: In the course of three days, besides routing the few German troops and police left in the city, they killed 30,000 German civilian residents, mostly women and children.

Citizens man a barricade in Prague with captured German weapons, including the Panzerfaust at right. The sandbagged bunker was an open declaration of the organized revolt that began at 3 p.m. on May 5, when the revolutionary Czech National Council broadcast an appeal to barricade the streets of the Czech capital.

government in Košice, which had counseled against the insurrection, hastened to stake a claim to it now that it was under way and doing well.

The Prague partisan leaders, most of them nationalists, were not unduly confident; Field Marshal Schörner had elements of two panzer divisions in the vicinity of Prague. The nationalist Czech partisans wanted an organized armed force to help them hold the capital until the arrival of the American Army, which reportedly was approaching fast. Vlasov's 1st Division of the ROA was just such a force. On May 5 the nationalist leaders made a compact with its commander, General Bunyachenko: In return for help against the Germans, the ROA men would be granted asylum in liberated Czechoslovakia.

On May 6, the scattered German troops in and around Prague launched counterattacks. Some Czech barricades were overwhelmed by SS units, which, though relatively weak by ordinary military standards, were better trained and equipped than the partisans, who were armed only with personal weapons and such small arms as they had been able to capture. In search of support, a hastily established

provisional government calling itself the National Council broadcast an appeal for aid over Radio Prague:

"A request from the city of Prague to all Allied armies! The Germans are advancing from all directions with tanks, artillery and infantry. Prague urgently needs help. Send aircraft, tanks and artillery. Help! Help us quickly!"

In Moscow, the Czech military mission relayed the appeal to the Soviet high command, which reported the news to Stalin. He ordered Marshal Konev to launch his offensive on May 6—a day ahead of schedule.

Konev responded with his usual celerity. He called for a heavy artillery bombardment along his front west of Dresden; on the afternoon of the 6th, two infantry armies and the Third and Fourth Guards Tank Armies drove southeast into the German lines. Later in the day a fifth Soviet army struck farther southeastward to assault Dresden and pin down two panzer divisions and one motorized infantry division in that area. Konev's first-day attacks were generally successful. But the Germans fought hard; they had orders from Field Marshal Schörner to hold at all costs so that his forces to the

183

east could retreat safely westward through Prague. The German defenders, aided by rain, mud and a dark night, slowed down Konev's armies and limited their deepest penetration to about 15 miles. Clearly the Soviets would not be able to enter Prague for a few days at least.

The insurgents in Prague did receive some immediate help—from the 1st Division of Vlasov's ROA. The renegade Russians were welcomed by enthusiastic crowds as they marched into the capital in their German uniforms, distinguished from the embattled German forces in Prague only by white shoulder patches bearing the blue cross of Saint Andrew, the patron saint of Russia. Their vehicles bedecked by the Czechs with early lilacs and tulips, the Russians moved out in combat teams to engage the pockets of German troops in and around the city. The heaviest fighting took place on the outskirts of Prague, especially at the airport, which General Bunyachenko took the next morning. According to the young Czech concentration-camp escapee, "The Russians fought well, for it was their last chance to make up for having fought in the German Army. Their losses were heavy."

The Czech nationalists, aware that Patton's army was approaching, now expected their liberation to come from the West. And so did the American GIs—until they came to a halt on the 6th of May at the agreed-upon line: Karlsbad-Pilsen-Budweis. An officer of the U.S. 16th Armored Division later reported that "hundreds of men in the command wanted and pleaded to go on to Prague, and could not understand why we did not go on."

In fact, just enough Americans had reached Prague to keep the Czechs' false hopes alive. On May 5, a jeep bearing an American flag pulled into Prague, carrying a U.S. Army intelligence team commanded by Captain Eugene Fodor. The Americans were escorted by a jubilant crowd of partisans to the headquarters of the insurgent leader, General Frantisek Kratochwil. The general formally offered to hand the city over to the Americans, and the team raced back to Pilsen to request permission for an advance on Prague. But the next day SHAEF reiterated orders to uphold the Allied agreement: Halt at Pilsen.

The failure of Patton's army to arrive worried Bunyachenko. Having learned that Germany had capitulated, that the Americans had definitely stopped their advance at Pilsen and, worse, that the Red Army was closing in on Prague from the north, Bunyachenko sent a delegation on May 8 to a committee of the National Council.

At the conference, Bunyachenko's delegation received more bad news. They were told that the council could not accept the help of turncoats and German mercenaries. Furthermore, the delegation was reminded that Marshal Konev's force would soon arrive to supplant the partisans with whom Bunyachenko had made his deal for amnesty. Josef Smrkovsky, leader of the Communist faction on the committee, dealt the final blow: "You yourselves confirm that you are fighting Communism. Many members of the council are Communists. Therefore, you are our enemies."

With the promise of sanctuary in postwar Czechoslovakia now revoked, Bunyachenko ordered his division to stop fighting the Germans and to pull out of Prague as fast as possible. Despite the hindrance of Czech partisan roadblocks the 1st Division managed to evacuate the capital and reach Vlasov's headquarters at Beroun. On May 9, Vlasov and his troops started westward toward the Americans.

Meanwhile, the Czech National Council was negotiating with General Toussaint, who also had received word of Germany's general capitulation at Rheims. Toussaint agreed to turn the capital over to the National Council, but insisted that his troops be guaranteed safe conduct out of the city. The council accepted the condition in order to get the Germans out of town before the Soviet forces arrived and renewed the battle, causing further damage to the city. The council even let Toussaint's men keep their small arms to defend themselves against any partisans or Soviet units they might meet. The Germans hastily began pulling out, still hoping, like Vlasov's men, to reach the American lines before their routes west were blocked by the Red Army.

The people of Prague were not nearly as lenient in their treatment of the Germans as were their leaders. They wanted to avenge six years of suffering. They attacked every German they could find, including their Sudeten countrymen.

Women and children bore the brunt of the Czech wrath. German women, many of whom had been taken prisoner by the Czech insurgents at the beginning of the uprising, were seized by maddened crowds from guards who were marching them to prison. The women were spat on, shorn,

Triumphant Czech freedom fighters ride through Prague aboard a Russian tank. When Soviet forces reached Prague on the morning of May 9, the Germans had largely evacuated the capital city. The Russians found themselves so swamped by ecstatic crowds that their commander, Marshal Konev, lost contact with them for several hours.

painted with swastikas and publicly raped. Some were stripped and forced to work, nude, dismantling barricades. Some had their Achilles tendons cut, and crowds jeered as they screamed and flopped about on the ground in helpless pain. German children were thrown from windows and drowned in horse troughs. Several hundred boys were taken out of their school and shot.

German men, women and children were bound together with barbed wire and rolled into the Vltava River. In twos and threes, the dead floated downstream into the Elbe. Two weeks later—after the last of 30,000 German civilians had been killed in Prague—thousands of bodies were still being pulled out of the river.

As vengeance ruled in Prague, Marshal Konev and his First Ukrainian Army Group labored successfully to slam the door on the German troops who, having abandoned their positions, were struggling in scores of thousands to flee through or around Prague into the American lines. On May 8, the units Konev had sent to assault Dresden captured the city. The bulk of his attack forces burst through the thinning

ranks of the Fourth Panzer Army, along the Czech border, and poured southward at will.

At 3 a.m. on May 9, after covering 50 miles in a day, the spearheads of Konev's Fourth Guards Tank Army broke into Prague from the northwest; a few hours later they were joined by the vanguard of the Third Guards Tank Army, storming down from the north. By 10 a.m. men of the First Ukrainian Army Group had cleared out the last German troops, occupied all of the Czech capital and were raping the women of Prague.

Units of the Second and Fourth Ukrainian Army Groups thrust into Prague from the south and east the following day, snapping shut the jaws of a pincers on a large part of the First Panzer Army. Russians also pushed westward in pursuit of those Germans who had escaped their trap.

Although the westbound Germans had succeeded in escaping for a while, they had a terrible time of it. Soldiers and civilians alike were subjected to bombing and strafing by Soviet warplanes. They then ran afoul of American roadblocks along the length of the Karlsbad-Pilsen-Budweis line. The roadblocks had been established to stem the westward

tide. At Pilsen several hundred German soldiers were allowed to enter American lines between May 5 and May 9, but beginning on May 10, the Americans required German fugitives to bivouac and wait for Soviet units to come up and take them prisoner.

Only a few thousand of Army Group Center's 600,000 troops reached Patton's army in Czechoslovakia, and the overwhelming majority of these were turned back to await the Russians. Among those who surrendered was Karl Hermann Frank. He was picked up by the Americans on May 9 and turned over to the Czechs, who quickly executed him. Field Marshal Schörner left his headquarters in northern Czechoslovakia on May 8, and flew in a small plane to western Austria. After drifting about the countryside until mid-May, he showed up, dressed as a Tyrolean peasant, at an American prisoner-of-war compound. The Americans delivered him to the Red Army on May 22.

Few dramas were more tragic—or more bizarre—than the fate of General Vlasov and his two divisions of Russian renegades. On May 10, Vlasov, General Bunyachenko and the ROA's 1st Division blundered into an out-of-the-way U.S. roadblock 30 miles south of Pilsen. The American officer in command had expected to see the Russians one of these days, but he was not prepared for a division of them in German uniform, led by a Lincolnesque general who wanted them all to be made prisoners of war.

Having no instructions on what to do in such an unlikley case, the American commander allowed the Russians to pitch camp outside the nearby town of Schlüsselburg. It seemed to Bunyachenko that his outfit was safely inside American lines.

Meanwhile the ROA's 2nd Division had been stalled since May 5 near Budweis, where its commanding officer, General S. A. Sveryev, had been trying to arrange a surrender to the U.S. Third Army. General Patton—who saw the ROA as "White Russians," anti-Communist holdouts from the 1917 Revolution—was not unsympathetic and offered to take Sveryev's men into his area. "These people," he said, "are in a pitiable state." But Patton, too, was unable to offer the Vlasovites what they desperately needed—status under American aegis as prisoners of war and protection against repatriation to the U.S.S.R. As of May 11, Sveryev had not yet decided to take up Patton's offer. By then, it wa too late. Soviet troops moved into the area that night.

Thereafter, it was every ROA man for himself. During the day, other Soviet units arrived at Schlüsselburg. The nex morning, U.S. officers informed Bunyachenko that at 3 p.m the Americans would begin leaving the area because the demarcation line between U.S. forces and Soviet forces wa being moved westward. An American captain named Donahue suggested that it was time for the division to break up and disappear piecemeal into Germany. Bunyachenko passed the word, informing his troops, "You will have to choose where you want to go. The Bolsheviks are coming from there"—pointing to the east. "The Americans are going there"—pointing to the west.

The men of the division got the idea, but by nightfall, Soviet detachments were on the hunt for the renegades. Approximately 10,000 men of the ROA's 1st Division were killed or captured.

General Vlasov himself, and what was left of his entourage, also ended up at Schlüsselburg. Orders that had come down from SHAEF rejecting the 1st Division's surrender to the Americans as a unit applied to Vlasov as its commander, but he was taken into custody anyway. Since he wore the uniform of a German general, he was subject to automatic arrest on war-crimes charges.

Vlasov was not in American hands for long. On the afternoon of May 12, he and his staff officers were riding in a small American convoy threading its way out of Schlüsselburg past incoming Soviet columns, on the way to Third Army headquarters in Pilsen for interrogation. A Soviet political commissar in a passing vehicle recognized Vlasov, stopped the U.S. convoy, and forced the renegade out of his car at the point of a submachine gun.

Vlasov held open his coat and said, "Shoot."

"Not I," answered the commissar. "Comrade Stalin will judge you."

The Americans drove on. Vlasov was sent to Moscow, along with Bunyachenko, who was captured a few days later. According to *Pravda*, Generals Vlasov and Bunyachenko and 10 other ROA officers were tried in 1946 on charges of "espionage and diversionist and terrorist activities." All were found guilty and were hanged.

The closing of the Czechoslovakian front, as Soviet troops

met the Americans west of Prague, doomed all German troops to the south who had not already beat their way westward and been accepted into American lines. Army Group South, occupying a line running from the Czechoslovakian border to southern Austria that had been largely inactive since the fall of Vienna on April 13, had fled westward on orders from Admiral Dönitz and, for the most part, was able to make good its escape. Farther south, in Yugoslavia, Army Group Southeast, which had lost one third of its 300,000 men in months of savage fighting against Tito's army, was concentrated too far east to gain the American lines; only a fraction made it to safety.

The fate of the remaining German troops in Yugoslavia was harsh in the extreme. At the time of the general capitulation order, some 175,000 of them surrendered to the Yugoslavs. They were marched for days through the countryside on their way to prison camps; 10,000 died on the road, and another 70,000 later perished in captivity. After the surrender order was issued, the army group's commander, General Alexander Löhr, was taken prisoner and shot.

Elsewhere during the second week of May, German surrenders and internments proceeded more smoothly. On May 9, May 10 and May 11, German units surrendered the Channel Islands and three isolated coastal garrisons—Dunkirk, Lorient and Saint-Nazaire. The end of the German presence in Denmark was complicated only by a few incidents in which resistance fighters attempted to disarm retreating German troops.

Even in Norway, where 10 days earlier the occupation force commander had been prepared to mount a last battle for the Third Reich, the Germans quietly turned over their arms to an Allied expeditionary force only 40,000 strong. The commander in chief in Norway, Lieut. General Böhme, reconciled his men and himself to surrender with a last order of the day: "Grit your teeth, maintain discipline and good order, obey your superiors and remain what you have always been—German soldiers who love their people and their country more than anything else in the world."

The Third Reich now survived only in the vestigial government of Admiral Dönitz at Flensburg. For that matter, the Western Allies had never considered it a government, merely a remnant of the German High Command. To take charge of this organism, a 25-man SHAEF control party arrived in Flensburg on May 12 and established quarters aboard the passenger ship *Patria*, moored in the harbor. Five days later, they were joined by a Soviet control party.

At any moment all the members of the Dönitz government might have been arrested on suspicion of being dangerous Nazis or war criminals. Indeed, General Keitel and Marshal Kesselring were taken into custody on May 13 and 15. That others were not arrested was at least partly due to the realization by the Western Allies that the instrument of military surrender did not provide them with a legal footing for the political control of Germany, but only stipulated a capitulation of armed forces. The Allies had set the European Advisory Commission to work to devise a document that would plug the loopholes. Until that was accomplished, they preferred to keep Dönitz and his ministers around just in case of some unforeseen emergency.

Taking itself seriously despite its powerlessness, the Dönitz government studied and discussed the German plight, pondering such problems as food shortages, the ruined transportation system, and the moral necessity of disavowing Nazi atrocities.

The Dönitz government cooperated willingly with the Western Allies; its policy was to urge all Germans to do the same—though some of Dönitz' men were rather cynical in carrying out the policy. Others were more fatalistic. General Jodl, who had replaced the arrested Field Marshal Keitel as commander in chief of the OKW, told a reluctant subordinate, "Like the rest of us, you have to lay a few eggs before you are turned into boiled fowl."

For all its relative earnestness, however, the Dönitz regime quickly became the target of angry accusations; the fact that it existed at all aroused concerns about Allied plans for de-Nazification and war-crimes trials. *Pravda* termed any acceptance of the Dönitz government "turning the poacher into the gamekeeper"; the *New York Herald Tribune* of May 16 called the rump regime a "grotesque comedy" and demanded to know why its members had not been arrested for war crimes. These and other attacks were instrumental in forcing the hand of the Western Allies.

Early on May 23, Admiral Dönitz, General Jodl and Admiral von Friedeburg were summoned to the *Patria* by the SHAEF control party. The Germans were told to consider

FINAL VOLLEY ON A BALTIC ISLE

Nazi Germany fought its final battle over the Danish island of Bornholm in the western Baltic Sea—a 227-square-mile piece of real estate that the Wehrmacht had occupied in 1940 and technically had already surrendered to the Western Allies. But the Soviet Union wanted Bornholm as a foothold in the Baltic.

As far as the German commander at Bornholm was concerned, he was still at war with the Russians. When a Soviet reconnaissance plane flew over the island on May 7, the Germans fired at it. The Russians in turn bombed the island towns of Nekso and Ronne that day and the next. Then on May 10, they landed shock troops and the German garrison capitulated.

A year later, after repeated complaints by the Danes and diplomatic entreaties by the Western Allies, the Soviets finally returned the island to Denmark.

The ferry Ostbornholm lies capsized in Nekso harbor, a victim of belated Russian bombing.

Gutted houses line a seaside street on Bornholm island. Russian planes wrecked some 3,000 dwellings and other buildings in the island's two towns.

themselves prisoners of war and to prepare to depart at 1:30 p.m. Their destination was not mentioned. Friedeburg went back to his quarters and committed suicide.

Then at 10 o'clock in the morning, during a regular conference at Dönitz' headquarters, British military police burst in shouting "Hands up!" The Germans were ordered to strip and were subjected to humiliating body searches for secret papers, concealed weapons, and for possible hidden poison capsules. Robert Murphy, who was General Eisenhower's political adviser, witnessed the event; he commented that as they performed these examinations the MPs, "in the manner of soldiers from time immemorial, simultaneously 'liberated' some souvenirs for themselves."

The Third Reich, whose existence had been extended by Dönitz for a little more than three weeks beyond the death of Adolf Hitler, was finally defunct. "The conquerors of the Nazis were in complete control," wrote Murphy, "and the administration of Germany was their responsibility." Dönitz, angered but not surprised, claimed that his government had been sacrificed by the Western Allies "in the interest of friendship with Russia."

"No sooner had the sound of gunfire faded," wrote General Charles de Gaulle, "than the world's appearance changed. The strength and spirit of the peoples mobilized for the War suddenly lost their unifying object, while the ambition of states reappeared in all its virulence. The Allies revoked those considerations and concessions they had necessarily granted each other in time of peril, when they were confronting a common enemy. Yesterday was the time for battle; the hour for settling accounts had come."

De Gaulle himself contributed substantially to the disarray he described. The general, his personal and national pride injured by the cavalier treatment he had received from the British and especially from the Americans throughout the War, spited the Allies by refusing to evacuate French troops from a section of Alpine northern Italy, an area not covered in any wartime Allied agreement. The French planned to annex the area, but SHAEF insisted that all such territorial questions were to be settled through diplomacy rather than military action. After an ugly exchange of communications—at first with SHAEF, later with President Truman—the French withdrew in late June.

More serious was the increasing ill will between the Soviet Union and the Western Allies. Soviet commanders at the working level were generally unfriendly, uncommunicative and downright obstructionist. The Soviet Union, its army ensconced in Berlin, deliberately put off the agreed-upon transfer of authority over the city to the Allied Control Council, the four-power military government organization that was to run the defeated country. President Truman, who was much more disposed than Roosevelt had been to "talk tough" to the Russians, gave them an excuse to continue their intransigence on May 8 by terminating unconditional Lend-Lease aid—the arrangement under which the U.S. shipped arms, food and other war supplies to the Soviet Union. Termination at the War's end was mandated by the 1941 act that had created Lend-Lease, but Truman's manner was almost provocatively abrupt.

In the atmosphere of rancor and disequilibrium that de Gaulle so accurately summarized, a dangerous new world was being created on the Continent. The balance of power that had stabilized Europe before the War had been destroyed along with Hitler's tyranny. France stood revealed as gravely weak, Great Britain as weakening. The virtually unchallenged world power of the United States loomed as an essential if unpredictable element in the future of Europe. The giant Soviet Union had emerged as the strongest European power, occupying or controlling more than half of the Continent. The U.S.S.R. was being welcomed into the world community of the United Nations, despite its notorious opposition to democratic process.

Most of these developments had been foreseen by that twisted genius who had precipitated World War II. On the 2nd of April, 1945, in a monologue transcribed in the *Führerbunker* by Martin Bormann, the leader of the Third Reich made a statement of frightening prescience.

"With the defeat of the Reich," Adolf Hitler said, "there will remain in the world only two great powers capable of confronting each other—the United States and Soviet Russia. The laws of both history and geography will compel these two powers to a trial of strength, either military or in the fields of economics or ideology. And it is equally certain that both these powers will sooner or later find it desirable to seek the support of the sole surviving great nation in Europe, the German people."

CELEBRATING THE PEACE

aze of rockets and searchlights illuminates the sky over Moscow's turreted Kremlin as thousands of cheering Russians jam Red Square to mark their victory.

"THE FLAGS OF FREEDOM FLY ALL OVER EUROPE"

Well before the documents were signed, everyone sense that peace was coming. Rumors of an impending surrende by the Germans sent jubilant crowds surging into the stree of Chicago's Loop on April 28—too soon by more than week. When at last the signing took place—at 2:41 a.m on May 7—the news leaked out a full day ahead of officia Allied announcements. By radio, the German governmer had urged its populace to accept the capitulation, an the Associated Press picked up the broadcast and broke th story: After 2,076 terrible days, the War in Europe was in deed finally over.

As the headlines appeared on front pages around th world, war-weary people poured into the streets in an ecsta sy of thanksgiving and relief. Half a million New Yorker gathered in Times Square. Londoners tore the blackout cur tains from their windows, and lit bonfires on street corner and in bombed-out buildings. For the first time in nearly si years, floodlights illuminated Buckingham Palace, Big Ben St. Paul's Cathedral and Trafalgar Square. Church bells i Rome rang a paean to liberty and peace. In Paris, which hac celebrated its deliverance the previous summer, crowd once again swarmed into the boulevards.

Official confirmation came on May 8. Winston Churchil delivered a V-E Day broadcast to his nation and spoke ir Parliament. President Harry Truman summoned the press to his White House office. "This is a solemn but glorious hour," Truman told the reporters. "The flags of freedom fly all over Europe." Then he could not help adding, with a characteristic twinkle, "It's . . . my birthday, too."

Moscow held off its celebration one more day, until the Russians had concluded surrender rituals in occupied Berlin and Prague. From the Kremlin, 1,000 guns boomed out. Rockets flashed overhead, and joyous Muscovites danced through the streets.

Then, quickly, the festivities waned as the victors turned to problems still ahead: in Europe, the monumental task of reconstruction; and in Asia, the final push against the forces of Imperial Japan.

A four-line banner headline in The New York Times proclaims victory in Europe—six hours before President Truman's official announcement.

Ecstatic Parisians crowd around the Arc de Triomphe after hearing of the German surrender. A searchlight silhouettes the banner-hung archway.

Anticipating the victory proclamation, thousands of New Yorkers flood Times Square beneath a replica of the Statue of Liberty marking a Red Cross kiosk.

Londoners, giddy with joy, mob a grinning Winston Churchill, who responds by giving his famed V-for-Victory sign before proceeding to Parliament.

Citizens of Prague cheer Soviet Marshal Ivan Konev as he rides triumphantly through the liberated Czech capital, ending six years of Nazi occupation.

On Okinawa, American soldiers of the 77th Infantry Division learn of V-E Day over a field radio, grimly aware that for them the fighting must go...

BIBLIOGRAPHY

Ambrose, Stephen E., *The Supreme Commander: The War Years of General Dwight D. Eisenhower*. Doubleday, 1970.

Atwell, Lester, *Private*. Simon and Schuster, 1958.

"Battle of Germany: 'Hello, Tovarish.'" *Time*, May 7, 1945.

Baumbach, Werner, *The Life and Death of the Luftwaffe*. Transl. by Frederick Holt. Coward-McCann, 1960.

Bergschicker, Heinz von, *Berlin: Bennpunkt Deutscher Geschichte*. Berlin, DDR: Deutscher Militärverlag, 1965.

Bialer, Seweryn, ed., *Stalin and His Generals: Soviet Military Memoirs of World War II*. Pegasus, 1969.

Biennial Report of the Chief of Staff of the United States Army to the Secretary of War, July 1, 1943, to June 30, 1945. U.S. Government Printing Office, 1946.

Blumenson, Martin, *The Patton Papers: 1940-1945*. Houghton Mifflin, 1974.

Boldt, Gerhard, *Hitler: The Last Ten Days*. Transl. by Sandra Bance. Coward, McCann & Geoghegan, 1973.

Bradley, Omar N., *A Soldier's Story*. Henry Holt, 1951.

Brett-Smith, Richard, *Berlin '45: The Grey City*. London: Macmillan, 1967.

Bryant, Arthur, *Triumph in the West: 1943-1946*. London: Collins, 1959.

"Bulgaria: To the Exit." *Time*, August 28, 1944.

Bullock, Alan, *Hitler: A Study in Tyranny*. Perennial Library (abridged ed.), 1971.

Butcher, Harry C., *My Three Years with Eisenhower*. Simon and Schuster, 1946.

Butler, J. R. M., ed., *History of the Second World War—United Kingdom Military Series*:
  Grand Strategy, Vol. 6: *October 1944-August 1945*, by John Ehrman. London: Her Majesty's Stationery Office, 1956.
  Victory in the West, Vol. 2: *The Defeat of Germany*, by L. F. Ellis. London: Her Majesty's Stationery Office, 1968.

Byrom, James, *The Unfinished Man*. London: Chatto and Windus, 1957.

Carell, Paul, and Günter Böddeker, *Die Gefangenen*. Frankfurt am Main/Berlin/Vienna: Ullstein Verlag, 1980.

Chuikov, Vasily I., *The Fall of Berlin*. Transl. by Ruth Kisch. Holt, Rinehart and Winston, 1968.

Churchill, Winston S., *Triumph and Tragedy*. Houghton Mifflin, 1953.

Clark, Alan, *Barbarossa: The Russian-German Conflict, 1941-1945*. London: Hutchinson, 1965.

Codman, Charles R., *Drive*. Little, Brown, 1957.

Davis, Kenneth S., *Experience of War: The United States in World War II*. Doubleday, 1965.

Deakin, F. W., *The Brutal Friendship: Mussolini, Hitler and the Fall of Italian Fascism*. Harper & Row, 1962.

Deane, John R., *The Strange Alliance: The Story of Our Efforts at Wartime Cooperation with Russia*. Viking, 1947.

Dedijer, Vladimir, *Tito Speaks: His Self-Portrait and Struggle with Stalin*. London: Weidenfeld and Nicolson, 1954.

De Gaulle, Charles, *The War Memoirs of Charles de Gaulle: Salvation, 1944-1946*. Transl. by Richard Howard. Simon and Schuster, 1960.

De Guingand, Francis. *Operation Victory*. Charles Scribner's Sons, 1947.

De Lattre de Tassigny, Jean, *The History of the French First Army*. Transl. by Malcolm Barnes. London: Allen and Unwin, 1952.

Delzell, Charles F., *Mussolini's Enemies: The Italian Anti-Fascist Resistance*. Princeton University Press, 1961.

Djilas, Milovan, *Wartime*. Transl. by Michael B. Petrovich. Harcourt Brace Jovanovich, 1977.

Dönitz, Karl, *Memoirs: Ten Years and Twenty Days*. Transl. by R. H. Stevens. World Publishing, 1958.

Dulles, Allen, *The Secret Surrender*. Harper & Row, 1966.

Eisenhower, Dwight D., *Crusade in Europe*. Doubleday, 1948.

Esposito, Vincent J., ed., *The West Point Atlas of American Wars*, Vol. 2, *1900-1953*. Praeger, 1959.

Essame, H., *The Battle for Germany*. Bonanza Books, 1969.

Farago, Ladislas, *Patton: Ordeal and Triumph*. Ivan Obolensky, 1964.

Feis, Herbert, *Churchill, Roosevelt, Stalin: The War They Waged and the Peace They Sought*. Princeton University Press, 1957.

Fest, Joachim C., *Hitler*. Transl. by Richard and Clara Winston. Vintage Books, 1975.

Fox, William J., *The Russian-American Linkup, April 25, 1945*. Unpublished interview with Albert L. Kotzebue. Office of the Chief of Military History, U.S. Army, 1945.

Franzel, Emil, *Die Vertreibung Sudetenland: 1945-1946*. Munich: Aufstieg, 1967.

Goerlitz, Walter, *History of the German General Staff: 1657-1945*. Transl. by Brian Battershaw. Praeger, 1957.

Goudsmit, Samuel A., *Alsos*. Henry Schuman, 1947.

The Great March of Liberation. Transl. by David Fidlon. Moscow: Progress Publishers, 1972.

Grechko, Andrei A., ed., *Liberation Mission of the Soviet Armed Forces in the Second World War*. Transl. by David Fidlon. Moscow: Progress Publishers, 1975.

Guderian, Heinz, *Panzer Leader*. Transl. by Constantine Fitzgibbon. E. P. Dutton, 1952.

"Hands across the Reich." *Newsweek*, May 7, 1945.

Harriman, W. Averell, and Elie Abel, *Special Envoy to Churchill and Stalin: 1941-1946*. London: Hutchinson, 1976.

Hoffmann, Peter, *The History of the German Resistance: 1933-1945*. Transl. by Richard Barry. MIT Press, 1977.

Italiaander, Rolf, Arnold Bauer, and Herbert Krafft, *Berlins Stunde Null 1945*. Düsseldorf: Droste Verlag, 1979.

Kennedy, Edward, "Germans Capitulate on All Fronts." *New York Times*, May 1945.

Kesselring, Albert, *Kesselring: A Soldier's Record*. William Morrow, 1954.

Knauth, Percy, *Germany in Defeat*. Alfred A. Knopf, 1946.

Konev, Ivan S., *Year of Victory*. Moscow: Progress Publishers, 1969.

Korbel, Josef, *The Communist Subversion of Czechoslovakia, 1938-1948: The Failure of Coexistence*. Princeton University Press, 1959.

Liddell Hart, B. H., *History of the Second World War*. G. P. Putnam's Sons, 1970.

Loewenheim, Francis L., Harold D. Langley, and Manfred Jonas, eds., *Roosevelt and Churchill: Their Secret Wartime Correspondence*. E. P. Dutton, 1975.

"London Goes Wild on V-E Day." *Life*, May 14, 1945.

Lukacs, John, *1945: Year Zero*. Doubleday, 1978.

MacDonald, Charles B., *United States Army in World War II: The European Theater of Operations—The Last Offensive*. Office of the Chief of Military History, U.S. Army, 1973.

Maclean, Fitzroy, *Eastern Approaches*. London: Jonathan Cape, 1949.

Manvell, Roger, and Heinrich Fraenkel, *Göring*. Simon and Schuster, 1962.

Mellenthin, F. W. von, *German Generals of World War II as I Saw Them*. University of Oklahoma Press, 1977.

Montgomery, Bernard Law:
  The Memoirs of Field Marshal the Viscount Montgomery of Alamein, K.G. Signet, 1959.
  Normandy to the Baltic. Houghton Mifflin, 1948.

Mosely, Philip E., "Dismemberment of Germany." *Foreign Affairs*, April 1950.

Mosley, Leonard, *The Reich Marshal: A Biography of Hermann Göring*. Doubleday, 1974.

Murphy, Robert, *Diplomat among Warriors*. Doubleday, 1964.

O'Donnell, James P., *The Bunker: The History of the Reich Chancellery Group*. Houghton Mifflin, 1978.

Panter-Downes, Mollie, *London War Notes, 1939-1945*. Farrar, Straus and Giroux, 1971.

Pash, Boris T., *The Alsos Mission*. Award House, 1969.

Patton, George S., Jr., *War as I Knew It*. Houghton Mifflin, 1947.

"The Peace at Hand." *Time*, May 14, 1945.

Pogue, Forrest C.:
  George C. Marshall: Organizer of Victory. Viking Press, 1973.
  The Meeting with the Russians, 25-26 April 1945. Unpublished memoirs. Office of the Chief of Military History, U.S. Army, 1945.
  United States Army in World War II: The European Theater of Operations—The Supreme Command. Office of the Chief of Military History, U.S. Army, 1954.

Rokossovsky, Konstantin K., *A Soldier's Duty*. Moscow: Progress Publishers, 1970.

Ruhl, Klaus-Jörg, *Die Besatzer und die Deutschen: Amerikanische Zone 1945-1948*. Düsseldorf: Droste Verlag, 1980.

Ryan, Cornelius, *The Last Battle*. Simon and Schuster, 1966.

Salisbury, Harrison E., *The Unknown War*. Bantam Books, 1978.

Scheel, Klaus, ed., *Die Befreiung Berlins, 1945*. Berlin, DDR: VEB Deutscher Verlag der Wissenschaften, 1975.

Schmidt, Dana Adams, *Anatomy of a Satellite*. Little, Brown, 1952.

Schwarzwälder, Herbert, *Bremen und Nordwestdeutschland am Kriegsende 1945*:
  Vol. 1, *Die Vorbereitung auf den "Endkampf."* Bremen: Carl Schünemann Verlag, 1972.
  Vol. 2, *Der Britischer Vorstoss an die Weser*. Bremen: Carl Schünemann Verlag, 1973.
  Vol. 3, *Vom "Kampf am Bremen" bis zur Kapitulation*. Bremen: Carl Schünemann Verlag, 1974.

Seaton, Albert, *The Russo-German War, 1941-1945*. Praeger, 1971.

"SHAEF Ban on AP Lifted in Six Hours." *New York Times*, May 8, 1945.

Shirer, William L.:
  End of a Berlin Diary. Popular Library, 1961.
  The Rise and Fall of the Third Reich. Simon and Schuster, 1960.

Shtemenko, Sergei M., *The Last Six Months: Russia's Final Battles with Hitler's Armies in World War II*. Transl. by Guy Daniels. Doubleday, 1977.

Smith, Bradley F., and Elena Agarossi, *Operation Sunrise: The Secret Surrender*. Basic Books, 1979.

Speer, Albert, *Inside the Third Reich*. Transl. by Richard and Clara Winston. Macmillan, 1970.

Steenberg, Sven, *Vlasov*. Transl. by Abe Farbstein. Alfred A. Knopf, 1970.

Stein, George H., *The Waffen SS: Hitler's Elite Guard at War, 1939-1945*. Cornell University Press, 1966.

Steinert, Marlis G., *23 Days: The Final Collapse of Nazi Germany*. Transl. by Richard and Barry. Walker, 1969.

Streit, Christian, *Keine Kameraden*. Stuttgart: Deutsche Verlags-Anstalt, 1978.

Sulzberger, C. L., "Moscow Goes Wild Over Joyful News." *New York Times*, May 10, 1945.

Thompson, John H., "How Yank Met Russ First Time on Elbe in 1945." *Chicago Daily Tribune*, April 25, 1949.

Thorwald, Jürgen:
  Flight in the Winter. Ed. and transl. by Fred Wieck. Pantheon Books, 1951.
  The Illusion—Soviet Soldiers in Hitler's Armies. Transl. by Richard and Clara Winston. Harcourt Brace Jovanovich, 1975.

Toland, John, *The Last 100 Days*. Random House, 1965.

Tolstoy, Nikolai, *The Secret Betrayal*. Charles Scribner's Sons, 1977.

Trevor-Roper, Hugh R.:
    Ed., *Final Entries 1945: The Diaries of Joseph Goebbels.* Transl. by Richard Barry. Avon, 1979.
    The Last Days of Hitler. Macmillan, 1947.
Truman, Harry S., *Year of Decisions (Memoirs by Harry S. Truman,* Vol. 1). Doubleday, 1955.
Tully, Andrew, *Berlin: Story of a Battle.* Simon and Schuster, 1963.
Viorst, Milton, *Hostile Allies: F.D.R. and Charles de Gaulle.* Macmillan, 1965.
Vyazankin, I. A., *Za Strokoi Boyevovo Donesenia.* Moscow: Ministerstvo Oborony, 1978.
"War in Europe Draws to Its End." *Life,* May 7, 1945.
Weigley, Russell F., *Eisenhower's Lieutenants: The Campaign of France and Germany, 1944-1945.* Indiana University Press, 1981.
Werth, Alexander, *Russia at War: 1941-1945.* E. P. Dutton, 1964.

Willkie, Wendell L., *One World.* Simon and Schuster, 1943.
Wilmot Chester, *The Struggle for Europe.* London: Collins, 1952.
Wolff, Robert Lee, *The Balkans in Our Time.* Harvard University Press, 1956.
Young, Peter, ed., *Atlas of the Second World War.* G. P. Putnam's Sons, 1974.
Zhukov, Georgy K.:
    Marshal Zhukov's Greatest Battles. Ed. by Harrison E. Salisbury; transl. by Theodore Shabad. Harper & Row, 1969.
    The Memoirs of Marshal Zhukov. Delacorte Press, 1971.
Ziemke, Earl F.:
    The Battle for Berlin: End of the Third Reich. Ballantine Books, 1968.
    Stalingrad to Berlin: The German Defeat in the East. Office of the Chief of Military History, U.S. Army, 1968.
    The U.S. Army in the Occupation of Germany: 1944-1946. Center of Military History, U.S. Army, 1975.
Zubakov, V., *The Final Assault.* Moscow: Novosti Press Agency, 1975.

ACKNOWLEDGMENTS

For help given in the preparation of this book, the editors wish to express their gratitude to Joergen H. Barfod, Director, and Bjarne Maurer, Research Fellow, The Museum of Denmark's Fight for Freedom 1940-1945, Copenhagen; Heinz Bergschicker, Berlin (DDR); Maréchal Jean de Lattre de Tassigny, Paris; Dr. Alfred M. De Zayas, Geneva; German Information Center, New York; Werner Haupt, Bibliothek für Zeitgeschichte, Stuttgart; Heinrich Hoffmann, Hamburg; Dr. Brooks Kleber, Deputy Chief Historian, U.S. Army Center for Military History, Washington, D.C.; Dr. Roland Klemig and Heidi Klein, Bildarchiv Preussischer Kulturbesitz, Berlin (West); Clarence Marshall, 69th Infantry Association, New Kensington, Pennsylvania; Olga Metlitsky and Victoria Edwards, Sovfoto, New York; Meinrad Nilges, Bundesarchiv-Bildarchiv, Koblenz; Lieutenant James Poole, Albert Simpson Historical Research Center, Maxwell Air Force Base, Alabama; Hannes Quaschinsky, ADN-Zentralbild, Berlin (DDR); Dr. William D. Robertson, Culver City, California; Wolfgang Streubel, Ullstein Bilderdienst, Berlin (West); Ladislav Svatos, Easton, Connecticut; Dr. Friederich Terveen, Landesbildstelle, Berlin (West); Paul White, Still Photo Division, National Archives, Washington, D.C.

The index for this book was prepared by Nicholas J. Anthony.

PICTURE CREDITS

Credits from left to right are separated by semicolons, from top to bottom by dashes.

COVER and page 1: Sovfoto.

HARD-BOOTED LIBERATORS—6, 7: Yevgeni Khaldei, Moscow. 8: G. Khomzor from Sovfoto. 9: Georgi Zelma, Moscow. 10, 11: Yevgeni Khaldei, Moscow; Novosti, Rome. 12, 13: TASS from Sovfoto; Yevgeni Khaldei, Moscow. 14, 15: Yevgeni Khaldei, courtesy Bureau Soviétique d'Information, Paris; Yevgeni Khaldei, Moscow. 16, 17: Fotokhronika-TASS, Moscow.

"WE SHALL NOT CAPITULATE"—20: Map by John E. Taktikos and Diana Raquel Vazquez. 22: Bildarchiv Preussischer Kulturbesitz, Berlin (West). 23: Bildarchiv Preussischer Kulturbesitz, Berlin (West), photo by Heinrich Hoffmann. 25: Map by John E. Taktikos and Diana Raquel Vazquez. 28: Ullstein Bilderdienst, Berlin (West). 30, 31: Drawing by Hanno Engler, courtesy Bildarchiv Preussischer Kulturbesitz, Berlin (West). 33, 34: Süddeutscher Verlag, Bilderdienst, Munich.

FORTRESS BERLIN—36, 37: Bildarchiv Preussischer Kulturbesitz, Berlin (West), photo by Heinrich Hoffmann. 38: Hilmar Pabel, Umratshausen, Federal Republic of Germany. 39: Heinrich Hoffmann, Hamburg. 40, 41: Ullstein Bilderdienst, Berlin (West) (2); Bildarchiv Preussischer Kulturbesitz, Berlin (West). 42, 43: Ullstein Bilderdienst, Berlin (West); Bildarchiv Preussischer Kulturbesitz, Berlin (West). 44, 45: Ullstein Bilderdienst, Berlin (West); ADN-Zentralbild, Berlin, DDR—Yakov Ryumkin, Moscow. 46, 47: Süddeutscher Verlag, Bilderdienst, Munich.

THE RUSSIAN ONSLAUGHT—48, 49: TASS from Sovfoto. 50: Mikhail Markov, Moscow. 51: Alexandr Ustinov, *Pravda*, Moscow. 52, 53: Fotokhronika-TASS, Moscow. 54, 55: Viktor Grebnev, Moscow; Süddeutscher Verlag, Bilderdienst, Munich. 56, 57: Alexandr Ustinov, *Pravda*, Moscow. 58, 59: Ivan Shagin, TASS from Sovfoto; Fotokhronika-TASS, Moscow. 60, 61: ADN-Zentralbild, Berlin, DDR.

THE BLOW DELIVERED—64: Map by John E. Taktikos and Diana Raquel Vazquez. 66: Sovfoto (2); Imperial War Museum, London. 67: Sovfoto. 71: Ullstein Bilderdienst, Berlin (West). 74: Yakov Ryumkin, Moscow. 78: Alexandr Ustinov, *Pravda*, Moscow.

ENCOUNTER ON THE ELBE—82, 83: Yevgeni Khaldei, Moscow. 84: Keystone Press, courtesy National Archives (No. 208-AA-38A-16). 85: Alexandr Ustinov, *Pravda*, Moscow. 86, 87: Black Star; National Archives (No. 306-NT-1343-2)—Wide World (2). 88, 89: National Archives (Nos. 306-NT-2921-V—208-AA-38A-2; 208-AA-38B-2—208-AA-38B-1). 90, 91: The Bettmann Archive.

MARKING TIME IN THE WEST—95: Margaret Bourke-White for *Life*. 96: Imperial War Museum, London. 98: Joe Pazen from Black Star, London. 99: U.S. Army; Wide World. 101: Imperial War Museum, London. 102, 103: UPI. 106: Courtesy Maréchal Jean de Lattre de Tassigny, Paris. 107: National Archives (No. 208-AA-210BB-1). 108: UPI.

DEATH STRUGGLE IN BERLIN—110, 111: Sovfoto. 112: ADN-Zentralbild, Berlin, DDR. 113: Süddeutscher Verlag, Bilderdienst, Munich. 114: Fotokhronika-TASS from Sovfoto. 115: Süddeutscher Verlag, Bilderdienst, Munich. 116, 117: Yevgeni Khaldei, Moscow. 118, 119: Landesbildstelle, Berlin (West). 120: Sovfoto. 121: Landesbildstelle, Berlin (West). 122, 123: Landesbildstelle, Berlin (West); Ivan Shagin, TASS from Sovfoto. 124, 125: Yevgeni Khaldei, Moscow.

LAST AGONIES OF THE REICH—128: Map by John E. Taktikos and Diana Raquel Vazquez. 132: Bildarchiv Preussischer Kulturbesitz, Berlin (West). 133: Ullstein Bilderdienst, Berlin (West). 134, 135: Maps by John E. Taktikos and Diana Raquel Vazquez. 137: Hilmar Pabel, Umratshausen, Federal Republic of Germany. 138, 139: Sovfoto. 141: Yevgeni Khaldei, Moscow. 142: TASS from Sovfoto.

A VAUNTED ARMY'S COLLAPSE—144, 145: Wide World. 146: UPI. 147: Imperial War Museum, London. 148, 149: UPI—U.S. Army (2). 150, 151: Black Star; Imperial War Museum, London—UPI. 152, 153: U.S. Army; Wide World—William Vandivert for *Life*. 154, 155: Wide World.

THE CONQUERED CITADEL—156-158: Yevgeni Khaldei, Moscow. 159: Dmitri Baltermants, Moscow. 160, 161: Sovfoto. 162, 163: Yevgeni Khaldei, Moscow; Novosti from Sovfoto—Süddeutscher Verlag, Bilderdienst, Munich. 164, 165: Süddeutscher Verlag, Bilderdienst, Munich—Sovfoto; William Vandivert for *Life*. 166, 167: *The Daily Mirror*, London.

A VIOLENT EPILOGUE—171: UPI. 173: Imperial War Museum, London. 174: The Bettmann Archive. 176, 177: U.S. Army; Yakov Ryumkin, Moscow. 180, 181: Pictorial Press Ltd., London. 182: Jiri Janovsky, courtesy Vladimír Remeš, Prague. 183: Václav Chochola, courtesy Vladimír Remeš, Prague. 185: Václav Chochola, Prague. 188: The Museum of Denmark's Fight for Freedom 1940-1945, Copenhagen.

CELEBRATING THE PEACE—190, 191: Novosti, Moscow. 192: © 1945 by The New York Times Co., reprinted by permission, courtesy The Bettmann Archive. 193: Ralph Morse for *Life*. 194, 195: Wide World. 196, 197: Popperfoto, London. 198, 199: TASS from Sovfoto. 200, 201: Wide World.